NATIONALISM, DEMOCRACY AND SECURITY IN THE BALKANS

J. F. (Jim) Brown was a Senior Researcher at RAND between 1989 and 1991. He was educated at Manchester University and the University of Michigan. He is a former head of Radio Free Europe (RFE) Research and between 1978 and 1983 was Director of Radio Free Europe. He has taught at the University of California at Berkeley and at the University of California at Los Angeles and has been a visiting research associate at Columbia University and St Antony's College, Oxford. He is the author, *inter alia*, of *Eastern Europe and Communist Rule* and *Surge to Freedom: The End of Communist Rule in Eastern Europe*, both published by Duke University Press. At present he is Distinguished Scholar in Residence at the RFE-RL (Radio Liberty) Research Institute in Munich and is working on a study of post-communist Eastern Europe.

Nationalism, Democracy and Security in the Balkans

J. F. BROWN

A RAND Research Study

Dartmouth

Aldershot • Brookfield USA • Hong Kong • Singapore • Sydney

RAND books are available on a wide variety of topics. To receive a list of RAND books, write or call Distribution Services, RAND, 1700 Main Street, P.O. Box 2138, Santa Monica, CA 90407-2138, (310) 393-0411, extension 6686.

Published by
Dartmouth Publishing Company Limited
Gower House
Croft Road
Aldershot
Hants GU11 3HR
England

Dartmouth Publishing Company
Old Post Road
Brookfield
Vermont 05036
USA

A CIP Catalogue record for this book is available from the British Library

Library of Congress Cataloging-in-Publication Data
Brown, J. F. (James F.), 1928–
Nationalism, democracy, and security in the Balkans / by J.F. Brown.
p. cm. – (A RAND research study)
Includes bibliographical references and index.
ISBN 1-85521-316-8 : $55.95 (U.S. : est.)
1. Balkan Peninsula–Politics and government–1945–1989.
2. Balkan Peninsula–Politics and government–1989– 3. Nationalism–Balkan Peninsula. I. Title. II. Series.
DR48.5.B698 1992
949.6–dc20 92-23927
CIP

ISBN 1 85521 316 8

Printed in Great Britain by
Billing & Sons Ltd, Worcester

To the memory of
Hugh Seton-Watson

Die Welt, November 23, 1990

'When you call for a public
discussion about democracy,
a couple of hundred intellectuals
come. When it's about nationalism,
you get tens of thousands
of all sorts.'

Alija Iszetbegovic
President of Bosnia-Herzegovina

Contents

Preface

This book is about six Balkan countries and their relationships with each other: Albania, Bulgaria, Greece, Romania, Turkey and Yugoslavia. In spite of themselves all six are entangled in a web of history, the complexities and dangers of which become more evident as old alliances collapse or show signs of becoming irrelevant. This book discusses the strength of nationalism in these countries, its impact on their stability and security, and the relative weakness of the liberal democratic tradition. Nationalism's strength affects and often destabilizes each country's internal order, as well as its international relations, with liberal democracy getting subordinated to or perverted by nationalist aims.

For many years these six countries, despite obvious differences, could be divided into three pairs: Bulgaria and Romania were part of the Soviet alliance, even if the latter was for many years hardly an integral part of it; Yugoslavia and Albania became two independent communist states, having broken away from Soviet domination; Greece and Turkey were members of the western political alliance. The pairings were, in different ways, a response to the post-Second World War international situation, to the East–West tension and the character of the different alliances arising from it. Together these alliances acted as a brake on national rivalries and centrifugal forces within the region as a whole. The Greek–Turkish hostility after 1964 is, of course, an exception to this. But alliance constraints and the threat posed by the Soviet alliance may have pulled Greece and Turkey back from the brink of war on more than one occasion.

Now, however, throughout the region, within countries and between them, the constraints have either disappeared or have greatly weakened. Nationalism, affecting nations or ethnic minorities within nation states, has become more virulent than ever and has already led to the bloody disintegration of Yugoslavia. Nor are the problems or the prospects discussed in this book solely regional; they are international, demanding the attention of the Western powers, including the United States. In fact, these Balkan problems could simply be part of a chain of instability, extending through Turkey into the southern parts of what was the Soviet Union, and beyond. Tragic though the situation in Yugoslavia has become it need not become an unavoidable pattern.

Part I of this book describes the Balkan setting and the interaction between nationalism and democracy in each country in the region. Part II deals with the disputes between Greece and Turkey and with potential crisis areas in the Balkans as a whole, pointing to the international importance of these problems and offering suggestions for Western policy.

This method of dealing with the subject has created some unavoidable repetition. Topics are introduced in their national settings in the chapters on each country and are then taken up in the key penultimate chapter on potential regional conflicts, with the aim of showing how they could degenerate into serious, even violent, conflict. If the region's problems are to be understood, the national individuality, variety, and differences of each country must first be emphasized. Only then can the importance of their interconnection be realized.

Research for this study began in 1987 when Greek–Turkish enmity was already a historical fact of life and when Western observers were beginning to understand the dangers of disintegration overtaking Yugoslavia. My assumption at that time was that the disintegration in Yugoslavia would continue and that the Soviet Union might try to make strategic and diplomatic use of it, threatening the balance of power that had existed for nearly 40 years in the region, even to the extent of drawing a weakened Yugoslavia back toward the Soviet alliance.

The assumption about Yugoslavia turned out to be as right as that concerning the Soviet Union was wrong, although the collapse of Soviet power in Eastern Europe followed by the collapse of the Soviet Union have contributed to the instability the entire region now faces. Obviously, the assumptions on which the research began in 1987 had to be reconsidered, and in August 1990 RAND agreed to sponsor my second attempt to come to grips with a region that had so rapidly changed.

* * *

I wish to thank Enid Schoettle and Paul Balaran at The Ford Foundation for their generosity, understanding, and forgiving spirit; Jim Thomson, Judy Larson, Jonathan Pollack and John Van Oudenaren at RAND for their encouragement and help; and Melissa Dawson and Ted Karasik for valuable research assistance. My thanks, also, to Linda Clark at RAND, who typed the manuscript and was a model of co-operation, skill and reliability; and to Sybil Sosin and her colleagues in RAND's Publications Department, for their efficiency and patience. RAND in Santa Monica provided the background for the work. It would be hard to imagine a better one.

J. F. Brown
Santa Monica,
California

Part I
The Regional and National Settings

1 The Balkan Background

The historical geostrategic paradox of the Balkans, a region of 800 000 square kilometres (roughly 500 000 square miles) in which about 120 million people live, is captured in this description:

> The far-flung mountain formations of the peninsula tended to divide the people of one valley from those of the next, and thus to foster local particularism and local hatreds. But the historic paradox of the Balkan region lay in the fact that the mountains served as a barrier chiefly to the settled inhabitants. For the travelers, for the army on the move, there were well defined lines of passage, main avenues of communication leading into the heart of the peninsula and across the rivers.[1]

One of the two main avenues began at Belgrade and followed important rivers south to Nis in what was Yugoslavia and then south-east across the Bulgarian border to Sofia, down to Plovdiv, on to Edirne in Turkey, and then to Istanbul. The other route had the same first leg from Belgrade to Nis but then moved south through Skopje and down to Salonika. In addition, the Romans had also built a road from Durres, in what became Albania, across to Salonika.[2]

Using these routes the Crusaders moved south toward the Middle East, and later the Ottomans moved north in their conquests of South-eastern Europe – conquests which, once in the early sixteenth century and again towards the end of the seventeenth, took them to the gates of Vienna. Better generals could have captured Vienna on either occasion. Had such leadership been available the history of Europe, and probably the world, would have been changed. In the nineteenth century, in both world wars, these routes played an important operational role. In the Second World War the Germans attributed their eventual defeat in the North African campaign to Yugoslav Partisan attacks which caused disruption of supplies on the rail link south to Salonika and then across the eastern Mediterranean.

Today, with the transformation of methods of warfare, the strategic importance of these historic routes has diminished. But as trade links between

Western Europe and South-eastern Europe and the Middle East have developed, their economic importance has increased. These routes were always important commercially: merchants as well as soldiers moved down them. But the recent increase has been dramatic. Statistics fully illustrating this cannot be obtained, but Yugoslav official publications give a glimpse of the development involved. Between 1957 and 1987 the number of trucks belonging to Yugoslav transport organizations, for example, rose from 3.3 thousand to 50.1 thousand. The volume of goods carried by Yugoslav carriers increased from 41 million in 1967 to 149 million in 1987.[3] These figures are for Yugoslavia alone.

The External Actors

The location of the Balkan countries on the routes between Europe, Turkey, the Middle East and beyond, together with the geostrategic paradox described above, have made these countries vulnerable to external influences, often predatory ones:

> On the one hand, the inhabitants were not able to unite to resist outside pressure; on the other, outsiders could easily enforce their will. ... They were, therefore, deeply affected by the radiations of military power and of political, economic, cultural, and religious influence which emanated from certain great centers of Europe, from which armies, diplomats, merchants, scholars, and priests always found it easy to penetrate into the heart of the peninsula.[4]

The penetration came from every direction – first by the Byzantines from the south, then from the fourteenth century on by the Ottomans who moved deep into the Balkans long before they captured Constantinople in 1453. During the late middle ages the Venetians, a commercial sea-faring power, pecked away at the western and southern fringes of the Balkans, becoming the strongest naval power in the south-east Mediterranean. But they penetrated only the mountain ranges lying close to the shores of the Balkan peninsula, and Fascist Italy, which aspired to be the new Venice and much more, also found itself largely confined to the same fringes. The first Western power to penetrate the Balkans proper was the Habsburg Empire. After turning back the Turks from Vienna in the late seventeenth century, Austrians and then Hungarians began their advances in earnest, the former getting almost to Belgrade, the latter over the Pannonian plain from Zagreb in Croatia to Timişoara in what is now Romania, as well as into Transylvania.

In the nineteenth century, the number of external actors increased dramatically, as the Ottoman Empire became the sick man of Europe, its possessions an obvious temptation for new predators. The Habsburg Empire was still there, an avid predator but no longer predominant. In the early nineteenth century, Napoleonic France appeared briefly on the eastern fringes of what became Yugoslavia and modern Greece, establishing a precedent for good government, the memory of which survived throughout the century. France also became the cultural beacon for the emerging elites in all the Balkan countries.

But the French influence was nothing compared with the Russian. Beginning early in the eighteenth century, the Russian drive through the Balkans toward the Mediterranean continued until the end of the twentieth. In addition to its military, political, and commercial aspects, this drive had ethnic, religious, cultural, and ideological dimensions. The Slavic peoples of the Balkans – especially Bulgarians, Serbs, and Montenegrins – looked with hope to their great Slav brother to support their aspirations for freedom. Moscow, too, as the most powerful centre of Christian Orthodoxy after the eclipse of Byzantium, had a powerful political, spiritual, and cultural appeal. But the Balkan Slavic nations were not the only ones attracted to Russia. During the second half of the eighteenth century and in the early nineteenth, many Greeks saw the Russians, not the Western powers, as their only hope against the Turks, and after liberation from the Ottoman Empire in 1829 the 'Russian party' continued to be important in Greek political life.

Immediately after the Second World War the strength of the Greek communists attested to the persistence of Russian influence in new circumstances, and in spite of Stalin's reluctance to support them, Greece would have become a Soviet satellite but for British and then American intervention. Despite this setback, after 1945 Russia (now the Soviet Union) did achieve its historic ambition by becoming master of most of the Balkan peninsula.[5]

Throughout the nineteenth century Great Britain played a crucial diplomatic role in the Balkans. Its aim was to protect the British connection with the Near East and India beyond by preventing the advance of Russia into the region. Britain's interest in what became known as the 'Eastern Question' led it to back a progressively weakening Turkey against Russia.[6] In the First World War, however, with Germany, Austria–Hungary, and Turkey in alliance, Britain was on Russia's side, as it also was against Germany and Italy in the Second World War. Briefly after that war, however, in the face of new Soviet penetration into the Balkans, Britain again opposed Russia, a task that was soon taken over primarily by the United States.

Germany assumed a dominant role only after it became Nazi Germany in 1933. Through a combination of economic power and skilful manipulation it reduced Yugoslavia, Romania and Bulgaria to the status of economic satellites. Military-political influence followed, supported by large ethnic

German minorities in both Yugoslavia and Romania. The culmination of this development was the German military occupation of the entire Balkan peninsula in the Second World War.

American political interest and influence began when the United States put forth a global foreign policy during and after the Second World War, although America was by no means unknown in the Balkans before then. It was the country of hope for many South-eastern Europeans. Although emigration was small compared with the huge outflow from East Central Europe towards the end of the nineteenth century and after, it was enough to build goodwill for America. So was the pioneering work done by American Protestant missionaries and the higher educational institutions they founded. Alumni of Robert College near Istanbul, for example, drawn from many parts of the Balkans, formed a small and well-connected pro-American freemasonry.[7]

But the United States became active in the Balkans – militarily, politically and, in the framework of the Cold War, ideologically – only after 1945. The Truman Doctrine of 1947 guaranteed the security of both Greece and Turkey against the Soviet threat and US support for Tito's Yugoslavia after its break with Stalin in 1948. In a sense, therefore, America stepped into Britain's shoes, emerging as 'the historic successor to British Balkan diplomacy and military action during the nineteenth century'.[8]

The Decline in the Soviet Position: First Phase – 1947–53

At the end of the Second World War Stalin had apparently achieved what had eluded previous Russian leaders: domination over the Balkans and access to the Mediterranean, to the 'warm water ports' of both ambition and imagination. Moscow controlled the victorious Partisan communist regime in Yugoslavia, and, through it, the new communist partisan regime in Albania. In barely two years it would break down the sham of democratic coalitions in Bulgaria and Romania, and install exclusively communist regimes there. In Greece, as just mentioned, the communists seemed to be winning the civil war. Stalin refused to help them directly, ready to let Greece go, at least temporarily, so as to soothe international fears about his capture of the rest of the Balkans. (In his famous Balkan carve-up with Churchill in October 1944, he had, after all, agreed to 90 per cent British 'preponderance' in Greece!) But if the Greek communists – aided and abetted by help from Albania, Yugoslavia and Bulgaria – could do it on their own, so much the better. At the same time Stalin put strong pressure on Turkey, not only for the surrender of the two Anatolian provinces of Kars and Ardahan on the Soviet border, but for Turkish approval of a

Soviet naval base in the Bosphorus. The Soviets seemed determined to impose on Turkey a 'quasi-Finnish' status.[9]

What followed over the next 20 years was one of the great international reversals in history. And, except for the bloody fighting of the last phase of the civil war in Greece, it came about without violence. First, Turkey, stiffened by US support, resisted Soviet demands and Stalin thought better than to press them. Then, also thanks to US support, the communists' strength in the Greek civil war ebbed and by 1949 they were defeated. Both Turkey and Greece, once in danger of becoming Soviet satellites, now became staunch Western allies. In 1952 both were admitted to the North Atlantic Treaty Organization (NATO).

Greece and Turkey were unachieved aims for Stalin, apples that did not fall into his basket. But worse was to come. Tito's Yugoslavia, regarded after the Second World War as the jewel in the Soviet Union's East European crown, broke with Moscow in 1948. This was the Soviet's first major post-war defeat in Europe, coming just as its East European empire appeared to be solidifying and less than four months after Czechoslovakia had become part of it.

The loss of Yugoslavia induced Stalin to tighten even more the Soviet grip on Eastern Europe. This he did through organizational means and through terror. But after his death the centrifugal forces he had temporarily checked asserted themselves once again, immediately in East Germany in July 1953 and then in Hungary and Poland in 1956. In the remaining three Balkan satellites – Romania, Bulgaria, and Albania – there were no such mass uprisings against communist rule. Control in these countries was too strict and efficient for popular feelings to express themselves, except to some extent in Romania immediately following the Hungarian Revolution.

But it was in the Balkans, much more so than in East Central Europe, that the phenomenon of *national communism* first emerged and then played a decisive role. This had already occurred in Yugoslavia in 1948. Within a decade it was affecting Albania, and shortly afterward Romania. The result was that, at the turn of the 1960s, Albania, first covertly and then overtly, bolted to the Chinese side in what was becoming the great schism in the communist world. By 1964 Romania, through nerve and skill, had achieved a remarkable degree of independence within the Soviet alliance and had the self-confidence to proclaim it. Bulgaria remained the only real Soviet dependency in South-eastern Europe. As the 1960s ended, although Moscow appeared to be strengthening its hold on East-Central Europe and was becoming more assertive in several other parts of the world, its position in the Balkans was in tatters.

The full story of this debacle has been told and interpreted many times,[10] but a brief explanation of why this happened and what the forces at work were that enabled this huge transformation to take place will be helpful.

In the first phase of the breakdown of Soviet power in the Balkans, two decisive factors interacted: the local will to resist and American willingness to support it. As already mentioned, Turkey resisted Soviet pressure from the start and its response called for a demonstration of American military support. The visit of the USS *Missouri* to Istanbul in 1946 was just the first step leading to Turkey's admission to NATO six years later. In Greece the domestic will to resist combined with American military and economic assistance led to the eventual defeat of pro-communist forces. The Americans' readiness to assume Britain's role in the region and the speed and determination with which they acted, shaped a historic turning point in world affairs. The Truman Doctrine in March 1947 not only saved Turkey and Greece, but signalled American determination to resist Soviet expansionism and marked the real beginning of the Cold War.

At the same time, in Yugoslavia Stalin was defied by a communist regime in power, not, as in the case of Turkey and Greece, by anticommunist regimes resisting communist encroachments. The Yugoslav leaders in 1948 also had no assurances or even apparent prospects of outside assistance in their struggle against the Soviet Union. In fact, their communist mind-set at the time may have excluded thoughts of Western assistance. But as the Soviet-led blockade began to bite and Yugoslavia became the object of every form of Soviet pressure except military attack, Yugoslav leaders began to change their minds. Western aid began first to seep and then to stream into Yugoslavia, enabling Tito to ward off Soviet pressure and later to mount his own political counter-attacks inside the Soviet bloc.

As Yugoslavia under siege became dependent on the US guarantee of its independence and territorial integrity, a change of US mind-set also became necessary. Helping anti-communist governments in Ankara and Athens was one thing, but intervening in a dispute involving two rigid communist regimes was another. But as the contours of the Cold War began to emerge more clearly, the position of the Soviet Union as the prime, even the only, enemy became clearer. As in the case of Nazi Germany in the Second World War, the victim of my enemy became my friend. Just as the Soviet Union had benefited from that dictum in the Second World War so now, in the changed circumstances of the Cold War, Yugoslavia was to benefit from it against the Soviet Union.[11]

The Decline in the Soviet Position: Post-Stalin Phase

The success of Yugoslavia's resistance against the Soviet Union was only really assured by Stalin's death in March 1953. In the cases of Turkey and

Greece, Stalin had probably resigned himself to his frustration as soon as it became obvious that to persist could mean a war in the eastern Mediterranean. But Yugoslavia was different: a communist state that had got away, and was to be reclaimed if at all possible. Outright attack was eventually ruled out; this also would most likely have led to a major war. But as long as Stalin lived, Tito's leadership could never feel safe from subversion.

After March 1953 the Yugoslav leaders could feel safe. Not merely that; they could feel confident. Stalin's successors adopted a new tactic of trying to entice rather than dragoon them back into the fold. Khrushchev's visit to Belgrade in 1955 began the long and sometimes zigzag course aimed at 'recovering Yugoslavia'. But, much as he desired a basic understanding with the Soviet Union, Tito insisted it be on the basis of independence and even equality. This attitude meant that the old satellite – even colonial – relationship could never be restored. The Soviets and the Yugoslavs knew it – and so did the United States and other Western powers.

Thus Stalin's death and the guarantee it meant for Yugoslavia marked the end of the *active* phase of US and Western involvement in the Balkans. After 1953 the erosion of Soviet power would result almost entirely from developments in the region, within the Soviet bloc and the world socialist camp, as a whole. It was caused by a combination of nationalism, ideology, and personality, and succeeded because of geography and the emergence of the Sino–Soviet dispute.

The Albanian leadership, under Enver Hoxha, felt that Albanian national integrity was threatened by Moscow's persistent courtship of Albania's historic enemy, Yugoslavia; it also clung tenaciously to 'Stalinism' in the face of Khrushchev's 'revisionist' onslaught. In any case, a deep personal antipathy developed between Hoxha and Khrushchev.[12] Once the conflict was joined, Albania could break with Soviet domination because it was too remote and, despite considerable strategic value to the Soviet Union, not important enough to be invaded. It could survive without the Soviet Union because, by the beginning of the 1960s, China had emerged as the great challenge to Soviet bloc leadership and was looking for allies. Albania became China's bridgehead in Europe, a relationship that lasted till 1978, enabling it to ward off the Soviet bloc's boycott.

The West played practically no role in Albania's defection from the Soviet Union. Although major Western powers like Italy and France maintained diplomatic relations with Tirana, as well as some economic relations, the 'capitalist' West, in general, was excoriated by Tirana in the same degree as the 'revisionist' Soviet Union. Both, in fact, were charged with being in collusion against Albania and other healthy Marxist-Leninist forces. No country was more excoriated than the United States. Assistance or support from that quarter was simply not wanted, and the many observers who predicted that Albania would follow the example of the Yugoslavs and become dependent on the West for survival were wrong. They had reckoned without Albanian stubbornness and China's will and capacity to help a distant ally.[13]

Romania's dispute with the Soviet Union involved a more complex process. In the first place, Romania was not geographically remote from the Soviet Union but adjacent to it and had been invaded many times by its eastern neighbour. Romania could not formally leave the Soviet-alliance; rather it sought the maximum manœuvrability inside it. In doing so it had recourse to a traditional Romanian strength, diplomacy – inside the world socialist movement, in the nonaligned world, and in the West. It exploited the Sino–Soviet dispute with remarkable success and sought safety in numbers in the Third World. But its most imaginative and rewarding forays were in the West, first in the Federal Republic of Germany and then in the United States. President Nixon's visit to Romania in 1969 and Ceauşescu's three visits to the United States during the 1970s symbolized what each side saw as an advantageous connection. Later, of course, the degeneration of Ceauşescu's domestic rule made Romania an embarrassment for the United States, but for several years Washington valued the connection. For Romania it provided support and reassurance. By the beginning of the 1980s, when the connection frayed and then broke, it was no longer crucial for Romania. The Soviet Union was no longer a danger.

It had probably ceased to be a direct danger long before that. The Soviets appear to have decided by the beginning of the 1970s that they had more to lose by trying to coerce Romania than by trying to contain it. Some evidence suggests that Khrushchev tried to unseat Ceauşescu's predecessor, Gheorghe Gheorghiu-Dej, in the early 1960s when the Romanian 'deviation' was getting underway, Ceauşescu himself later complained about Soviet commercial pressure several times after he had become party leader in 1965. Immediately after the Soviet invasion of Czechoslovakia in August 1968 there were widespread fears that a strike was being prepared against Romania, too, which had not only refused to join in the invasion but had also roundly condemned it. But by the turn of the 1970s it became evident to Moscow that the Romanian 'deviation' was not going to be contagious and that its own consolidation efforts in the Warsaw Pact alliance might succeed. In addition, the Sino–Soviet schism had become complete and confirmed; Romania could do little harm to the Soviet position by trying to manipulate the schism. As for relations with the capitalist West, these became standard operational procedures for the whole Soviet bloc during the 1970s; Romania was no longer the defiant exception. In fact, for the Western powers, now that the whole of Eastern Europe was opening up to them, Romania was no longer the attractive proposition it had once seemed to be. Its value had lain in its uniqueness. Take that away and its Western ratings tumbled.

Moreover, the serious deterioration in Romania's domestic condition neutralized its disruptive threat in Soviet eyes. In 1965 Ceauşescu had begun his rule promising to continue and broaden the tentative de-Stalinization begun under Gheorghiu-Dej. For at least five years he appeared to fulfil his promise. Improvement at home, together with a popular foreign policy – climaxed by his defiance of the Soviet Union in August 1968 – brought domestic support and even a certain legitimacy for the communist regime. From the early 1970s, however, for reasons not relevant here, the promising legacy of the 1970s steadily dissipated. By the end of the 1970s the Romania regime had become a byword for tyranny and misrule, a threat to nobody except its own people. Moscow, therefore, could sit back and wait. In an inverted way, even, Ceauşescu was an advertisement for Brezhnev's brand of 'real existing socialism', making it look good by comparison.

Finally, there was the geostrategic factor. Romania, tucked away in south-eastern Europe, bordering only communist states, was the least important to the Soviet Union of all the Warsaw Pact countries. Had any other member of the alliance attempted what Ceauşescu did, Moscow would have prevented it. In some respects, Ceauşescu was more a threat to Soviet hegemony than Dubček was in the Prague Spring in 1968. But Czechoslovakia, in the heart of central Europe where NATO and the Warsaw Pact directly faced each other, was coerced; Romania was not.[14]

Contrasting the situation and the fate of Czechoslovakia and Romania leads into the familiar 'Southern Tier' – 'Northern Tier' syndrome in Eastern Europe. This, of course, covers not only Romania but the other three Balkan communist countries as well. Until the appearance of Mikhail Gorbachev and the revolution in Soviet East European policy in 1989, the Warsaw Pact's Northern Tier states (the German Democratic Republic [GDR], Czechoslovakia, Poland, and Hungary) were considered indispensable to the Soviet Union, on the other hand, the quadrilateral of the Southern Tier came to be viewed as expendable, less valuable by every criterion than the states to the north. Although a persuasive enough proposition, it carries assumptions warranting debate in light of developments in Eastern Europe as a whole after 1988. Even here, though, it can be asked whether the retrospective rationalizing of Soviet setbacks in the Southern Tier did not influence the subsequent depreciation of the region's importance. Immediately after the Second World War, Soviet chances in south-eastern Europe looked distinctly promising, and, to repeat, this region had been the target of Russian ambitions for two centuries. Less vital to the security of the Soviet Union than the Northern Tier region and less economically valuable, it presented opportunities for expansion and, in general, was more important than it later became or was considered to be. It was later disparaged chiefly because the Soviet Union lost most of it and, for various reasons, could not get it back.[15]

The External Impact

For 20 years after the Second World War the politics of the Balkan countries – Turkey and Greece, as well as the communist states – were largely *outer-directed:* external factors played a major role in affecting their security and domestic stability. This was more true for some countries than for others, in terms of both degree and the time frame involved. The two noncommunist countries, Turkey and Greece, were externally secure by the beginning of the 1950s, and their security was assured by their entry into NATO in 1952. Yugoslavia's independence and integrity were assured by Stalin's death in 1953. But the tremors caused by the revolution in neighbouring Hungary in 1956 and the zigzag course of Tito's relationship with Khrushchev and the world communist movement in general continued to have a destabilizing potential on Yugoslav affairs – much less so than before 1953, but still enough to be distracting.

In the case of Albania, small and vulnerable, whose very creation in 1913 had been disputed by its neighbours, and yet important because of its location at the entrance to the Adriatic, it was inevitable that external factors would weigh heavily on its existence before and after the Second World War. Between 1945 and 1948 Albania, whose communist party had been founded by the Yugoslav Partisans in 1941, was practically a colony of Yugoslavia. When Tito broke with Stalin in 1948, the Albanian leadership, anxious to shake off Yugoslav control which they identified with historic Serbian expansionism, became a direct Soviet satellite. A remote patron was better than one next door. As long as Stalin was alive and Yugoslavia's pariah status continued, the Hoxha regime in Tirana could feel safe. But as soon as his successors began mending fences with Belgrade, Hoxha quickly perceived a new threat to Albania. There followed several years of unease and insecurity while the Albanian regime manœuvred away from Moscow and toward Beijing. After 1961, when the Soviet Union began openly criticizing Albania and the Sino-Soviet split solidified, Albania's evolution from Soviet to Chinese satellite was completed and confirmed. A remote patron had been changed for the remotest possible one. Although the relationship perhaps could not last, while it did it was a sustaining one for Albania, allowing the country to become more inner-directed than ever before in its brief history.[16]

This leaves Bulgaria, the blood-red incorruptible among the Balkan states. Sofia's loyalty to Moscow was not just set in bold relief by contrast with the policy of the other three communist states in the region; it drew attention in its own right. The cringing protestations of allegiance to Moscow, not only as the centre of the world communist movement but as the capital of Mother Russia, the beacon for all Slavs, gave Bulgaria – first under Georgi Dimitrov, then Vûlko Chervenkov, and finally under Todor Zhivkov's rule between 1954 and 1989 – the reputation of being the most loyal of all the East European satellites. In its economic development Bulgaria allowed itself to become tied to the Soviet economy to a much greater extent than any other East European country. In most foreign policy issues, too, the Sofia regime appeared at all times to toe the Soviet line.

For over 40 years, therefore, apparently content and comfortable, Bulgaria appeared to be the big Balkan exception. Its devotion to the Soviet Union, and Soviet willingness to cosset it economically, relieved Bulgaria of many of the external challenges that tested its neighbours. This did not mean that Bulgaria was inactive in foreign affairs. From the end of the 1950s to the 1980s it played an active role as a Soviet diplomatic agent, mainly but not exclusively in the Balkans. And since there was often a complementarity between the Soviet and Bulgarian *raison d'état,* the Bulgarian leadership could often argue that its policy was both in the national interest and that of world socialism as a whole.

It should not be assumed, though, that there was never anything but harmony between the master and the servant. There were several cases during the period of communist rule in Bulgaria when, through misunderstanding, faulty assumptions, or over-eagerness on Sofia's part (and occasionally a Schweik-like evasiveness) Soviet and Bulgarian policies were anything but identical. After 1985, there were clearly policy differences, especially over Bulgaria's treatment of its Turkish minority. In economic policy there must occasionally have been quite serious differences. For example, at the turn of the 1960s, when the Soviet Union, backed by Czechoslovakia and the GDR, was pressing for rationalization in COMECON (the Council for Mutual Economic Aid), Bulgaria, like Romania, must have been under considerable pressure to divest itself of much of its heavy industrialization programme. And while it was the Romanians and, typically, not the Bulgarians who carried the banner of national sovereignty, the latter must have supported them. In any event, the Bulgarians shared the fruits of victory with the Romanians and both went ahead unimpeded with comprehensive industrialization. Later, on the key issue of relations with West Germany, Bulgaria's eagerness for contacts with Bonn was clearly at variance with Soviet policy.

Still, allowing for the differences, Bulgaria's external relations, taking place against the stable background of Soviet protection, were relatively ordered and calm. They never took on an existential dimension in the way that the foreign policy of all five other Balkan countries did. In this regard, Bulgaria was always the exception.[17]

Instability from Within

By the end of the 1960s the immediate decisiveness of external influence on all six Balkan countries had become markedly reduced. The principal external constraints, the threats to their national integrity, and the independence of their governing processes had largely been removed.

This independence, of course, was relative. External influences could probably have been ultimately decisive. Until recently the whole history of the region since the end of the Second World War has developed under the sign of East-West confrontation and the Cold War. Turkey and Greece were both members of NATO, held the status of 'quasi front-line states' and were strongly under the political and military influence of the United States.[18] Economically both countries were moving into the West European economic orbit. Albania became economically dependent on China. Romania, despite its successful manœuvring against Moscow, was still a member of both the Warsaw Pact and COMECON and could do nothing about its inhibiting geographical adjacency to the Soviet Union. Bulgaria was sitting in the Soviet Union's lap. Yugoslavia, with its correct relations with the Soviet Union underpinned by a common ideological outlook (however great the differences), its relations with both Western Europe and the United States steadily improving, and its prestige in the nonaligned movement at its pinnacle, probably suffered the fewest constraints on its independence of action. But economic weakness and, in its southern part, sheer economic backwardness, still left it vulnerable and, in any case, subsequent developments would show just how precarious Yugoslavia's unity was.

But, still, all the countries concerned, with the partial exception of Bulgaria, had acquired a degree of inner direction that enabled them to conduct their domestic affairs and, in the framework of the different alliances to which all except Yugoslavia adhered, with a large degree of independence in foreign policy. The Balkan countries were not 'on their own', but, with the exception of Turkey, they were probably more in control of their own destinies than ever in their history.

It is in this context that subsequent Balkan developments are examined in the following chapters. This is done on two levels: At the national level, the efforts of the states concerned to achieve domestic stability, progress and legitimacy will be discussed; at the regional level the most significant multilateral and bilateral aspects. What emerges is the interplay between liberal democracy and nationalism, or the weakness of the former and the strength of the latter. It is the strength of nationalism and its grip over the body politic in all the countries of the region – albeit in varying degrees – that produces the instability for which the Balkans are historically notorious. And now that the stabilizing factor of the Cold War and the alliances it helped create are a matter of history, this instability has re-emerged with all its vigour, threatening not only the region concerned but possibly the peace of Europe.

Notes

1 Robert Lee Wolff, *The Balkans in Our Times* (Cambridge, MA, Harvard University Press, 1956), pp. 18–19.
2 Ibid., p. 19.
3 *Statistical Pocket Book on Yugoslavia* (Belgrade, March 1989).
4 Wolff, pp. 19–20.
5 Together with Wolff's book the following are highly recommended for background on Balkan history: Barbara Jelavich, *History of The Balkans*, 2 volumes (Cambridge, Cambridge University Press, 1983). For a most valuable collective work, see Charles and Barbara Jelavich (eds), *The Balkans in Transition* (Berkeley, University of California Press, 1963).
6 See M. S. Anderson, *The Eastern Question, 1774–1923* (London, Macmillan, 1966).
7 See James F. Clarke, *Bible Societies, American Missionaries, and the National Revival of Bulgaria* (New York, Arno Press, 1971).
8 Wolff, p. 23.
9 See F. Stephen Larrabee, *Balkan Security*, Adelphi Papers, No. 135 (London International Institute for Strategic Studies, 1976).
10 The best book on the subject is Paul Lendvai, *Eagles in Cobwebs: Nationalism and Communism in the Balkans* (New York, Doubleday, 1969).
11 The best analyses of Tito's break with Stalin, and its wider consequences, are Adam Ulam, *Titoism and the Cominform* (Cambridge, MA, Harvard University Press, 1952), and John C. Campbell, *Tito's Separate Road: America and Yugoslavia in World Politics* (New York, Harper and Row, 1967); on Yugoslavia after 1948 the best is Denison Rusinow, *The Yugoslav Experiment 1948–1974* (London, C. Hurst, for The Royal Institute of International Affairs, 1977).
12 See William E. Griffith, *Albania and the Sino–Soviet Rift* (Cambridge, MA, MIT Press, 1963); J. F. Brown, 'Albania, Mirror of Conflict', *Survey* (London), No. 40, January 1962.
13 See Michael Kaser, 'Albania under and after Enver Hoxha', in *East European Economies: Slow Growth in the 1980s, Selected Papers Submitted to the Joint Economic Committee, Congress of the United States* (Washington, DC, US Government Printing Office, 1988), Vol. 3, pp. 17–21. See also Paul Lendvai, *Das Einsame Albanien*

(Zurich, Edition Interfrom, 1985), pp. 73–6; Brown, *Eastern Europe and Communist Rule*, pp. 370–83.

14 See Brown, *Eastern Europe and Communist Rule*, pp. 263–93.

15 Ibid., pp. 33–6.

16 See note 13.

17 See J. F. Brown, *Bulgaria under Communist Rule* (New York, Praeger, 1970); Brown, *Eastern Europe and Communist Rule*, pp. 316–35.

18 See Monteagle Stearns, *Updating the Truman Doctrine: The U.S. and NATO's Southeastern Flank*, International Security Studies Program, Working Paper No. 86 (Washington, DC, The Wilson Center, 1989).

2 Turkey: Giant Re-emerging

A country of over 780 000 square kilometres (over 300 000 square miles), Turkey in 1990 had a population of about 55 million.

In A.D. 2000 the population is expected to be about 70 million, reaching about 100 million by about 2025.[1] (In 1923 its population was 13 million.) It is bordered by six important but widely different neighbours: Syria, Greece, Bulgaria, the former Soviet Union, Iran and Iraq. Reciting the names of those neighbours gives in itself some idea of how strategically important Turkey is. It stands at the crossroads between Europe and Asia and astride the Turkish Straits, the series of waterways connecting the Black Sea with the Mediterranean. In the course of the 1980s about half of the Soviet Union's total imports and about 40 per cent of its exports passed through these Straits.[2] Turkey shares a border with the former Soviet Union 620 kilometres long and, as a member of NATO with strong defences, stood for 40 years as an obstacle to whatever aggressive intentions the old Soviet Union may have had toward the Near East. It stands adjacent to the now unstable, possibly explosive, Caucasian republics of the disintegrated Soviet Union. At its south-eastern tip it is about 800 kilometres (500 miles) away from the Persian Gulf, 400 kilometres away from Bagdad. Its border with Iraq is about 300 kilometres long.

For 500 years Turkey was a European power, but solely by virtue of conquest. By every religious, cultural, political, administrative and economic criterion the Ottoman Empire was *sui generis*. It was only toward the end of the eighteenth century, with the Empire shortly to be diagnosed as the 'sick man of Europe', that farsighted Sultans realized that, only by taking Europe as a model, could there be any hope of recovery. In the first three quarters of the nineteenth century basic modernizing reforms were designed to achieve this, and military officers were in the vanguard of these reforms. Thus, as Turkey was being pushed physically out of Europe, it tried to draw more closely to the culture of Europe through its domestic reforms.[3] But the 'sick man' could not be cured. The remedies applied were superficial and only served to expose further the basic weaknesses. But these modernizing reforms of the nineteenth century paved the way for Mustafa Kemal ('Atatürk') and his followers in their building of the new Turkey to replace the Ottoman Empire after the First World War. Atatürk then instituted a political and cultural revolution that, in a far less violent way, paralleled the revolution taking place in neighbouring Russia. His ambition was to make the new Turkey indelibly European. He certainly made an immense impact.[4] But whether the imprint of his reforms went deep enough to survive the subsequent reaction, whether modernization could prevail over resurgent tradition, secularization over religion – these are the questions now preoccupying Turkey at the end of the twentieth century.

Atatürk's aim was to Europeanize Turkey domestically. But Turkish foreign policy between the two wars was preoccupied with settling problems lingering from the past – with Greece, for instance, and the new Soviet Union. It was the aftermath of the Second World War that projected Turkey westward, into a mainstream dominated not by Europe but by the United States.

Turkish relations with the Soviet Union before the Second World War had been correct, often cordial. Atatürk and Lenin admired each other, and Ankara's relations with the Soviet Union under Stalin were relatively unalarming. Much was made on each side during the interwar period of the fact that both were in the throes of revolution. But after the Second World War the relationship changed. Turkey found itself under strong Soviet expansionist pressure. Some of Stalin's demands were clothed in a spurious historical legitimacy: Kars and Ardahan, for example, had been part of the Tsarist empire until late in the nineteenth century. But his demand for a naval base in the Straits, first made during the war, was clearly aggressive although, again, he could argue that the Straits were more vital to the Soviet Union than they were to Turkey. This at least made his insistence on the revision of the Montreux Convention of 1936 regulating passage through the Straits appear reasonable.

Moscow's view of the Straits had in fact changed radically as Soviet naval ambitions grew. As a weak naval power Russia's aim had been to prevent foreign warships from getting out of the Mediterranean and into the Black Sea. But after 1945, as their naval programme expanded with their global ambitions, the Soviets' main aim was to get their *own* warships out of the Black Sea and into the Mediterranean. Hence, their efforts at loosening what they considered Turkey's fortuitous stranglehold on the crucial waterway. The Soviet Union was not alone in wanting the Montreux Convention revised, but because Moscow's proposals were made in the context of its threatening behaviour toward Turkey and at the beginning of the Cold War, they were bound to be rejected.[5]

Turkey's determination to resist Soviet pressure met with a ready response from Washington. In 1946 the U.S.S. *Missouri* visited Istanbul. In March 1947 the 'Truman Doctrine', guaranteeing the security of both Turkey and Greece, was announced in Washington. Realizing that Soviet pressure made its alliance with the United States irreversible, Turkey sent a crack brigade to Korea to fight with United Nations' (UN) forces. In 1952, along with Greece, it entered NATO, where because of its size, its strategic location, and its military strength, it soon assumed importance in the Western military alliance. During the 1950s the Turkish government strongly supported all American and Western initiatives in Europe and in the Near and Middle East. During the same period US and NATO bases were established on Turkish territory. The Turkish armed forces were expanded and re-equipped with more modern American weapons.

Turkey became both a bastion and an outpost, important on sea, land, and in the air. It controlled the Straits. It eventually deployed an army of about 800 000 men, thus holding down 21 Soviet divisions that could otherwise have been used on the Central European front. The NATO and American air bases and intelligence installations in Turkey in the 1970s accounted for 25 per cent of NATO's *hard* intelligence. After the loss of Iran in 1979, Turkey's already great importance in this regard correspondingly increased. Large American air bases, most notably that at İncirlik, near Adana, close to the eastern Mediterranean coast, allowed forward deployment of US tactical bombers and put them in striking distance of the Soviet Caucasus. Access to Turkish air bases came to be considered critical in case of emergency in the Persian Gulf. (This proved to be the case in 1991 when American planes used İncirlik as a base from which to bomb northern Iraq.) Turkey also provided early warning, using regional and sea surveillance capabilities that could warn the American Sixth Fleet in the case of attack.[6]

Diversifying Foreign Policy

Turkey's strongly pro-American foreign policy was supported by the main political groupings in the country. The Republican People's Party (RPP), founded by Atatürk, lost power in 1950 in the first democratic elections ever to be held in Turkey, but on foreign policy there was little difference between it and the Democratic Party that held office throughout the 1950s. The Turkish government's stance was as pro-American as that of the Greek government during this period, so much so that the rising generation in both countries, many of them drawn to left-wing politics – especially in Greece, where the legacy of the civil war hung heavily over political life –

charged that their governments had become American satellites, just as bound to their masters as the communist East European states were to theirs. As the Soviet threat receded, many Turks (as well as Greeks) began questioning the wisdom of putting all their eggs in the American basket. They agreed that, while the United States was Turkey's almost exclusive source of support, Turkey's rating was not all that high on the US priority list and might even go lower. Turkey would then have to start seeing its position in the world in proper perspective.

The need to do this became evident early in the 1960s. In October 1962, as part of the package settling the Cuban missile crisis, President Kennedy agreed to remove Jupiter missiles from Turkey, without having consulted the Turkish government. This caused serious misgivings among the Turkish military and in politically articulate circles generally, but the public-at-large was not greatly affected by it.[7] Then came President Johnson's warning to President İnönü in June 1964 that, if Turkey invaded Cyprus, NATO would not automatically come to its aid if the Soviet Union took the opportunity to move against it. The whole basis of Turkey's alliance with the West was shaken. For many Turks, Johnson's warning also offended their well-developed sense of *amour propre*. They felt that a national institution in the person of President İsmet İnönü – Atatürk's right-hand man, one of the heroes of the liberation war against the Greeks in 1922, and a great historical figure by any reckoning – had been treated by President Johnson as if he were an insignificant Third World upstart. Conversations with Turks some ten years later showed how fiercely the matter still rankled.[8]

It was then that Turkey began putting its eggs in more than one basket. It reopened a dialogue with the Soviet Union that had been interrupted at the end of the Second World War. In 1965 Soviet President Podgorny visited Ankara, symbolizing the start of a new era in Turkish foreign policy. Turkish–Soviet exchanges – military, political, but, above all economic – became numerous and brisk particularly during the 1970s.

The improvement of relations with the Soviet Union was only one part of the process of 'diversifying Turkey's foreign portfolio'.[9] At the same time relations were improved with East European countries. Turkey had enjoyed good relations with Yugoslavia since Tito's break with Stalin in 1948. In 1954, when relations with Greece were still cordial, Turkey, Yugoslavia and Greece joined in the so-called Balkan Pact, a defensive alliance forming, a link in a tenuous chain of alliances extending from Western Europe through to the Middle and Far East.[10] But as the historic Turkish–Greek enmity resumed after the middle of the 1950s and Soviet–Yugoslav relations eased as a result of Khrushchev's initiatives, the Balkan Pact fell into desuetude. In the 1960s, while maintaining its good relations with

Yugoslavia, Turkey also initiated better relations with the Soviet Union's East European satellites. With Bulgaria, for example – with which relations had been strained since Bulgarian independence in 1878, especially over the issue of repatriating members of the large Turkish community in Bulgaria – agreement was reached in 1964 on further repatriations, and for a time relations between the two neighbours improved.[11]

Turkey also expanded its relations with Western Europe, becoming an associate member of the European Economic Community in 1964, letting it be known that it aspired to eventual full membership. But even more important was the impact made by the *Gastarbeiter* phenomenon. The hundreds of thousands of Turkish workers and their families who came to Western Europe – most of them to West Germany, where 1.8 million were still living in the middle of the 1980s – made a solid if often unacknowledged contribution to Western Europe's economic progress.[12] But in Turkey, as one expert put it, they 'broke the old middle class monopoly on direct contact with the West – with social and cultural implications apparent only in future generations'.[13] They brought Europeanization into Turkey far more pervasively and effectively than Atatürk's revolution had done. Culturally, economically, and socially they spread their experiences into Anatolian towns and villages where that revolution had hardly penetrated. The returning *Gastarbeiter* were not necessarily pro-European. Many still smarted from the discrimination, often racism, they had experienced. But they all brought something of Europe back with them.

Subsequently, in the course of the 1970s and the 1980s, Turkey began to cultivate better relations with the Arab countries of the Middle East. Considerable distrust, at times tension, had always existed between the two sides. The Arab states resented Turkey as the former Ottoman overlord, and their religious sensibilities had been offended by the Atatürk's secularism. But economic complementarity began to bring the two sides together. Turkey was dependent on the Arab states – Iraq, Kuwait, Saudi Arabia and Libya – for oil and in return could export a whole array of products, including machinery, textiles, and processed foods.[14] Also, Turkish contractors and export-import traders became active throughout the Middle East. Thus, while the largely proletarian *Gastarbeiter* were breaking new ground in Western Europe, Turkish commercial representatives were restoring direct contacts between the educated elite and the Muslim Middle East that had been cut with the fall of the Ottoman Empire. In the 1980s, when Beirut collapsed due to civil war, Istanbul became headquarters for many Arab businesses and an increasing number of wealthy Arabs lived there.[15]

But Turkey's restored contacts with the Middle East began to extend beyond the commercial. The Muslim religion began its revival in Turkey after the Second World War as the impetus of Atatürk's revolution weakened and the Republican People's Party, the political arm of the revolution, lost its monopoly on power in 1950. By the 1980s Islam, including Islamic fundamentalism, had become important not only in the religious sense but also politically, socially and culturally. This process facilitated the strengthening of Turkish–Arab ties. Turkey joined the Islamic Conference Organization (ICO) which established headquarters in Istanbul. Although a moderate Islamic organization originally, many feared it could become a centre for Muslim extremism.[16]

Turkey's foreign policy after 1964, particularly its 'turn to the East', alarmed some Americans, who saw in it a weakening of Turkey's loyalty as a Western ally. But what Turkey was doing in the 1960s was reverting to the kind of multilateral diplomacy it had practised for centuries during the Ottoman Empire. For 500 years it had been an active player on the world diplomatic scene. This experience had developed a long-term perspective, a sharpness of perception, a realism of assessment, and a maturity of judgement that rarely deserted the diplomats of the Sublime Porte. There was no reason to fear it would falter now. In particular, Turkey was used to dealing with Moscow and parrying its aggressive tactics.

The Domestic Background

In 1992 the Turks were still trying to decide what kind of a state, polity, society and orientation they wanted. Nearly 70 years after the beginning of Atatürk's 'shock therapy' of Europeanization and secularization both Turkish state and society were still trying to adjust to it, recover from it, and modify it. In increasing numbers they were beginning to reject it. In the meantime enormous changes had affected the country: a huge population increase, social upheaval, massive economic development and a flood of diverse Western influences. For over 40 years this had taken place against a background of East–West tension in which Turkey played a front-line role. And, finally, in 1990, when East–West tension had largely disappeared, the Middle East was caught in crisis. Turkey was pitchforked into the world's dispute with Iraq; its external relations and its domestic situation would be affected for a long time to come.

Although emerging from almost total collapse after the First World War, the new Turkey still possessed important historic advantages. 'More than any "new nation" of the twentieth century, Turkey emerged in 1923 with both a tradition of government and a firm sense of self.'[17] In sharp contrast to the Ottoman Empire, it was largely homogeneous in both nationality and religion: 90 per cent Turkish; 98 per cent Muslim. But the new state had also taken over from the empire a strong governmental and diplomatic experience. And its struggle to be born, against the intentions of the great powers, and its victory in arms against the Greeks, gave the new Turkey a national myth that inspired and sustained.

What Turkey had always lacked was a tradition of representative government that could evolve into democracy. Moreover, Atatürk, imposing a revolution from above, had little empathy with democracy. (He toyed with the idea of introducing political competition but soon backed off through fear of anarchy.) The first phase of Turkey's post-Ottoman history was revolutionary, not democratic. It lasted beyond Atatürk's death in 1938, through the Second World War, and until 1950.

Atatürk's successor, İnönü, also had little instinctive sympathy with democracy, some of his associates considerably less. In addition the political, military, social and economic vested interests in the *status quo* were very strong. İnönü agreed to political democracy and free elections in response to two factors: to the growing domestic pressure from the urban intelligentsia and the growing economic entrepreneurial class; and to pressure from the West, particularly the United States. Even in an international situation inspired by fear of Soviet intentions many influential figures in the West, though recognizing Turkey's unique importance, were uneasy about its undemocratic internal order and many of its domestic procedures. These reservations have persisted – despite Turkey's strides toward democracy – and have dogged Turkey's relations with the West throughout the second half of the twentieth century. But in 1950 İnönü was able to oblige with free elections. Even more, he accepted their outcome, which was a staggering defeat for his own party. The newly formed Democratic Party under Adnan Menderes came to power and stayed there for ten years.[18]

The result of the election revealed in some respects the superficiality of Atatürk's revolution, especially in the sphere of secularization. The Democratic Party's victory in 1950 and Turkey's subsequent history have demonstrated the tenacity of Islam, the main divisive force in Turkish society and the body politic. But there were other divisions and sharpening conflicts: between classes, for example, the urban bureaucracy, landowners, peasants, the growing urban working class. Economic development in Turkey was now proceeding with great speed, providing many opportunities but also causing much hardship. Turkey simply lacked the social and economic structure to contain these 'contradictions', as the growing number of Marxists, of various shades, began to call them. These 'contradictions' have not led to the revolution these Marxists anticipated (and which some tried to foment), but they have caused the young Turkish democracy more than once to falter and to lurch into chaos. Even in 1992 it is still not certain that

Turkish democracy can stand on its own feet without the support and sometimes the guidance of the military.

The Military in Politics

The importance, the sacrosanct character of the military in modern Turkey is difficult to portray. Some aspects were inherited from the Ottoman Empire where the military caste was synonymous with government. But, in periods of almost continuous conflict, its exclusive task was to fight, often leaving administration to lesser orders. From the middle of the nineteenth century, however, a growing number of officers – Atatürk was the outstanding example – became the spearhead of change, eventually the makers of revolution. Atatürk's revolutionary Turkey saw the culmination of this process whereby the military became the integrating force of state, responsible in the last analysis for the whole of public life: the true and comprehensive national guardian.

Most people supported the army's three well-executed military interventions in 1960, 1971, and 1980 because many Turks associated politicians with chaos and corruption. The army they associated with patriotism and honesty. Politicians disturbed them, soldiers reassured them. As a Turkish journalist wrote in 1982:

> The Turkish armed forces are an integral part of the Turkish people ... When problems were at their worst and hopelessness spread among the people, these same problems and feelings affected the armed forces. At this point [i.e., in September 1980, when the most recent coup took place] the armed forces intervened to perform what the people were powerless to do.[19]

The Turkish officer corps continues to be a meritocracy representing the brightest and best from the main sections of society. A 1980 survey of students at the Ankara military academy showed that '29 per cent were sons of workers or peasants, 24 per cent sons of civil servants or teachers, and 18 per cent sons of officers or noncommissioned officers and the rest of a variety of other backgrounds'.[20]

The three military interventions were designed to 'cure' democracy, not to set it aside permanently. The officers intervened – at least ostensibly – not to take power, but to help democracy back on to its feet. The first time was in May 1960 against the Menderes government, though then, despite serious student disorders in Istanbul, it was not so much chaos that prompted the action as the alleged economic, political, and personal misdeeds of Menderes and his associates. These misdeeds certainly occurred: the country was drifting towards bankruptcy and Menderes seemed intent on perpetuating his party's corrupt rule. But many observers believed that the army was also bent on a personal vendetta against Menderes, the man whose party ten years before had broken the one party rule they supported. Certainly his subsequent trial and execution damaged Turkey's international reputation and created a bitterness in Turkish politics that lasted many years.

In March 1971, the issue was more clear-cut: political anarchy and social chaos did threaten. This military action was less a full-scale intervention and more a 'rap over the knuckles' for the Turkish political establishment. In view of what was to come, it would have been better for Turkey had it been more radical. It only temporarily slowed the massive drift toward anarchy.

In the late 1970s, when the 'contradictions' mentioned earlier came to a head and the economic situation was rapidly deteriorating, Turkey seemed on the brink of civil conflict. The military intervention in 1980 – this time a full-scale *coup d'état* – therefore had widespread support and was by common consent the most 'necessary' of the three military interventions in the democratic era.[21]

The new military government, led by army chief of staff General Kenan Evren, though not bent on permanent power, was determined to produce systemic change, a new situation that would preclude the necessity for future interventions. At first the new military administration seemed unwilling to surrender power. Whereas in 1960 and 1971 the officers were quick to leave politics, after 1980 they showed every sign of hanging on. As *The Times* of London wrote as late as August 1983, 'it looks as though what is planned is not, after all, the restoration of democracy but the legitimation of military rule'.[22] Such speculation turned out to be groundless, but the military determined to take their time about handing power back to the civilians and to avoid the mistakes of their predecessors in 1960 and 1971. But in some ways, the military had only themselves to blame for the political instability between 1961 and 1980. In 1963 they gave up power after having earlier approved a constitution that permitted a political situation to develop like that in the Weimar Republic in inter-war Germany. The new 1961 constitution made for both a weak executive and legislature. The electoral procedure was governed by a system of proportional representation that made a stable government impossible. Although changes were made after the second military intervention in 1971, the constitution still remained too 'loose' an instrument in a country where a frail democracy was beset by a severe economic crisis.

The new constitution, approved by a referendum in November 1982 by well over 90 per cent of the population, emphasized the strength of the executive and was a typical military response to the 'looseness' of its predecessor. It made General Evren president for seven years. It preserved the National Security Council (NSC), established under the 1961 constitution, and a Presidential Council was formed to advise the president and the cabinet. The NSC had its powers both enlarged and more sharply defined. For some time afterward it was the key to the whole governing structure. This body, in which military officers played an important role, passed on its views to the president on any matter it considered important to Turkey's external and internal security.

The new constitution was also strongly presidential. The president could dissolve parliament and call new elections if the government lost a confidence vote in parliament. He appointed the chief of the general staff, the members of the constitutional court and all university rectors. He could preside, if he wanted, over both the NSC and the Council of Ministers. Together with the Council of Ministers he could proclaim a partial or a full state of emergency, although parliament had the authority to rescind such an emergency decree. The acts of the president were not subject to judicial review. Trade unions, professional organizations, and university faculty members were not allowed to engage in political activity, and political parties could not form auxiliary organizations. The ban on Marxist, Islamic, and Kurdish national parties continued. There were provisions for a rigorous press censorship.

Generally there was a strong bias against political parties in the new constitution. Evren himself said that political parties should not be the pivot of political life but should rather concentrate on making for a more effective administration. This prejudice was shown in the constitutional provisions that received much attention in the West: those prohibiting the former political parties and banning 100 of their best known members from politics for ten years.[23] Former premiers like the conservative Suleiman Demirel and the socialist Bulent Eçevit were therefore barred from public life.

The intervention of the generals in 1971 had been prompted by the inability of the civilian authorities to cope with a mounting terror mainly organized by Marxist-Leninist students in the universities, technical colleges, and high schools. The military remained a watchdog authority until 1973 and then withdrew from politics. What followed was certainly the most degrading and lawless period in the Turkish republic's history.

By 1980 the country was practically in a state of civil war. Over 13 000 people had been killed or wounded. More than 20 political killings occurred each day.[24] The executive was practically powerless to intervene, partly because of the feebleness of the 1961 constitution, and partly because neither of the two big parties – the Justice Party (Demirel) and the

Republican People's Party (Eçevit) – had an absolute majority in parliament. Not only Demirel, the conservative, but also the left-wing Eçevit had become dependent on extreme *right*-wing groups, many of whose followers were responsible for some of the bloody violence. Add to this a bitter personal and destructive animosity between Demirel and Eçevit, and it is small wonder that disillusionment with civilian rule had become overwhelming.

By its decisive ability to stop the slaughter in 1980, the Turkish military emerged with enhanced credibility, in spite of its mistake in 1973 in leaving so flawed a constitution. It not only ensured stability at home but left no doubt that it would keep Turkey firmly on the side of the West. General Evren, in particular, was known to be strongly pro-American.

But amid the approval, both at home and in the West, for the army's action and the continuing respect for it as an institution, serious misgivings were expressed about the military government's attitude towards human rights. In Turkey itself the concern was largely among intellectuals, many of whom were the victims of human rights abuse, but from the West came a mounting outcry. The Council of Europe suspended Turkey's membership in early 1984, thereby eliciting an unconciliatory and uncharacteristically tactless response from General Evren himself. Some reports about judicial breaches and atrocities in Turkish jails may have been exaggerated. But, allowing for all the exaggerations and for specific Turkish conditions, there were far too many violations of human decency to be ignored.[25]

What seemed like totally unnecessary purges in the government bureaucracy and particularly in higher education occurred. In the spring of 1983 the universities were purged, not just of Marxists but of many liberal or left-leaning professors, including some of Turkey's most distinguished scholars. In some areas in public life a vendetta atmosphere was allowed to generate and, again, the Turkish response was hardly that of a government seeking to reassure a basically sympathetic but increasingly perturbed outside world. It often seemed to be another case of the military venting its spleen against sections of society it misunderstood or despised.[26]

And overshadowing these issues was the question whether the Turkish military's own view of itself and its role might not be changing, whether military rule might now be seen not as a means to save democracy but rather as an end in itself. Unquestionably, some Turkish generals enjoyed power. But even some of those who viewed their situation more modestly began to ask questions about the suitability of Western democracy for Turkey. Many civilians were asking the same question too. But the point at issue here was that the army seemed to be claiming for itself the exclusive right to answer it. As one observer put it, the army had 'for decades arrogated to itself a residual power in the constitution, in accordance with

Kemalist principles'.[27] This was the crux of the matter: the military, not the civilian authority, would decide when and whether it should act. In the last analyses, therefore, the army was above the civil authority, even above the law – the guardian answerable only to itself and its traditions. Atatürk himself did not believe in military rule. He sought, and received, wide civilian support. But he did see the military as the self-appointed and self-motivating guarantor of civilian rule.

As late as 1988, when democracy in Turkey looked stable, President Evren repeated this historic Kemalist view of the army's role: The military had the *right,* not just the duty, of political supervision. Political leaders across the spectrum were incensed. Some admitted that military intervention might still, at some future date, be necessary. But it must be for the *political* leaders to decide if, when, and how, this should take place.[28] This could still become a crucial constitutional issue in Turkey. In a situation of political, social, and economic chaos, complicated, even caused, by a burgeoning Islamic fundamentalism, it could again be the military that reserves for itself the decision of whether and when to act.

Misgivings about the military's view of its role were hardly quieted by the carefully prepared, restrictive general elections it allowed in November 1983, after three years of military government. But the results of those elections restored everybody's faith in the independence of the Turkish electorate. For the military it was the same kind of miscalculation that İsmet İnönü and his associates made in allowing the first free general elections in 1950. The officers were simply out of touch with the electorate. Of course, the miscalculation this time was not as momentous as it had been then. What had seemed an earthquake in 1950, was only 'one in the eye for the generals' 33 years later.[29]

The election scenery was also quite different than it had been previously. The old parties had been disbanded and new ones rather laboriously created. And in the place of the old barred political leaders new, largely unknown, figures emerged. The military clearly favoured the National Democratic Party, led by one of their own, retired General Turgut Sunalp. But the decisive winner was Turgut Özal's Motherland Party (ANaP). It was a huge personal triumph for Özal and a humiliating defeat for Evren, who had strongly backed Sunalp.[30] But, like his predecessor in 1950, Evren accepted the result with constitutional propriety and good grace personally.

The Özal Decade

Turgut Özal dominated the political life of his country in a way no other recent politician did except Margaret Thatcher in Britain. Like Thatcher, he brought about a revolution. Whether it will be a lasting revolution is open to question. What cannot be questioned is the impact it made.

Özal began his political career as an unsuccessful local candidate for the National Salvation Party, a Muslim grouping that played a considerable role in the political manœuvrings of the 1970s. This party was clearly outside the post-Ottoman political mainstream of secularism, tolerance and Westernism – in fact, it was partly a reaction against it. But it had nothing to do with Khomeini's Islamic fundamentalism, although Islam has been an essential part of both Özal's public and private persona. In him two key elements in Turkish political culture during the last quarter of the twentieth century found their expression. The first was the Islamic revival or, more correctly, the re-emergence of Islam after Atatürk's efforts to relativize it. The second was the development of the entrepreneurial spirit and the growth of a capitalist class. He was not exactly an originator in the latter. This entrepreneurial-Islamic duality had begun with Menderes and was developed by Suleiman Demirel. But it was Özal who did in economics what Atatürk had tried to do 50 years before in politics, education, science, and culture. He broke the existing mould.

The end of the 1970s brought an entrepreneurial milieu smart and self-confident enough to stand up to a deeply entrenched governmental bureaucracy. Özal was their spokesman. He was helped not only by the domestic situation but also by the international environment. With President Reagan in the United States and Margaret Thatcher in Britain, the successes of the newly industrializing countries of the third world, and the terminal illness of Soviet-style socialism, the 'market' had become almost *de rigueur.*

But the modern side of Özal's political makeup should not be stressed at the expense of the traditional. He is known to have expressed admiration for Japan with its mix of technology and tradition. He has taken the *hajj* (pilgrimage) to Mecca at least once and is a member of an Islamic religious order that is still officially banned. For him there is no incompatibility between Mecca and the market: the two are complementary and mutually reinforcing.[31]

Özal, put in charge of the military government under Evren, faced an economic crisis to which he responded with a tough austerity programme which the military supported. As Evren himself said in the summer of 1983: 'We cannot rely on foreign credit or worker's remittances anymore ... the only way is to export. We have to search for markets at the furthest corners of the world, in China, Korea and elsewhere.'[32] This policy inevitably caused social dissatisfaction, but because of civil restrictions imposed by the military government, it was seldom expressed. In fact, Turkey's move to the market in the 1980s was not accompanied by the expansion of democracy but was facilitated by its denial. Yet in its early stages the majority of Turks preferred the order of the generals to the chaos of the politicians they had endured in the 1970s. In March 1984, Özal's government won strong backing in the Turkish local elections.

The policy began to show results. Exports rose by over 60 per cent in 1981 and over 20 per cent in 1982. Inflation dropped from about 130 per cent in 1980 to just under 30 per cent in 1982. The previous negative economic growth was reversed by a 4.4 per cent rise in the Gross National Product (GNP) in 1982 – this mainly the result of greatly increased exports. Turkey, therefore, moved from a position of not being able to service its foreign debt – estimated at $18 billion in early 1983 – into one of being able to repay over $2 billion in 1982 and in 1983 it was able to pay off another $2.4 billion. These successes improved Turkey's world credit rating and in July 1983, for the first time since 1976, an unconditional syndicated bank loan of $200 million was secured on the international money market.[33]

After his election victory in 1983, the positive side of Özal's policy began to function. Briefly, the principles he and his Motherland Party (ANaP) espoused were: encouragement of the private sector; encouragement of private capital flow; a competitive market economy; the privatization of the existing State Economic Enterprises, and the restriction of public sector investments to projects relating to the infrastructure. The general strategy to be adopted was one of an open economy and export-led growth, as opposed to domestic-market orientated or import-substitute industrialization.

These policies achieved some striking results. The Turkish economy in the 1980s grew at an average annual rate of about 8 per cent, one of the highest growth rates in the world. By the end of the 1980s the Turkish Chamber of Commerce claimed that 75 per cent of Turkey's industry was 'ready or nearly ready to compete with Europe's'. Turkish exports during the 1980s, especially of industrial goods, had strongly increased. The foreign debt had been paid off to the point where extra credit was now easy to obtain. Özal himself was quoted by *The New Yorker* in June 1989 as saying that 'the combination of political stability, infrastructural improvements and economic reforms had brought in 2 billion dollars in foreign investment'.[34] He claimed that Turkey was ready for Europe. It had a 'young economy'. With a population of 70 million by the turn of the century, 'we will offer a huge market to Europe'. Turkey would also bring a 'new dimension to the European community'.[35]

The achievements of this liberal–capitalist approach, evident in the outward modernization of Turkey, won great international acclaim, particularly in the United States. At the same time considerable weaknesses began to show, and serious questions began to be asked, similar to questions being asked about the performance of other liberal–capitalist economic programmes, especially in Great Britain. The great weakness of Özal's policy was always its inability to control inflation. The haste to modernize the country had caused big budget deficits which had, in turn, stoked inflation. In 1982 the inflation rate was just over 36 per cent. In 1984 it had jumped to 53.5 per cent. It then dropped quite dramatically to 24.6 per cent in 1986, but after that began to climb alarmingly. In 1988 it was nearly 70 per cent and, after a slight drop, was over 75 per cent at the beginning of 1989.[36]

But the rising inflation rate was not the only criticism levelled at Özal. Some critics had prepared a comprehensive indictment of his whole policy. These critics included not only those who still clung to the *étatist* policies of Atatürk and his successors, but also some strong supporters of liberal capitalism. These 'capitalist' critics doubted the genuineness and permanence of what Özal claimed he had achieved.

They tended to concentrate on the obvious weaknesses: inflation, budget disequilibrium, and rising deficits. They accepted that striking increases had been made in GNP growth rates and in exports, as well as decreases in the current account deficit, but they argued that these achievements were superficial in several key aspects. The increase in the growth rate of GNP, they said, had affected unemployment and the labour surplus problem only slightly and, in any case, these problems were much greater than official statistics dared admit. Regarding one of the government's proudest achievements – export growth – they argued that the figures had been highly inflated because of the relative decline in the value of the dollar. These critics were also skeptical about claims that the government had substantially reduced the historically swollen public sector. They argued that, whatever might have been achieved in privatizing the State Economic Enterprises (SEEs), the *total* public sector, comprising the consolidated budget, local administrations, various social funds, as well as some newly created SEEs had actually increased.[37]

Such criticisms of Özal's economic policy, accompanied by serious charges levelled against his style and manner of government, increased toward the end of the 1980s. As one commentator wrote, 'many fields of achievements are suspect with waste, corruption, partisanship as well as nepotism; an exaggerated "spoils system" at its very worst'.[38] There were also charges of statistical manipulations and, occasionally, downright falsifications.

On corruption and nepotism Özal was undoubtedly vulnerable. Whether there was more corruption in the 1980s than in some previous decades since the death of Atatürk was open to question. The Menderes decade, for example, with which the Özal decade has some similarities, was inordinately corrupt. But as Özal became more successful and confident and, as the prospect of renewed military intervention became much less likely – causing *inter alia,* the memory of the vengeance wreaked on Menderes to recede even further – he appeared to become indifferent to questions of public probity.

Although Özal himself lived relatively modestly and seemed personally untouched by financial scandal, the same could not be said about many of his associates. In any case big businessmen and contractors close to the government, as well as mayors of big cities and smaller cities, and businessmen and contractors close to them, reaped big profits in terms of various export, credit, and tax privileges. As for nepotism, Özal seemed totally unconcerned about the criticism. He placed unqualified relatives in important governmental positions. Towards the end of the 1980s it appeared that he was grooming his brother Korkut, already a wealthy banker, to succeed him as prime minister while he made his bid for the presidency to succeed General Evren. He later, however, dropped Korkut whose Islamic fundamentalism proved an embarrassment and who in any case had fallen foul of Özal's wife, Semra, a robust personality in her own right and much more Kemalist (loyal to the Atatürk tradition) than her husband.[39]

Even more serious was Özal's view of his own relationship to the political process. The 1982 election law, designed to prevent the governmental instability of the 1960s and 1970s, imposed a 10 per cent total vote threshold at the national level as well as limits at the local level. In the November 1983 general elections these limitations enabled Özal's Motherland Party (ANaP) to get an absolute majority of 53 per cent of the seats in the new parliament with only 43 per cent of the total votes cast. Although governmental stability resulted, some Turks privately expressed their concern about the extent of the safeguards. During the course of this newly elected parliament even further safeguards in the electoral system were introduced to 'reinforce' this stability. The intended electoral manipulation was here so transparent that two opposition parties led by former premiers Bulent Eçevit and Suleiman Demirel, recently allowed to return to politics after the ban on them was lifted, wanted to boycott the next elections, which took place in November 1987. But the largest opposition party, the Social Democratic Populist Party (SHP) led by Erdal İnönü, son of the late President İnönü, refused to join any boycott. Eçevit and Demirel felt obliged to take part in what they considered a prearranged election.

ANaP, with only 36 per cent of the popular vote, got 65 per cent of the parliamentary seats, giving ANaP the number of seats necessary to decide singlehandedly in the parliament on a referendum to change the constitution. It was just a few seats short of the two-thirds majority needed for parliament to change the constitution without having recourse to a referendum. Few would deny, as one observer commented, that this result went 'much further than an effort to maintain political stability ... or a compromise between the principle of proportional representation and a desire to avoid coalitions'.[40]

On the face of it this general election of 1987 put Özal and his Motherland Party in an impregnable position. But this election, in fact, signalled a sharp downward turn in Özal's popularity. The electoral system had obviously become fixed in the interests of the Motherland Party, however the electorate might vote. The opposition parties, taking nearly two-thirds of the countrywide vote, had finished up with only one-third of the parliamentary seats. Resentment grew over Özal's apparent contempt for democratic practice combined with his obvious attempts to manipulate the media. In the meantime, economic dissatisfaction continued to increase. At the local municipal elections in March 1989, the Motherland Party came in a humiliating third with only 21 per cent of the votes behind the Social Democrats and Demirel's conservative True Path Party. Opinion polls taken during the following spring and summer indicated only about 15 per cent support for it.[41]

Özal was obviously at the lowest point of his political career in terms of public acceptance. But despite this, or because of it, he announced his candidacy for the presidency of Turkey to be vacated by Evren at the end of October 1989. Since the president is elected by parliament, Özal's success was assured because of the Motherland Party's absolute majority there. But the majority of the electorate clearly opposed his election, and the opposition parties declared that if they won the next parliamentary elections in 1992, they would not accept his presidency. Apart from Özal's waning popularity in the country at large there were two other serious objections to his becoming president: first, the head of state was supposed to be politically impartial – and Özal could never be that; second, he was not supposed to interfere in a whole range of political activities – and Özal was also clearly incapable of such self-denial.

Many Turks felt affronted by Özal's succession to the presidency, an office which to them was something historically special. As David Barchard wrote:

> Mr. Özal's election ... is a watershed in the country's history. The Turkish President plays a pivotal figurehead role in the state and the position has traditionally been occupied by retired military commanders, beginning with Atatürk and İnönü in the 1920s and 1930s. The President acts as the repository of the values of the higher bureaucracy and is expected to be the guardian of the state and its values against challenges from below by elected politicians.[42]

Immediately after his election as president it became obvious that Özal was not going to accept the traditional or even the statutory limitations on the activity of its incumbent. He chose his own successor as prime minister, Yildirim Akbülüt, a colourless figure distinguished only by his loyalty to Özal. He also made it clear that he would be his own foreign minister.[43] In visits to the United States and France, in February 1990, for example, Özal behaved as head of government rather than head of state. He also actively interfered in the affairs of the Motherland Party although, as president, he should have officially severed all links with it. In short, Özal considered himself above the constitution, that the presidency made no difference to his activities and powers. Rather, it gave him extra powers, plus the institutional prestige he had never had as prime minister. The Gulf crisis in the summer of 1990 only enhanced his role and his view of it. For the time being, because of both the seriousness of the crisis and the important role it gave Turkey in world politics, most Turks seemed willing to let Özal, with his undoubted ability, experience and world standing, speak for them. But when the crisis passed he would face internal and international consequences which could seriously weaken him.

The internal consequences were not long in coming. In the parliamentary elections held in October 1991 the Motherland Party lost its majority and Prime Minister Mesut Yilmaz, who had recently replaced Akbülüt, submitted his resignation. The Motherland Party finished second behind the True Path Party (Demirel) and only slightly ahead of the Social Democrats (İnönü). Though it was not as resounding a defeat as many had expected, the poll result was still an expression of widespread dissatisfaction with Özal. Worse still, it threatened another period of instability and bitterness in Turkish politics. The election victor, Suleiman Demirel, was a sworn personal enemy of Özal, and during the election campaign his declared aim was to topple Özal from the presidency. After the election Demirel was more cautious, but few Turks believed in the possibility of these two men working together for long. Few Turks also considered that the new coalition government of the True Path Party and the Social Democrats could work effectively. True Path stood for free enterprise and the market, while the Social Democrats, though also espousing market principles, also stood for a strong element of state ownership and intervention. Perhaps even more ominous was the strong showing at the polls of the Islamic and national parties. They were not in government, but they could be if the present coalition failed to work. And the military? Some Turks were not so confident now that it was out of politics permanently.

Historical Problems Returning

The weaknesses that have just been discussed were serious and growing by the middle of 1992. Nevertheless, despite the dangers Turkey was still stronger and healthier politically and economically than it had been since democracy was introduced in 1950. The situation with regard to human rights was incomparably better than it had been ten years earlier. In 1980, immediately after the military coup, there were conservatively estimated to be about 200 000 political prisoners. Additional repressive measures were also taken that affected hundreds of thousands more citizens. Trade unions were forbidden; strikes were punishable. Whatever legal safeguards that did exist for the individual in Turkey were often disregarded. Detention without trial had become a common feature of life. Education, intellectual life and journalism were most gravely affected. Torture of prisoners, suspects, and even temporary detainees was used to an extent that suggested calculated policy. Only Albania and Romania in Europe presented a grimmer picture than Turkey. As a *New Yorker* reporter wrote:

> If the positive side of the [military] "intervention" was that the Army gave Turgut Özal the authority to modernize the economy, the negative is that it unleashed a downward spiral of contempt for human rights ... [44]

By the end of the decade there had been clear improvement. In July 1989 the number of political prisoners had shrunk to an estimated 5000.[45] After the restrictiveness of military rule political life had become much freer. Extreme left-wing activity was still officially banned, but some left-wing groups operated with relative freedom. Considerable pressure was growing for the legalization of an official Turkish communist party. There was generally a more mature attitude to dissent, which itself had become more mellow, more restrained and peaceful. Many of the young extremists who had caused the chaos of the 1960s and 1970s had now matured. Certainly, the collapse of communism in Eastern Europe and the changes in the Soviet Union at the end of the 1980s had deprived many left-wing activists of their potential support as well as their own psychological and intellectual *raison d'être*.

Much of the militant left-wing activity in Turkey during the 1980s focused on the Kurds in south-eastern Anatolia. On the Kurdish issue, communism and frustrated nationalism coalesced, as it had done in parts of Eastern Europe in the 1920s and 1930s. The Kurds, a people numbering about 20 million, spread themselves through northern Iraq, Syria, Iran, the Soviet Union, and Turkey. There are believed to be more than 10 million of them in Turkey, accounting for about 15 per cent of the total population.[46]

Because they are Muslims, they have never been granted minority status, or even cultural autonomy. Most Turks still refuse to regard them as ethnically different from themselves and dub them 'Mountain Turks'. Many Kurds strongly resent this description. A large number, though, have submitted with varying degrees of readiness to the integration process. Some 30 members of the Turkish parliament in 1989 were Kurds. Moreover, there has been much racial intermingling over the centuries. Many Turks are partly Kurdish. Özal himself readily admits that he may have Kurdish blood.[47] Most Kurds would be satisfied with cultural autonomy, with safeguards for the use of their language. Many Turkish political figures had begun to support them and considered it only a matter of time before this was granted. But, though there was considerable moderation to be found on the issue, there was also much implacability. Kurdish militancy generated Turkish intolerance.

The Kurdish question re-emerged with a vengeance during and after the Gulf War in 1991. The Kurdish uprising in northern Iraq in the aftermath of Saddam Hussein's defeat in Kuwait led to the poring over into Turkey of tens of thousands of Kurdish refugees. This exposed the raw nerve of Turkey's own seemingly intractable Kurdish problem. At the same time, in efforts to silence foreign critics of Turkey's attitude to the problem, but also with a degree of sincerity on his part, Özal publicly lifted the previous ban on the speaking of Kurdish in public. It was a long overdue concession but it was furiously opposed by many Turks and became an important political issue.[48] Suleiman Demirel, however, appointed premier in October 1991, was offering even greater concessions to the Kurds. At the same time Kurdish agitation, and acts of terrorism by militant Kurdish groups, increased, provoking Turkish military reprisals that to many seemed excessive. By the end of 1991 the 'Kurdish problem' was growing rather than receding.

This is the background to the increased official repression throughout the 1980s, often accompanied by illegalities, brutality, and even atrocities on the part of the police and army. These were ostensibly in response to guerrilla activity, instigated and often led by the Kurdish Workers' Party (PKK), a Marxist-Leninist group operating in the Taurus Mountains and across the border of Syria, Iraq, and Iran. These guerrillas often terrorized Kurdish villages into giving them at least passive support and presented a small but serious problem to the military authorities in south-eastern Turkey. The problem still remained unsolved. In the meantime it had had two important consequences; one for Turkey's international reputation and the other for its domestic political situation. As the human rights situation in Turkey generally improved during the 1980s, international attention focused more on the Kurdish situation. Turkey's refusal to grant the Kurds minority status as well as the repressive measures used against them were condemned as serious breaches of human rights. The extreme left's association with the violence and terrorism of the Kurdish fringe alienated many Turks from leftist politics.

In March 1992 the Kurdish problem exploded to the very forefront of Turkish domestic politics and Turkey's international relations. Conciliatory gestures by the new Demirel government were exploited by the PKK, which incited some sections of the Kurdish population in the extreme south-east of Turkey to demonstrations that the government had forbidden. The government's response was massive and brutal, involving the use of force often against innocent civilians. The government rejected Kurdish demands for autonomy, and its policy and actions were supported by the vast majority of the Turkish population. But the goal, set by Atatürk, of assimilating the Kurds had been shown to be unattainable and more tension was expected. Abroad, Turkey was severely criticized, especially by Germany, with which relations took a sharp turn for the worse. This only increased the Turks' conviction that Europe was against them.

As industrialization and urbanization became the two dominant economic and social trends in Turkey in the 1960s, the different Marxist groups that dotted the Turkish political landscape had greatly increased their strength and support. Now, some 30 years later, with the social effects of Turkey's economic development so much more serious, with large-scale destitution and pauperization presenting a stark contrast with the growing general prosperity, it was not the political left but Islam that derived advantage from the situation. Islam had moved into the vacuum left by the eclipse of the Turkish left.

Islam, therefore, became not just a religious and cultural force in Turkey but also a political, economic, and social one. It was not just traditional but also modern, appealing not only to the ageing and conservative, but to the young and progressive. Mention has already been made of the Muslim revival after the Second World War. It had then been considered a reaction against the Kemalist cultural revolution, the past weighing against the present, the countryside striking back at the cities, the East reasserting itself against the West. In the early 1990s it was still all those things. But the true significance of the Islamic revival in Turkey was that, while still retaining its spiritual and traditional values, it also addressed some of the most pressing material problems of the present. Nor was it now essentially a rural phenomenon. It was present in the burgeoning slums and shanty towns of the big cities, especially Istanbul, full of migrant peasants from Anatolia. As Graham Fuller describes it, 'urban discontent and the psychological dislocations that come with rapid urbanization lie at the heart of the Islamic challenge'.[49]

But contemporary Islam also appealed to intellectuals, and the economic and technical intelligentsia. It had a growing following among older school children, students, and the central and municipal bureaucracies.[50] Religious political parties were still banned, but the Muslim influence in the Motherland Party and Demirel's True Path Party was strong. There were many religious newspapers, although officially they were not allowed to engage in political propaganda. There were 65 000 mosques in the country, one for every 800 citizens.[51] Classes in the Muslim religion were taught in state schools, and many private Islamic schools had recently been established. The 'Westernizing secularists' in Turkey showed particular concern about Islamic inroads on the university campuses, once considered a bastion of 'modernism'. This encroachment was dramatized by the issue of women's headscarves on campuses – a badge of their Islamic loyalties. In 1986 the Higher Educational Council forbade the wearing of scarves. In the fall of 1989 parliament passed a law allowing it. President Evren vetoed the law on the grounds that it violated Atatürk's 'modernizing principles and reforms'. The crux of the matter, of course, lay in its symbolism. As Evren wrote, 'modern garb is an unalienable requisite of the modernizing principles and reforms of the founder of the Republic'.[52]

Eventually Evren's presidential veto was overridden by the Higher Education Council. Students could now cover their heads and necks 'according to their religious beliefs'. The 'modern style' headscarf was seen to be 'civilized'. This was by no means the storm in a teacup it might have seemed to some outsiders. Nor was it just a trial of strength between modernizers and traditionalists – although it was that, too. It was a case of the traditionalists demonstrating that they were also modern.

Growing Islamic influence in the central bureaucracy had also shaken the complacency of many 'Westernizers'. In several governmental ministries in Ankara there were said to be Muslim 'cells', members of which protected each other and tried to make their departments Muslim 'closed shops'. Many of these recruits were members of Dervish orders still ostensibly banned. Even more unsettling was the apparent increase in Muslim activism in the military, the bastion of Kemalist secularism. Some feared that the army could become a 'doubtful quantity' in the not too distant future. With largely Muslim recruits and more self-consciously Muslim officers, the whole balance of power within Turkey could be drastically altered.

The resurgence of Islam should not be instantly identified with Islamic fundamentalism of the Iranian variety. Muslims like Özal and Demirel, at the top of the political pyramid, were representative of scores of thousands in all walks of public life whose religion may permeate their attitudes and activity but not dominate them. They saw no incompatibility between Islam and modernization based on Western practice. Although they understood Islam fundamentalism better than the secularists, most probably distrusted it just as much. Neither they nor the secularists were complacent about the fundamentalist 'threat'. It was real and growing. It appealed to all classes, but its most dangerous inroads were likely to be among the poor, forming a symbiosis between social and religious revolutions. If Marxism was the most dynamic force in Turkey in the 1970s, liberal capitalism in the 1980s, it would probably be Islam in the 1990s.

During the 1990s Turkey's contacts with the Islamic world in the former Soviet Union seemed likely to increase dramatically. Azerbaijan, Uzbekistan, Kazakhstan, Turkmenistan, Tadzhikistan, and Kirgizia all had Muslim majorities except, narrowly, Kazakhstan, and were, except Kazakhstan and Tadzhikistan, made up of peoples who were mostly Turkic. With the collapse of the Soviet Union Turkey was already extending its ties with these countries, especially in the economic sphere. Most of the leaders of the newly independent republics looked to Turkey as a model of development – economically, culturally, and politically – and as a counterweight to the fundamentalist Islamic influence of Iran. This new relationship seemed eventually to offer several possibilities. A prosperous Turkey could be a democratic and secularist influence. In doing so it could become a great, dynamic, power again, the extent of its influence assuming Ottoman dimensions. Whether it entered the European Community or not it would become a link between Europe and this part of Asia. It could, however, be drawn into a never-ending Asian imbroglio, with Iran a potentially serious enemy. Perhaps Iran's brand of Islam might be more immediately attractive to the newly emancipated nations of former Soviet Asia. Domestically, too, the growing 'Asian connection' could prove detrimental to Turkey. It could tend to weaken European influence, thereby further undermining the democratic foundations of Turkish life. In that sense Turkey would become more 'Eastern' and Islamic, more 'Ottoman' than it had been for over a century. As such, it could become a negative influence internationally. Much would depend on how democracy, secularization and the economy withstood the comprehensive rigours of the 1990s.

Notes

1 See, for example, 'Too Many Young Turks', *The Economist*, 23 August 1986.
2 For a brief discussion of Turkey's strategic importance, see Dankwart A. Rustow, *Turkey, America's Forgotten Ally* (New York, Council on Foreign Relations, 1987).

3 See Roderic Davison, *Reform in the Ottoman Empire: 1856–1876* (Princeton, NJ, Princeton University Press, 1963); Stanford Shaw and Ezel K. Shaw, *History of the Ottoman Empire and Modern Turkey*, Vol. II: *Reform, Revolution, and Republic: The Rise of Modern Turkey* (Cambridge, Cambridge University Press, 1977).

4 On Atatürk, see Lord Kinross, *Atatürk: The Rebirth of a Nation* (New York, Morrow, 1965); Bernard Lewis, *The Emergence of Modern Turkey* (London, Oxford University Press, 1968).

5 See Jesse W. Lewis, Jr., *The Strategic Balance in the Mediterranean* (Washington, DC, American Enterprise Institute, 1976), pp. 70–72, 155–69; also Barry Buzan, 'The Status and Future of the Montreux Convention', *Survival*, Nov.–Dec. 1976.

6 F. Stephen Larrabee gives excellent, succinct analyses of American involvement in both Turkey and Greece in 'Balkan Security', Adelphi Papers, No. 135, op. cit.; and 'The Southern Periphery: Greece and Turkey', in Paul W. Shoup (ed.) and George W. Hoffman (project director), *Problems of Balkan Security: Southeastern Europe In the 1990s* (Washington, DC, Wilson Center, 1990), pp. 174–204.

7 Larrabee, op. cit.; p. 17.

8 Author's private conversations. See also Larrabee, pp. 17–18.

9 See Udo Steinbach, 'Türkei – Diversifizierung der Aussen-politik', *Aussenpolitik*, No. 4, 1973, pp. 436–46.

10 See Aurel Braun, *Small-State Security in the Balkans* (London, Macmillan, 1983), pp. 44–6; also John O. Iatrides, *Balkan Triangle: Birth and Decline of an Alliance Across Ideological Boundaries* (The Hague, Mouton, 1968).

11 Brown, *Bulgaria under Communist Rule* (New York, Praeger, 1970), pp. 293–7.

12 For an excellent discussion of contemporary Turkey, including the *Gastarbeiter* factor, see Milton Viorst, 'A Reporter at Large: Crossing the Straits', *The New Yorker*, June 5, 1989.

13 Rustow, op. cit., pp. 32–3.

14 Wolfgang Günter Lerch, 'Wohin treibt die Türkei?', *Frankfurther Allgemeine Zeitung*, 30 June 1990.

15 Viorst, loc. cit.

16 Joseph Kraft, 'Letter from Turkey', *The New Yorker*, 15 October 1984.

17 Rustow, op. cit., p. 17. On the Turkish sense of identity, see S. D. Salamone, 'The Dialectics of Turkish National Identity' and 'Ethnic Boundary Maintenance and State ideology'. This article appeared in two parts in *East European Quarterly*, XXIII, No. 1, March 1989, and XXIII, No. 2, June 1989.

18 See Kemal Karpat, *Turkey's Politics. The Transition to a Multi-party System* (Princeton, NJ, Princeton University Press, 1959), passim. See also Feröz Ahmed, *The Turkish Experiment in Democracy, 1950–1975* (London, C. Hurst, 1978), pp. 177–212.

19 Nicholas S. Ludington and James W. Spain, 'Dateline Turkey: The Case for Patience,' *Foreign Policy*, No. 50, Spring 1983.

20 Ibid.

21 For an excellent review of the military's role since 1960, see A. H., 'Die Schwächen der türkischen Demokratie', *Neue Zürcher Zeitung*, 3 October 1986 (Fernausgabe, Nr. 228).

22 *The Times*, 15 August 1983.

23 Ludington and Spain, loc. cit.

24 Ibid.

25 There has been a voluminous literature on Turkey's human rights record. The situation is well summed up by Viorst, loc. cit. For examples of the government's efforts

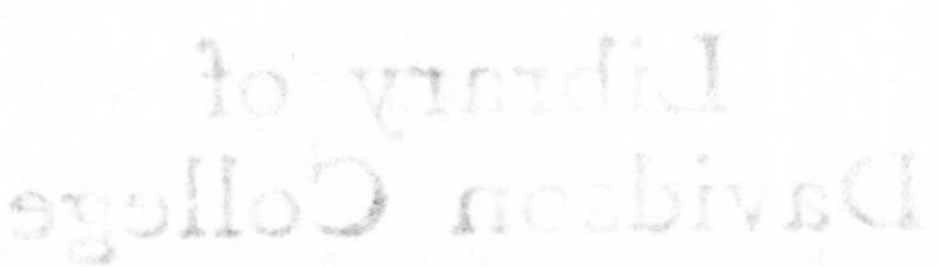

to improve the situation see, I. T. 'Grössere Meinungsfreiheit in der Türkei?', *Neue Zürcher Zeitung*, 7 December 1989 (Fernausgabe, Nr. 284).

26 Viorst, loc. cit.

27 Kenneth Mackenzie, 'Turkey After the Storm', *Conflict Studies*, No. 43 (London, Institute for the Study of Conflict, 1974).

28 See A. H., 'Vergangenheitsbewältigung in der Türkei: Stehen die Streitkräfte hinter oder über der Verfassung', *Neue Zürcher Zeitung*, 18 June 1988 (Fernausgabe, Nr. 139).

29 See *The Times*, 8 November 1983.

30 See Heiko Flottau, 'Eine Lektion fur die türkischen Militärs', *Süddeutsche Zeitung*, 8 November 1983.

31 Özal has been the subject of much discussion and analysis. For insights into his personality and motivations, *The New Yorker* articles by Kraft and Viorst, already cited, are excellent. See also the discussion in the special survey of Turkey in *The Economist*, 3 November 1984.

32 Associated Press, 10 August 1983.

33 Ibid., 12 December 1983. See also 'Soll und Haben der türkischen Wirtschaft', *Neue Zürcher Zeitung*, 8 September 1983.

34 Viorst, loc. cit.

35 Ibid.

36 See Mükerrem Hiç, 'Weaknesses and Risks of Turkey's Economic and Social Policies' (Ebenhausen, Stiftung Wissenschaft und Politik, May 1989), p. 52.

37 Ibid., pp. 11–14, 39–74. See also G. T., 'Die Türkei zwischen Planung und Markt', *Neue Zürcher Zeitung*, 20 August 1986 (Fernausgabe, Nr. 190); B. E., 'Galoppierende Inflation in der Türkei', *Neue Zürcher Zeitung*, 19 October 1988 (Fernausgabe, Nr. 243); Ahmet and Janine Sahinoz, 'Coûteuse facture du libéralisme en Turquie', *Le Monde Diplomatique*, July 1990.

38 Mükerrem Hiç, op. cit., p. 19.

39 On Semra Özal, see Viorst, loc. cit. On nepotism and Özal's retreat from it, see C-1, 'Kabinettsumbildung in der Türkei: Zurückstutzen des Özal-Klans', *Neue Zürcher Zeitung*, 2–3 April 1989 (Fernausgabe, Nr. 75).

40 Mükerrem Hiç, op. cit., p. 18.

41 See A. H., 'Özal's Konsequenzen aus der Wahlniederlage', *Neue Zürcher Zeitung*, 30 March 1989 (Fernausgabe, Nr. 72).

42 David Barchard, 'Turkey's Troubled Prospect', *The World Today*, Vol. 46, No. 6, June 1990.

43 C-1, 'Aussenpolitischer Aktivismus Präsident Özal's', *Neue Zürcher Zeitung*, 8 June 1990 (Fernausgabe, Nr. 129).

44 Viorst, loc. cit.

45 Reuters, 11 September 1989.

46 Of the huge volume of reporting on the Kurds, perhaps the best single piece is by Michel Farrère, 'Kurdes de coeur, Turcs par raison', *Le Monde*, 3 August 1989.

47 Viorst, loc. cit.

48 For background, see Christiane More, 'Les Kurdes, une fois encore oubliés', *Le Monde Diplomatique*, December 1990. On Özal's removal of the ban on speaking Kurdish in public, see Hugh Pope, 'Turkey Lifts Ban on Speaking Kurdish', *The Independent* (London), 13 April 1991. Pope called this and other basic reforms announced at the same time, 'a sweeping stroke worthy of a reforming Ottoman sultan'.

49 Graham Fuller, personal communication, December 1988.

50 A well-balanced discussion of Islam in Turkey appears in the 'Islamic Renaissance in Turkey', *Swiss Review of World Affairs*, Vol. 39, No. 5, August 1989.

51 Viorst, loc. cit.
52 Ibid.

3 Greece: Politics and Patronage

In April 1990 Greece held its third general election in ten months. The two previous, in June and November 1989, had both produced hung parliaments. The April 1990 election gave the right of centre New Democracy a working majority, but only by the narrowest of margins. The election had given it exactly half the seats in the new parliament, but promised support by the one member returned from a rightist party tipped the scales in its favour. Under Prime Minister Konstantin Mitsotakis the New Democracy government began with a bold programme of financial stabilization and economic regeneration.[1] It had considerable public sympathy, but in a political atmosphere so historically volatile and with a parliamentary majority so slim, few were confident it could anywhere near fulfil the promises it was making.

Some of the sympathy for the new government stemmed from relief after the squalor and uncertainty that had characterized the end of the 1980s. It was a decade that had begun so promisingly. In 1981 Greece entered the European Community, anchoring itself decisively in the European mainstream and completing a process that had begun nearly 30 years before with membership in the North Atlantic Treaty Organization in 1952.

The clear victory of Andreas Papandreou's Panhellenic Socialist Movement (PASOK) in October 1981 was also a hopeful sign for Greece's political development. This may sound like a perverse judgement in view of what PASOK was threatening at the time: neutrality, withdrawal from NATO, elimination of American military bases, even possible withdrawal from the European Community. Domestically, too, some of PASOK's more radical spokesmen were urging political, economic, and social changes more in tune with eastern socialism than western social democracy.

But, in any event, few if any of these changes materialized. Greece under Papandreou proved a fractious and irritating Western ally. It did, however, stay in the alliance, and the American bases remained on Greek soil. Greece remained, without the promised referendum, inside the European Community, quickly discovering that the material benefits offset the dangers it was originally alleged to present, either to Greek sovereignty or the purity of PASOK's socialism.[2]

In terms of Greek political history the promise of PASOK's victory was more in what it symbolized than what it actually was. First of all, it showed that a genuine opposition could come to power without a political or national upheaval. It was a triumph, therefore, for modern Greek democracy. But even more profound was the fact that it went a long way to bridging the national schism that had characterized twentieth century Greece and which, in the civil war after the Second World War, had become an open and almost fatal wound. The communists and extreme left were not the only ones excluded from political life after the right-wing nationalists triumphed, with American help, in 1949. They were *formally* excluded for a quarter of a century until Konstantin Karamanlis re-legalized the Communist Party in 1974 after the downfall of the military junta. But the left of centre forces, by no means communist, had been effectively excluded from political power almost continually since the civil war except for a short period in the 1960s, between 1964 and 1967. The liberal Centre Union under George Papandreou, Andreas's father, did then achieve a shaky hold on political power, but its prospects of real power were cut short by the military coup in April 1967.

Now, in October 1981, the Greek left had won a clear victory through the democratic political process. No matter how distasteful this was for many Greeks (and for many Americans) this victory was essential for the health of Greek politics. The entry into Europe and the PASOK victory were, therefore, mutually reinforcing: the one put Greece in democratic company, the other stimulated Greece's own democratic impetus.[3]

Breaking the Pattern

The PASOK victory deepened the consolidation of Greek democracy begun by Karamanlis and his new Democracy party after the fall of the junta. The years 1974 and 1981 were in fact two of the most important in Greek history since the achievement of independence from the Ottoman Empire in 1830. They broke the established historical patterns that had slowed constitutional development and hindered national unity.[4] The return to democracy in 1974 under Karamanlis and then its strengthening because of what the PASOK victory in 1981 signified, changed the pattern of Greek politics that had existed for almost a century. This pattern had been established by the interaction of several forces, among them: the historic political parties; the monarch; the army; foreign power interests; the church; a small native economic and financial oligarchy; and the Greek diaspora in Western Europe and subsequently in the United States.

By the end of the 1980s some of these forces had ceased to be serious factors in Greek politics. The importance of others had decreased or their character and significance had changed. It is worth while briefly to examine each one in turn:[5]

The Political Parties. Since the early years of the twentieth century, especially since the First World War, the political divide in Greece had been between royalist and republican. After the Second World War the divide was between the conservative nationalists and the 'left'. The world war, and especially the civil war after it, made important changes in the political climate and its configurations. The post-war political groupings were by no means identical with those before the war.[6] In fact, important modifications occurred during the Metaxas dictatorship established in 1936. After the Second World War many pre-war republicans supported the nationalist cause; this they associated with anti-communism. They opposed the 'left' because they loosely identified it with communism and the prospect of Soviet domination, although the official Communist Party was, as just mentioned, proscribed till 1974. But, still, despite the differences and the fact that the post-Second World War groupings were new political entities, some of the basic philosophical and political differences from before the war carried over into Greek politics after it.

The Monarch. Greece had been a monarchy since regaining its freedom in 1830. This institution became, however, not the unifying element that was intended but, especially during the twentieth century, a sharply divisive one – not above politics but deeply embroiled in them. In view of the royal prerogatives contained in the constitution, or inferable from it, this was inevitable. In the First World War the first great schism in Greek politics occurred when King Constantine I demanded a pro-German neutralist policy, whereas the liberal government of Premier Eleftherios Venizelos was strongly pro-allies.[7] The royalist–republican split continued throughout most of the inter-war period. It was resumed in the middle 1960s between King Constantine II and the newly elected liberal–centre government under George Papandreou. This led indirectly to the military coup of April 1967, the king's unsuccessful counter-*coup* a few months later, and the eventual abolition of the monarchy by referendum in 1974. Today royalist sentiment has some emotional but no significant political expression.

The Army. The army's historical role in Greek politics was even greater than that of the monarch. Its importance, in fact, is difficult to exaggerate. Military intervention in politics was almost the rule rather than the exception. In the nineteenth century, when Greek politics were often subordinated to myth of the 'Megali Idea' – the irredentist drive to reunite all Greeks in one nation-state and to restore the Byzantine Empire with its capital at Constantinople – the army was seen as the guardian of the nationalist ideal.[8] Between 1912 and 1920, the period of the Balkan Wars, the First World War, and the post-war treaties, much of the promise was fulfilled and even greater hopes were kindled at the expense of a prostrate Turkey. The military, therefore, was at the peak of its reputation. But the staggering Greek defeats in Asia Minor at the hands of a resurgent Turkish nation in 1922 killed any hopes of fulfilling the 'Megali Idea'. With it the role of the Greek military sank from national guardianship to political jobbery.

The political general *par excellence* emerged, he and his coterie of subordinates tied to one or another political figure, their fortunes tied to those of their patron. During this period the officer corps was divided between royalists and republicans. In 1936 the military dictatorship of General Metaxas was established, but this division continued throughout the Second World War. The civil war and the subsequent Cold War between East and West then led to a fundamental realignment of officer allegiance. The military now became identified with the royal house and the American alliance. The officer corps was put on a new pedestal and was showered with official prestige and material benefit. It was bitterly opposed to Papandreou and the liberals in the 1960s and many Greeks, as well as foreign observers, considered it only a matter of time before the army again interfered massively in the political process.

But the *coup* of April 1967 was not the orthodox kind many had expected, but rather a variant of it. The ruling junta that emerged was not composed of generals espousing predictable values, but was mostly made up of either brigadiers or colonels with an ideology not unlike that of the Metaxas military dictatorship of the late 1930s or the original Falange ideology of Francoist Spain. Their fiercely anticommunist, Manichean view of world politics made them pro-American as long as Washington appeared to hold the same view. Some members of the junta had a fanatical bent that differentiated them from many Greek officers, who were 'easy-livers' rather than crusaders. Their attitude towards the monarchy was also equivocal and it changed to downright hostile when King Constantine tried his abortive *coup* towards the end of 1967, which resulted in his exile. But, whatever its philosophy and twisted idealism, the junta's record in office was so disastrous that it almost certainly ended the military's historically decisive role in Greek politics.[9]

Foreign Power Interests. Foreign influence, sometimes amounting to domination, has been a constant in Greek politics ever since liberation and has made a deep impression on the Greek political psyche.[10] Independence from the Turks was won not so much by Greeks, heroic though some of their efforts were, but by a combination of great powers – France, Britain, and Russia – acting in their own interests. Independent Greece was given a Bavarian king and a German governing and legal system. At the Greek court there was an English, French, and a Russian party. The pattern, therefore, for decisive foreign influence was set right at the beginning. Nor was the influence just political. Greece's poverty made it a hostage to foreign economic interests.[11] Moreover, as long as the Greeks pursued the 'Megali Idea' they made themselves even more dependent on foreign interests.

After the First World War, in spite of the different circumstances, foreign influence continued, and the Second World War and the ensuing civil war made Greece dependent first on Britain and then massively on the United States. This dependence has continued in some degree right to the present. But Karamanlis, on his return to power in 1974, was determined to reduce it, not only because of the support Washington had given to the military regime but mainly because of the *lack* of American support for Greece against Turkey in the Cyprus crisis of that year. Under Karamanlis Greece began, as Turkey had done several years earlier, to 'diversify its foreign portfolio', to look for other allies and associates, both lessening dependence on Americans and strengthening Greek leverage in dealings with them.[12] Papandreou continued and broadened this policy, adding personal, ideological, and nationalistic dimensions to it that often led to serious tension with the United States.[13]

The Church. The Greek Orthodox Church traditionally represented conservatism at home, and irredentism and the 'Megali Idea' abroad. The presence of the Greek Patriarchate in Istanbul symbolized the continuity of the Byzantine tradition, and Greek policy in relations with Turkey is still coloured by a desire to keep it there. It is the sole remnant of the Byzantine Empire and of the 'Megali Idea' itself. Domestically, the Church's relations with successive governments have been based on the Erastian principle of subordination to the state. Its preference for conservative regimes, always more inclined to leave its privileges and property alone, was taken for granted.[14] Nowhere was this more evident than during the military dictatorship of 1967–74. The colonel's crusade for 'Christian civilization' and its defence of 'traditional virtues' won it the support of the Church as an institution and of the majority of the clergy. Subsequent attempts to explain this support have remained unconvincing to most Greeks. The Church's role in politics has now substantially declined, as has religious practice and church attendance, especially in the towns. But Orthodoxy still plays a considerable role in the psychology of most Greeks. The Church is also very rich and will continue to be so despite the Papandreou government's expropriation measures in 1988 against the bulk of its huge land holdings.[15]

The Native Economic and Financial Oligarchy. Both individually and, in some cases, collectively this small group of native magnates, with international shipping and financial interests, have exerted considerable influence on twentieth century Greek politics. Though only rarely participating directly in public life, they have strongly supported conservative politicians and the American alliance. (Again, many, like the Church, sympathized with the military junta.) Not surprisingly, their relations with a movement like PASOK have been marked by mutual antipathy. Generally, though, this oligarchy's success contributed considerably to the Greek economy's remarkable progress from the 1950s to the 1980s. The global economic downturn in the late 1980s, however, which particularly affected Greek shipping and insurance interests, affected both the Greek economy and the political power of this oligarchy.

The Greek Diaspora. First in Western Europe and in cities like Odessa, Varna, Trieste and Vienna the Greek diaspora played a major part in securing Greek independence in the early nineteenth century. More recently it has been the diaspora in North America that has exerted the strongest influence – politically, economically, and culturally. The Greek lobby in the United States, representing about three million Americans of Greek descent, has been the strongest single source of international support for Greece over the last 40 years, particularly in its hostility with Turkey.[16] Historically, the diaspora's influence on Greek politics has gone through different phases since liberation. At first the incompatibility of the liberalism of the foreign Greek merchant communities with a native population moulded by four centuries of Ottoman rule led to severe tension, and elements of this tension continued well into the twentieth century. The diaspora, though, was generally supportive of the 'Megali Idea'. When this myth collapsed in Asia Minor in 1922 the diaspora contributed generously to subsequent relief work and the huge resettlement operation of Greeks from Asia Minor to Greece itself. Since the Second World War Greek-Americans have backed the conservatives in Greek politics and sympathized with the military dictatorship. For the left-leaning Papandreou, especially for his anti-American rhetoric, there was almost universal hostility. On Greek–Turkish relations many Greek–Americans have distinguished themselves by their militancy.[17]

The New Political Landscape

By 1992 the combination of six factors outlined above in Greek political life had been modified considerably. The monarchy had disappeared. The army remained but its political role appeared to have ended. The vast majority of both its senior and junior officers accepted (or were resigned to the fact) that their exclusive task was to defend Greece's territorial integrity. The fact that the military never made any attempt to intervene during the decade of PASOK rule was proof to most Greeks of its new nonpolitical role.[18] Most observers now agreed that, except in a case where the civilian authority was guilty of 'national betrayal', the military would not be tempted to intervene in politics again. Just what would constitute 'national betrayal' and who would define it remained a moot question: cession of parts of Western Thrace, certainly; surrender of certain Cypriot–Greek positions, possibly. But these are unlikely eventualities. The Greek military, much more so than the Turkish, now looks resigned to its political subordination.

Any meaningful role of the Church in national politics could also now be discounted. The big international issue involving the Church in the future was likely over whether the Patriarchate would remain in Istanbul. Its continuance there is a nationalist issue, a matter of the Greeks' pride in themselves and their history. But it is also a flagrant anachronism. The danger is that, as Turkish nationalism increases, a future Turkish government might decide that it must go. In recent years the Muslim (mainly Turkish) minority in Greek Thrace, numbering about 200 000, and the Greek Patriarchate in Istanbul, plus the tiny Greek minority remaining there (250 000 in 1923; some 7–8000 in 1991) have been seen by Athens and Ankara as counterbalancing, or interactive, factors. Disturbing the one would mean disturbing the other. The Greeks have been careful, therefore, with the minority in Thrace so as not to provoke the Turks on the Patriarchate. The Turks have tolerated the Patriarchate so as not to affect the situation of their compatriots in Thrace.[19] But the future might not lend itself to restraint. If it does not, the Church in Greece could still become the focus of intense nationalism over the Patriarchate and other issues.

Regarding political parties, the change in the political landscape since 1974, and particularly since the first PASOK victory in 1981, has been considerable. Despite the polemics, the polarization that was a legacy of the civil war has now narrowed. A middle ground has been created and confirmed after its quick life and death under George Papandreou and the Centre Union in the 1960s. During the 1980s, both New Democracy and PASOK moved toward the middle, becoming essentially right-of-centre and left-of-centre parties. New Democracy's move toward the middle began under Karamanlis from 1974 and accelerated under Konstantin

Mitsotakis, premier since April 1990. In PASOK's case, those listening only to its rhetoric would be slow to accept its basic moderation. Yet in practical politics, it has been appropriately described as the 'prodigal son' of the 1960s Centre Union with Andreas Papandreou as the political son of his father, George.[20] As for the real left, the KKE (Communist Party of the Exterior) has existed legally since 1974. It is based on the hard core of communist support that survived the civil war and the subsequent persecutions and has usually been sure of 10 per cent of the vote. Andreas Papandreou's decision, during his first term of office, to allow the thousands of exiled communists from the civil war to return certainly helped in its regeneration. But, more important, it was also a gesture of healing and reconciliation symbolizing the shift to political moderation and perhaps even compromise.[21]

The new political groupings have continued to be influenced – sometimes directly, more often indirectly – by the domestic financial and economic oligarchy. Important sections of this oligarchy, for example, made large contributions to the New Democracy. Important clandestine or semi-clandestine contributions went from business interests into the coffers of all political parties. Often, as will be discussed below, these practices degenerated into rampant corruption. But, generally, the plutocratic influence on Greek politics had begun to diminish by the end of the 1970s. PASOK won its decisive victory in 1981 partly on a platform of curbing such interests and mutual relations often became tense. In any case, as mentioned above, world economic conditions had begun to sap the strength of this once powerful sectional interest.

Finally the influence of foreign powers. Since the Second World War this has meant the influence of the United States. From the end of the 1940s to the middle of the 1960s American influence was direct, comprehensive, and pervasive, not only directing Greek foreign policy but touching on key aspects of domestic policy as well. It was seriously threatened by the Centre Union victory in 1963, and the United States made little secret of its hostility. Over this, many American officials subsequently made no secret of their relief over the coup in 1967. This led many Greeks to believe (and many still believe) that the United States did not just approve of the coup but also engineered it. The United States did not engineer the coup, but the demonstrative sympathy subsequently shown toward the junta did little to correct this erroneous impression.[22]

It was after 1974, the collapse of the military junta and especially the Greek humiliation over Cyprus, that American influence declined. Karamanlis began his more multi-directional foreign portfolio, and then after 1981 PASOK began its noisy efforts to withdraw further from the American embrace. Economically and, to some extent, politically the European Community began to replace the United States as the principal external factor in Greek domestic and foreign affairs. Greece, of course, remained a member of NATO but for most Greeks the Cold War had ended many years before. But the growing perception of Turkey as the main foreign danger actually increased the *military* importance of the United States to Greece. It also galvanized the Greek lobby in the United States to successful efforts to gain increases in military assistance to Greece, at least to the proportionate level (7 to 10) in relation to the aid the United States was giving to Turkey. Greek military dependence, therefore, continued, even increased. But, as in the case of Turkey, as this military dependence grew, political dependence on the United States actually lessened. The more American arms poured into both countries the less influence Washington had on the political and even diplomatic behaviour of either country. American military influence, therefore, became neutered.

PASOK's Wasted Opportunity

As already mentioned, most of the signs were auspicious for Greece's first ever socialist government in 1981. Internally and internationally the stage seemed set for the 'new dawn' that PASOK's supporters were now claiming had arrived. True, many aspects of the economic situation were negative: the second Organization of Petroleum Exporting Countries (OPEC) oil price explosion of 1979 had shaken the global economy yet again. But in the early 1980s some countries, by dint of good husbandry, had shown a considerable resilience in adversity. In any case, Greece's accession to the European Community (EC) was soon to bring good results for the Greek countryside and the promise of extensive help for the country's poorer regions.

The 2 750 000 Greeks who voted for Papandreou and PASOK in 1981 and the nearly three million who, giving both the benefit of the looming doubt, did so in 1985, were responding to a dream for their country that Papandreou brilliantly articulated. The watchword was *allaghi* (change), which even many of those who did not vote for PASOK thought was urgently necessary. As one commentator put it:

> Most voters read *allaghi* ... to signify primarily a commitment on the Socialists' part to manage Greece's successful economic, social and political entry into the developed European mainstream. These voters had come to feel that the Conservatives who had ruled the country for decades were ill-equipped, in terms of both technocratic skills and ideology, to accomplish this task, despite having negotiated Greece's accession to the EC in January 1981.[23]

Eight years later many Greeks who had seen *allaghi* in these terms had become profoundly disappointed. In the first place, far from putting Greece's economic house in order, Papandreou in his first term of office almost bankrupted the economy through a 'socialist' policy of handouts and subsidies. This was done largely through foreign loans, so much so that by the middle of the 1980s Greece was threatened with a foreign lending freeze. After re-election in 1985 Papandreou introduced an abrupt change of policy just as the Mitterrand government in France had done earlier and as Turkish premier Özal had done the first years of the Turkish military regime's rule after 1980. But the new 'Thatcherist' policy was only briefly and inconsistently applied in Greece.

In 1987, for purely electoral considerations, the policy was reversed back to expansion and handouts. By the end of the decade the results were clear. The economy had developed to nowhere near the extent Papandreou had promised. The hopes for private investment in particular had failed miserably. The debts of public enterprises weighed on the whole economy. The inflation rate, at nearly 15 per cent, was the highest in the European Community. (It was still very low, though, compared with the Turkish.) Both the public and the foreign debt threatened, as they had done in 1985, to destroy the economy's credit-worthiness. In terms of industrial productivity Greece stood lower than either Turkey or Portugal. Between 1980 and 1988 Greece topped a list of 19 industrialized states for the number of days lost through strikes.[24]

But Papandreou's failures were not just in the realm of public policy. What had prompted many Greeks, particularly of the younger generation, to support him was the crusading image that he and his movement projected. But by 1989 his government was up to its neck in the kind of corruption he had promised to eliminate. Its details made compulsive reading in many parts of the world. The Bank of Crete scandal involving George Koskotas was the most spectacular. It led to a judicial investigation that began in October 1988. Papandreou tried to brazen his way out of the crisis by offering his own scenario: the whole Koskotas scandal was a foreign plot designed to discredit him, concocted by the CIA in league with his right-wing opponents at home. This was vintage Papandreou, but while this version of events might have made some impression at the beginning of the 1980s, it made considerably less at their close. Many Greeks used to blame the CIA for everything; now they were inclined to blame Papandreou. Anyway, the Bank of Crete scandal not only led to a serious loss of political credibility; it also led to the resignation or dismissal of six governmental ministers and the imprisonment of a growing number of bureaucrats and PASOK officials. One of Papandreou's closest political associates, Agamemnon Koutsogiorgas, was eventually imprisoned for his role in the affair.[25]

The Bank of Crete affair was only the best known and the most far-reaching scandal. There was also one involving defence contracts and several minor ones.[26] Koskotas tried to involve Papandreou personally in the scandal but there was no direct evidence linking him with it. But it was quite clear that he had presided over a sink of corruption. Nor was this the only source of public disappointment in him. He was charged with authorizing wiretaps on public officials and political opponents.[27] In many respects he virtually ruled like a dictator, bending laws, parliamentary rules, and election procedures according to his interests of the moment. His scant respect for parliament was reflected in his increasingly infrequent attendances there. All this and Dimitra Liani, too! Many Greeks did take umbrage at his deserting his wife and going for an Olympic Airline hostess half his age. But many more would have been prepared to overlook this as an old man's private peccadillo had his conduct been unexceptional otherwise. His crushing illness and near death in the summer of 1988 seemed to be a tragic culmination of what could have been a triumphant, historic career.

Papandreou's Support and the Greek Political Culture

In the late summer of 1988 Andreas Papandreou's political – if not his personal – obituary was being written in Greece and around the world. So was that of PASOK, the movement he had founded and led into office. But what was remarkable about the ten months between June 1989 and April 1990, a period during which three general elections were held, was that PASOK clung tenaciously to about 40 per cent of the vote. PASOK was forced out of office, but the rout at the polls that so many predicted certainly did not take place.

Why? Many analysts offered explanations, none more coherently and convincingly than Heinz-Jürgen Axt, an expert on Greece who teaches at the Technical University of Berlin. Writing in *Südost-Europa*,[28] Axt gave seven reasons for PASOK's remarkable showing in defeat, and the following analysis is based almost entirely on his findings. Seven types of Greek voters, according to Axt, stayed loyal to PASOK:

(1) *The political 'camp followers'*. The Greek electorate has always been fairly solidly divided into three 'camps' or blocs. Today these are: the right and centre-right, represented by New Democracy; the centre and centre-left, represented, though with many notable left-leaning exceptions, by PASOK; and the hard-left, now mainly represented by KKE. Except in the crisis year 1989 to 1990 when one Greek government was a New Democracy–PASOK coalition (without Papandreou) and the other a conservative–

communist coalition, each with a politically neutral prime minister, these camps have been generally incapable of co-operation. Although each camp, especially New Democracy and PASOK, has different political currents and is, in fact, a coalition in itself, there is a strong unity in loyalty. The flexibility within each camp actually facilitates loyalty. This camp-loyalty has been particularly strong in PASOK. Therefore, whatever its failures in governance and policy, PASOK has continued to count on this solid support.

(2) *The die-hard 'anti-rightists'*. The civil war has been over for more than 40 years and considerable success has recently been achieved in diluting its bitter legacy, but the loyalties, habits of mind, and hatreds engendered by it remain a force in Greek politics. This is particularly true among leftists, defeated in the civil war and victimized afterward. For them New Democracy, for all its 'pretence' of moderation, is still the 'hard-right' of Marshal Papagos in the early 1950s and of Konstantin Karamanlis in his first premiership between 1955 and 1963. (Karamanlis was for many years considered the supreme symbol of conservatism.)[29] For such stalwarts the 'right' could never change its spots.

(3) *The Greek farmers*. These have been described as PASOK's *real* voting constituency, a fact that needs some explaining. The rural districts in many countries are usually identified with conservatism. But in Greece where, despite massive migration to the towns, 30 per cent of the voters are still engaged in agriculture, the farmers have benefited appreciably from membership in the European Community. The Community's Common Agricultural Policy (CAP) has guaranteed Greek farmers a stable income even when they were forced to destroy their produce. In addition, the agricultural development projects under the Community's integrated programme for the Mediterranean region have helped bring an unprecedented prosperity to the Greek countryside. All this helps to explain why, when many workers in the towns, formerly strong supporters, were becoming disillusioned with PASOK, its support in the countryside generally held firm. As for the governmental scandals in the late 1980s, despite the penetration of television into almost every nook and cranny of the Greek countryside, their political repercussions were largely confined to the towns. This was partly because most of the juicy details about them appeared, not on television or radio, but in the metropolitan press, which does not penetrate deeply into the countryside.

(4) *PASOK 'clients'*. PASOK, for which many Greeks originally voted in the hope that it would reduce historic 'clientism' and political patronage, did in fact perfect the system. The spoils went to the victors to an unprecedented degree. This applied both to positions in the government and in the public sector of the economy, both of which expanded greatly under

PASOK. Some estimate that employment in the overall public sector increased by between 300 000 and 400 000 people. Thus a pyramid of self-serving support was created. The bureaucracy became needlessly swollen.[30] Many of its new members were relatively well qualified, but many more were not. It was the latter that realized they owed everything to PASOK.

(5) *Papandreou's personal following – the 'Andreas phenomenon'*. The subordination of politics to personality is common enough in any political system but nowhere more so than in Greece. Andreas Papandreou, especially, had the charisma, the ability, and the opportunity to create and inspire a large personal following that endured despite everything. He not only inherited the following of his father George, but expanded it greatly. And, for many, 'Andreas' still remained untouchable in 1992.

(6) *The 'victims' of political opportunism*. PASOK as an organization and Papandreou personally amassed a very large client following. The PASOK government, as mentioned above, also got solid electoral support from the rural community. But this would probably not have been enough to win the 1985 election handsomely and to do quite well in subsequent elections. What was needed to maintain PASOK support through failure and disappointment was *opportunist tactics,* zigzag populism, changes of policy, always with an eye on the voting booth. The best example of this in domestic policy was the switch after 1985 from Keynesianism to Thatcherism and then back to Keynesianism to face the elections in 1989. In foreign policy there were more numerous and egregious examples.

Many Greeks, regardless of political persuasion, soon realized that Papandreou's anti-American bark was worse than his bite. It was therefore necessary to titillate PASOK's big anti-American constituency with anti-American rhetoric and gestures. The most notorious of these was the Greek government's refusal to join the world condemnation over the Soviet shooting down of the South Korean jumbo jet in 1982. Even more popular, of course, were gestures against Turkey. PASOK's decade of the 1980s was studded with them.[31]

(7) *Supporters of the old 'left-centre'*. This factor has already been referred to in a different context. PASOK inherited *en bloc* the Centre Union voters of the middle 1960s. This group contained much of the old personal following of George Papandreou but was not identical with it. PASOK began to attract a left-centre following in increasing numbers after its foundation in 1974, filling a historic gap in Greek politics. This liberal–social democratic following disposed of much more public spirit and constructive political motivation than any other segment of PASOK's support. Perhaps amounting to about a quarter of PASOK's total support, it could, in the opinion of some experts, form the nucleus of a future Greek social-democratic party. PASOK without Papandreou is not easy to imagine. But a

strong social–democratic party could emerge, especially now that the far-left, represented mainly by the KKE, has been discredited through the collapse of communism in Eastern Europe and in the Soviet Union.

The Persistence of Tradition

This breakdown of the sources of PASOK's support helps explain the resilience of a powerful Greek political movement. It also illustrates the persistence throughout modern Greek history of traditional social, cultural, and moral factors on which much of Greek public life continues to be based.

One Greek historian has summed up his nation's development as follows:

> Formally, Greece is a European country, but it comprises a society that in perceptions, values, and social and cultural attitudes, remains essentially Near Eastern and Ottoman. Yet it is not Muslim or Turkish. Nor is it Western; its Europeanism is a euphemism made possible by the accident of geography.[32]

It follows from this that the entire civic culture in Greece is quite different from that in parts of Western Europe and North America. Whether, in fact, a civic culture can be said to have existed at all in modern Greece is open to question. The primary, often the exclusive, loyalty of most Greeks – and here there are still some strong similarities with some parts of Italy – is to family, kinsmen, and related groups. Their loyalty to a body politic is largely non-existent. In politics their support for a public figure is given largely in the expectation of place, preferment, or patronage for themselves and their family.[33] This loyalty to a single public figure has been a dominant feature throughout Greek history: Eleftherios Venizelos, for example, between 1910 and 1935, was probably the best historic example of all. So has nepotism – at the top and running downward. Andreas Papandreou succeeded his father George; now many are expecting Andreas's son, George, already a prominent politician, to take up Andreas's mantle. One of Karamanlis's sons is prominent in New Democracy.

PASOK's burgeoning 'clientism' was, therefore, only the continuance of tradition. So, unfortunately, was the corruption into which it descended in the late 1980s. The movement that promised to clean out the Augean Stables became part of them. In short Greek history, its political tradition and practice were still strong in the 1980s. PASOK had become only its latest victim. It had indeed taken some steps to fulfil its promise of modernization: in social legislation – for example, toward greater equality for women; in easing the grip of the Church in social and cultural life; in helping to break down class and social distinctions. Its contributions had been considerable. But, in the end, the 'new road' it had taken turned out to be quite similar to the old one. This was not liberal democracy. It was the kind of populism that could subvert it. It is too early still to judge the Mitsotakis government. It was undoubtedly well meaning. It would be almost miraculous, though, if it can break the hold that tradition and culture has always had on Greek politics since independence from the Ottomans. The early signs were not promising. The government, and the country with it, were running into a political, economic, and social swamp. Modern Greek history was catching up with it quickly.

Notes

1 See Kerin Hope, 'Mitsotakis Patience Pays off at Last', *Financial Times*, 12 April 1990. On the previous stalemate, see 'Greece: The Stalemate Continues', *The World Today*, February 1990; also 'Try Again', *The Economist*, 31 March 1990.

2 On Papandreou's defence of Greek national interests see the two excellent articles by F. Stephen Larrabee: 'Dateline Athens – Greece for the Greeks', *Foreign Policy*, No. 45, Winter 1981–2; 'Papandreou: National Interests are the Key', *Atlantic Monthly*, March 1983.

3 On overcoming the legacy of the civil war, see P. J. Vatikiotis, '*Greece: a Political Essay*', The Washington Papers, Vol. II, The Center for Strategic and International Studies, Georgetown University, Washington, DC (Beverly Hills and London, Sage Publications, 1974); P. S., 'Griechische Bürgerkriegsbewältigung', *Neue Zürcher Zeitung*, 3–4 September 1989 (Fernausgabe, Nr. 203).

4 George Th. Mavrogordatos, 'The Emerging Party System', in Richard Clogg (ed.), *Greece in the 1980s* (London, Macmillan, 1983), pp. 70–94.

5 Vatikiotis, op. cit., p. 51.

6 Ibid., p. 31. See also S. Victor Papacosma, 'The Historical Context', in Clogg (ed.), op. cit., pp. 30–69.

7 On the monarchy see Richard Clogg, *A Short History of Modern Greece* (Cambridge, Cambridge University Press, 1979), *passim*.

8 On the Megali Idea see Papacosma, loc. cit., pp. 31–2.

9 On the junta see Peter Schwab and George D. Frangos (eds), *Greece under the Junta* (New York, Facts on File, 1973). See also Thanos Veremis, 'Greek Security Issues and Politics', Adelphi Papers, No. 179 (London, International Institute for Strategic Studies, Winter 1982); also the same author's 'Security Considerations and Civil Military Relations in Post-war Greece', in Clogg (ed.), op. cit., 173–82.

10 See Theodore A. Coloumbis, 'The Structures of Greek Foreign Policy', in Clogg (ed.), op. cit., pp. 95–122; also Betty A. Dobratz, 'Foreign Policy and Economic Orientations Influencing Party Preferences in the Socialist Nation of Greece', *East European Quarterly*, XXI, No. 4, January 1988, pp. 413–30.

11 Clogg, *A Short History of Modern Greece*.

12 Karamanlis's career spans practically the whole of Greek history after the Second World War. The best brief analysis of his career is by Pavlos Tzermias, 'Karamanlis – der strenge Makedonier', *Neue Zürcher Zeitung*, 14 March 1985 (Fernausgabe, Nr. 60). In May 1990 Karamanlis returned as president of Greece.

13 Relations probably reached their lowest point in 1984. At a PASOK party congress in May of that year Papandreou had praised the Soviet Union as an agent of détente and had castigated the United States as an imperialist power; see Andriana Ierodiaconou, 'Greek-U.S. Relations Take Another Dive', *Financial Times*, 11 July 1984.

14 See Kallistos Ware, 'A Time of Transition', in Clogg (ed.), op. cit., pp. 184–207. On the background to US–Greek relations, see John O. Iatrides, 'Greece and the United States: the Strained Partnership', in Clogg (ed.), pp. 150–72.

15 Alan Cowell, 'Greek Bill Would Take Church Land', *The New York Times*, 14 March 1987; 'All Hellas Could Break Loose', *The Economist*, 5 September 1987.

16 On the Greek lobby, arguing against 'demonizing' it, see Sallie M. Hicks and Theodore A. Coloumbis, 'The "Greek Lobby". Illusion or Reality?' in Abdul A. Said (ed.), *Ethnicity and U.S. Foreign Policy* (New York, Praeger, 1977), pp. 83–116.

17 These are mainly personal impressions the author has derived from conversations with Greek-Americans in the course of the 1980s. They would be confirmed by most observers.

18 The Papandreou government was extremely sensitive to any signs of opposition within the armed forces. In April 1985, for example, three naval officers were transferred from a base at Piraeus for having 'warmly greeted' the then opposition leader Konstantin Mitsotakis. They apparently ignored an official order that only government officials should be 'warmly received' (Radio Free Europe internal report from Athens, 19 April 1985). Papandreou carried out a considerable modernization of the armed forces. In 1985 he approved a plan to spend $2.8 billion on new armaments, justifying it by 'the danger from the East' (that is, Turkey). Support for a strong military and high defence spending is likely to continue in Greece in spite of the decline in tension between East and West. The perceived Turkish threat, while the most important reason, is not the only one. The very unstable situation in the Balkans generally is also taken into account. Writing in the October 1990 edition of the periodical *Amina Kai Tekhnologia* (Weapons and Technology), Lt. Gen. Anghelos Lazaris said that Greece had five potential operational sectors: Thrace and Eastern Macedonia; Central Macedonia; Epirus; the Aegean; and Crete (FBIS-WEU-90-247, 24 December 1990, p. 39).

19 P. S., 'Politische Aktivität der Muslime Westthräkiens', *Neue Zürcher Zeitung*, 7 June 1989 (Fernausgabe, Nr. 128).

20 See Heinz-Jürgen Axt, 'Wandel und Kontinuität in Griechenland', *Aus Politik und Zeitgeschichte* (Beilage zur wochenzeitung Das Parlament, 29 June 1985), esp. pp. 26–9; Robert McDonald, 'Greece after Pasok's Victory', *The World Today*, July 1985.

21 The Greek Communist Party of the Exterior (KKE) had always been notable for a strong orthodox, pro-Moscow orientation. It suffered severely from the 1989 revolutions in Eastern Europe and the debacle in the Soviet Union; see P. S., 'Erschütterungen in der KP Griechenlands', *Neue Zürcher Zeitung*, 14 July 1989 (Fernausgabe, Nr. 160); and P. S., "Krise bei Griechenland's Kommunisten," *Neue Zürcher Zeitung*, 26 September 1989 (Fernausgabe, Nr. 301).

22 See Iatrides in Clogg (ed.), op. cit.

23 Andriana Ierodiaconou, 'Greece's Dying Socialist Dream', *Financial Times*, 24 April 1989.

24 See Anke Weig, 'Ein hilfloser Papandreou', *Frankfurter Allgemeine Zeitung*, 17 De-

cember 1987; P. S., 'Öffentliche Defizite belasten griechische Wirtschaft: Jahresbericht der Zentralbank', *Neue Zürcher Zeitung*, 29 May 1990 (Fernausgabe, Nr. 121); P. S., 'Der Sozialkonflict in Griechenland', *Neue Zürcher Zeitung*, 13 July 1989 (Fernausgabe, Nr. 159).

25 The Koskotas, Bank of Crete, scandal attracted enormous world-wide publicity, as did Papandreou's marital problems and his personal illness. One of the best summaries of, and commentaries on, the whole sequence was 'A Greek Tragi-comedy', *The Economist*, 14 January 1989.

26 Clyde Haberman, 'In Trouble, Papandreou Strikes Back', *The New York Times*, 14 February 1989.

27 I. G., 'Papandreou soll wegen des Abhörskandals vor ein Sondergericht gestellt werden', *Frankfurter Allgemeine Zeitung*, 22 September 1989.

28 Heinz-Jürgen Axt, '2.7 Millionen fanatische Griechen?' *Südost-Europa*, No. 2, 1990, pp. 119–36.

29 The return of Karamanlis as head of state (see note 12) was seen by many of this group as 'proof' that the right had not changed.

30 For specific examples of this patronage at the senior level in the public sector, see P. S., 'Mutationen im öffentlichen Sektor Griechenlands', *Neue Zürcher Zeitung*, 22 July 1989 (Fernausgabe, Nr. 167).

31 For a perceptive article on Papandreou's zigzag populism, see Viktor Meier, 'Papandreou macht zuviele Umwege', *Frankfurter Allgemeine Zeitung*, 8 March 1989.

32 Vatikiotis, op. cit., p. 1.

33 The influence of the Ottoman tradition is paramount here. See *Banquiers, Usuriers, et Paysans* (Paris, Fondations des Treilles, 1988). This book consists of a series of essays under the direction of Georges B. Dertilis. Especially valuable in this context are Dertilis's introduction, 'Structuration sociale et spécifités historiques (XVIIIe – XXe siécles)', pp. 11–32; 'Le village et le marchand: le cas de Rapsani' by Eugenie Bournova, pp. 105–77; and 'Marchands, banquiers et financement industriel' by Titsa Kalogri, pp. 118–27. My attention was drawn to this book by Olog Higlon's insightful review 'Mangelnde politische Substanz in Griechenland', *Neue Zürcher Zeitung*, 15 June 1989 (Fernausgabe, Nr. 135).

4 Yugoslavia: Approach to Disaster

At the end of 1991 Serbia and Croatia were at war. In mid-1992 war had destroyed many parts of Bosnia-Herzegovina. Probably more than 40 000 people had been killed in 18 months, and over 1.5 million made homeless. All this amid scenes of often indescribable brutality. Slovenia had left the federation and other republics had declared their independence. Yugoslavia, born after the First World War, recreated after the Second World War, existed no longer.

The immediate origins of this conflict and disintegration are discussed in Chapter 9. But they are incomprehensible without some attempt to analyse their historical context and background since the origins of Yugoslavia's disintegration lay in its very creation. Nationalism in Yugoslavia was always too strong for unity and for whatever type of government its rules imposed on it: quasi-democracy, royal authoritarianism, Stalinist communism, or reform communism. In the end Yugoslavia was an unnatural creation.[1]

Between the two world wars, Yugoslavia, whether as the Kingdom of the Serbs, Croats and Slovenes or, after 1929, as the Kingdom of Yugoslavia, was Serb-dominated. Most Serbs and non-Serbs, though from conflicting perspectives, regarded it as essentially an extension of Serbia. The second Yugoslavia, after the Second World War, seemed for some years to be on the way to solving, or at least containing, the problem of nationalism that had bedevilled and eventually helped to destroy its predecessor. But in the end it turned out to be just as unsuccessful. The subsequent question, whether a third Yugoslav variant was possible had, by the end of 1991, been answered in the negative. Yugoslavia was a matter of history.

The speed with which Yugoslavia began to disintegrate in the course of 1990 was, of course, affected by the avalanche of revolution that had swept through Eastern Europe the year before. But the *basic* reasons for it were domestic, and the symptoms of disintegration had been developing and multiplying for several years. In fact, the very pillars on which this Yugoslavia was built eventually contributed to its fatal weakness.

The Six Myths of Titoism

After the Second World War the new Yugoslavia was built on six myths. At first these myths were powerful and sustaining and appeared to give Yugoslavia a vigour and legitimacy the Soviet satellites in the rest of Eastern Europe – as well as pre-war Yugoslavia – manifestly lacked. But the myths faded into impotence and illusion. In the end independent Yugoslavia was to prove only slightly more durable than the most dependent of Moscow's satellites.[2]

The six myths were:

(1) *Tito himself.* Tito's personality, leadership, wartime victory, establishment of Yugoslavia, and successful defiance of Stalin secure his place in history, despite recent unconvincing attempts, inside Yugoslavia and outside, to disparage them.[3] But his achievements, together with his own personal inclinations, invested him with an aura of sacred indispensability that eventually harmed rather than helped Yugoslavia. For Yugoslavia's future it was self-defeating.

(2) *The 'Club of 41' myth: The wartime partisan legend.* Again, as an inspirational force in the early days of the republic, this was a creative, binding force.[4] The break with Stalin – the very thought of it, let alone its achievement – would have been impossible without this myth. But in the ensuing years what had once been a living legend, and a force holding the federation together, now became a fossilized relic, a cramping, not a creative, tradition.

(3) *The socialist myth.* There was nothing specifically Yugoslav about this: the myth that socialism represented the shortest, surest route to human prosperity and happiness. In Yugoslavia, 'reformed' though it claimed to be, it did nothing of the sort.

(4) *The myth of federalism.* This was the notion that federalism, combined with socialism, could overcome ethnic differences in a multinational state by making them irrelevant. In 1962 Tito was saying that the national problem in Yugoslavia had been overcome.[5] In his own lifetime there would be ample evidence that this was not true. After his death the tragic absurdity of this claim became manifest.

(5) *Self-management: The ideological myth.* This was Yugoslavia's own contribution to the 'treasure house' of Marxism-Leninism. It was a short-lived propaganda triumph and a long-lived economic catastrophe.[6] Its deficiencies could be hidden in the artificial prosperity of the 1960s and 1970s. Later, when it was too late, they could not. Self-management gave Yugoslav socialism a global reputation for enlightenment it did not deserve. In its own way it was as dogmatic as anything in either Eastern Europe or the Soviet Union.

(6) *The myth of non-alignment*. This was Tito's illusion, a mixture of geopolitics and grandeur. Even before his death most Yugoslavs recognized it as unsustainable.[7] It became a choice between East and West – and most Yugoslavs, collectively or severally, were in no doubt that the choice would be the West, in general and Western Europe, in particular.

All these myths, except the Tito myth, lost their potency several years before Tito's death in 1980, but his charisma prevented the fatal effect of this deterioration from becoming obvious, although signs of it had been evident for many years. They began to appear in the early 1970s with the Croatian crisis and were greatly exacerbated by the global economic downturn that began with the first OPEC energy price increase in 1973. Like all the East European communist countries Yugoslavia never recovered from this.

Although Tito, by his very survival, could mask the symptoms of disintegration, his basic conservatism prevented them from being tackled in a way that might have slowed their progress. Tito himself was by no means unaware of the dangers. But his response was not to advance toward systemic change and democracy but, however spectacular some of his reorganizations were, to retreat to the 'safe' haven of Leninism. Tito remained true to Leninism throughout his life. He could broaden its framework and in the minds of the purists play fast and loose with some of its tenets, but he could never break that framework. In his last years he became its prisoner. The single remark that best revealed his true political convictions was made regarding the Sixth Congress of the Yugoslav League of Communists in 1952. It was this congress that recommended the party withdraw from active, everyday direction of the political life of the country into a guiding, teaching, arbitrational role, persuasive rather than coercive. Some 18 years afterward Tito said he had 'never liked the sixth congress'.[8] It went against the grain of everything that meant sense and order to him.

In the Croatian crisis that came to a head in December 1971, the first liberal–national challenge to the concept of a socialist–federal Yugoslavia, Tito responded by the only means he knew: the force of his personality and the threat of force, insinuations that the Russians might come, and massive purges. But having temporarily overcome the crisis in Zagreb with these means, Tito then adopted a policy, right up to his death, of restoring party control at the expense of all other potentially competing centres of authority. He also purged the liberal communist leadership in Serbia as well as in other republics. In the case of Serbia his hard-line policy in the early 1970s helped pave the way for the dogmatic nationalist leadership in the late 1980s. In 1976 he helped break the self-management system by fragmenting it. The system was doomed to ineffectiveness anyway, but the main beneficiary of its destruction was the Communist Party. Communist parties at the *republic level* now recovered some of the power they had lost in the previous quarter of a century. Thus, as Yugoslavia moved from a federation toward a *de facto* confederation, the credo that benefited was nationalism, and the institutions that benefited were the republican communist parties.[9]

The Resurgence of Nationalism

Tito's claim in 1962 that the national problem in Yugoslavia had been solved seems, in retrospect, a preposterous claim, but it was not wholly irrational at the time. The Leninist in Tito made it axiomatic that socialism could make nationalism irrelevant. More practical was the fact that, since the bloody reprisals against 'fascist' and 'nationalist' enemies inside Yugoslavia after the Second World War, and the unity engendered by the stand against Stalin in 1948, national differences had certainly dissipated. The economic prosperity, too, that had begun to be evident after the hardship of the 1940s and the early 1950s, was having its soothing effect.

But within a few years what had once been thought banished began to re-emerge as Yugoslavia's most intractable problem. In 1968 came the first serious Albanian demonstrations against Serbian rule in Kosovo, and in 1970 the Croatian crisis began. Leninist though he was, Tito was realistic and experienced enough to understand that the Kosovo and Croatian crises signalled the return of the national problem. The devolution, therefore, contained in the new constitution of 1974 was meant to pre-empt it. So was his promulgation in 1978 of the collective leadership system, to take effect after his death. This system's main aim was to establish and perpetuate strict equality between the nations of Yugoslavia in party posts and in the executive organs of federal government. After Tito's death his own posts of president of the Yugoslav state and of the League of Communists of Yugoslavia (LCY, the party) would be rotated annually on an ethnic basis. Hence, a new state and party leader from a different republic or province would be elected every year. It proved a singularly ineffective expedient, not solving the problem but rather demonstrating its insolubility. But it was an attempt; it was also further evidence of how Yugoslavia's chronic historical problem was preying on Tito's mind in the last years of his life.[10]

The Economic Debacle

It was Yugoslavia's economic decline that boosted nationalism beyond containment. As this decline cut more deeply, nationalism appeared as both a chimeric remedy and an appealing diversion. Since the beginning of the

1980s the economy had been in serious difficulties; living standards in all parts of the federation had been falling. These difficulties only exacerbated ethnic tensions.

The basic reasons for Yugoslavia's economic decline have been analysed elsewhere. What is worth emphasizing here is that the different attitudes towards tackling this decline brought to the fore the struggle between socialist 'liberalism' and 'conservatism', between reformers and reorganizers in Yugoslavia after 1965. The struggle turned out to be indecisive, but the fact that the liberals did not win meant that, not only the Yugoslav economy, but also Yugoslav democracy lost. The only winner was Yugoslav nationalism or, more correctly, nationalism in Yugoslavia. In 1982 a serious (though hardly audacious) economic reform programme was launched. Called a Stabilization Programme so as not to alarm anybody, the programme provided for a market economy and a wide range of free enterprise activity. Although not as far-reaching as some liberals (or the state of the economy itself) demanded, it would have involved important changes.

Had it been implemented seriously, it might have provided a basis for further capitalist-type reforms and put the economy back on the road to recovery, thereby not only hastening the fall of communism but also cushioning the budding democracy by stemming the nationalist tide. But the Stabilization Programme foundered on political and bureaucratic resistance, the triumph of which was assured by Branko Mikulić's appointment to the premiership in 1986. Mikulić substituted reorganization for genuine reform, and the liberal elements of the Stabilization Programme were lost in a welter of pointless bustle.

Mikulić's policies sent the economy plummeting further and only hastened Yugoslavia's disintegration. He resigned at the end of 1988.[11] It was ironical that his successor, in the twilight of the Yugoslav federation and as it turned out of Yugoslavia itself, was one of the most competent officials in the country's history. Ante Marković a successful Croatian economic official, and former factory director, instituted a programme of economic reform that resembled the shock therapy reform of the Mazowiecki government in Poland at the beginning of 1990.[12] (Both Marković and Leszek Balcerowicz, the Polish finance minister, had the same American adviser – Professor Jeffrey Sachs of Harvard.) The early period of Marković's programme was severe. The first few months of 1989 were almost as disastrous as anything under Mikulić.[13] But by the end of the year there was real promise. Trust between Belgrade and the International Monetary Fund (IMF) had been established, based on Marković's financial draconianism. Yugoslavia's hard currency debt went down slightly, there was a marked improvement in foreign trade, and foreign investments began to increase. Marković's most radical step was to make Yugoslavia's currency, the *dinar,* convertible, pegging it to the German Mark. His most dramatic success was in fighting inflation. By the end of 1990 it was down to around 13 per cent; at the beginning it had been in the thousands.[14]

These successes generated some optimism in the West about Yugoslavia's prospects. Within Yugoslavia itself there was for a time more optimism than at any time since Tito's death ten years before. Despite the hardships caused by the shock therapy, many Yugoslavs then respected Marković for his courage and principle. He became the symbol and the energetic proponent not only of economic but also of political liberalization. The pressure for the latter was certainly growing. The multi-party system began to sprout in different republics even before it was approved by the federal government in April 1989 – a sign of the latter's loss of authority. But Serbia, under Slobodan Milošević, continued to resist and became for a time the leader of Southern conservatism against Northern liberalism, a familiar enough divide throughout Yugoslavia's history.

But the Marković-generated optimism evident at the beginning of 1990 began to evaporate by the middle of the year. Inflation began to rise again, unemployment started to bite – some estimated it would hit two million by 1992 – and shortages increased.[15] Yugoslavia's international financial position also looked less encouraging than it had a few months earlier. Part of the general downturn could be explained in purely economic terms, but the growing force of nationalism was also beginning to erode the effectiveness of the reforms. Marković's reforms, radically market-orientated, even capitalistic, still hinged on the concept of a unified Yugoslav market. But the nationalist avalanche was ruining that prospect. Marković realized that an all-Yugoslav political, as well as economic, movement was necessary and founded in the summer of 1990 the Alliance of Reform Forces of Yugoslavia. It was a movement that tended to attract well-educated liberal men and women – some of the 'best and the brightest', like him. There were still quite a number of these in Yugoslavia at the end of 1990. But the ethos they reflected was fighting a losing battle.

The Serbian Revolt

Tito died in May 1980, and the next year serious riots in Kosovo resulted in considerable bloodshed. These riots, which proved to be a catalyst in the history of Yugoslavia's disintegration, brought the nationalist 'threat' to the top of the Yugoslav agenda. Most Yugoslavs associated this threat during the 1980s with the dissatisfaction and ambitions of Serbia; the Serbs associated it first with Albanian nationalism in Kosovo, and then with other Yugoslav nations they claimed were in league against them. The basis and background of Serbian nationalism need not be discussed here at any length. Its current manifestation was prompted by the provisions of the new Yugoslav constitution in 1974 which gave Vojvodina and Kosovo, the two autonomous provinces of Serbia, a degree of freedom amounting to virtual independence.

Vojvodina, with its population dominated by Serbs, presented few practical problems. But the Serbs saw Kosovo, with an Albanian majority approaching 90 per cent 'trespassing' on 'hallowed Serbian ground', as an existential problem. Behind their anger over the constitutional elevation of Kosovo was many Serbs' increasingly voiced conviction that Tito's Yugoslavia had sold them short throughout its history. It was now claimed that one of Tito's main aims from the beginning had been to cut Serbia down to size and strip it of its former pre-eminence.[16] Most Serbs had never doubted that, even if Yugoslavia could no longer be considered an extension of Serbia, or the Serbs its exclusive 'nation of state', they should still be accorded a special status. They believed this because of their numerical strength (about 40 per cent of the entire population), the extent of their territories, their historical sacrifices for the freedom of nations throughout south-eastern Europe, and (though fewer were now claiming this *openly*), their sheer superiority to everyone else. What they found (or thought they found), however, was just the opposite. To them Tito's concept was 'strong Yugoslavia, weak Serbia' – the federation could only flourish, even survive, at Serbia's expense. It was an ironic illustration of the chasm separating the Yugoslav nations that while the Serbs had this view of Yugoslavia, most of the other nations viewed the federation as Serb-dominated. Strengthening the federation, therefore, meant strengthening Serbia. Belgrade they regarded as the capital of Serbia first and as the capital of Yugoslavia second.[17]

Serbian resentment focused on Kosovo increased, exacerbated by their contempt for Albanians, inferior 'interlopers' – and Muslims to boot. As for the Albanians, they contributed their share to the mutual antipathy. Their behaviour was often brutal and primitive, although Serb reports of terror, rape, robbery, and the like in Kosovo were often exaggerated. But, underlying all the charges and countercharges, was the ineluctable fact that the Serbs in Kosovo, already a small minority, were still diminishing in number, while the Albanians there had the highest birthrate in Europe. The Serbs were living on borrowed time, while the Albanians were sensing their hour had struck.[18] And bordering on Kosovo was Albania itself, its birthrate the second highest in Europe. The Serbs did not just *suspect* Albanian intentions: they were sure of them. Hence the desperation of a proud nation determined to arrest what others saw as the course of history.

Serbian nationalist grievances, seething for many years, only needed a leader who could articulate them. Slobodan Milošević became that leader.

Milošević came, in a very short time, to dominate Serbian life in a way no other leader had since King Alexander in the inter-war period. He got to the top of Serbian politics by ruthless tactics, purging his opponents and subordinating the media to his own brand of populist nationalism.[19] In retrospect the Yugoslav civil war of 1991 was the logical culmination of Milošević's rise to power in 1987, though few suspected it at the time.

Milošević's attention first focused on Kosovo. He wanted to grind down the virtual independence the province had achieved through the new Yugoslav constitution of 1974. This could not be done at the federal level, since only Montenegro would have given Serbia full support on this issue. It could only be done through subverting the elected government in Kosovo itself – by intimidation both on the streets and in the corridors of power – and replacing it with a motley collection of Albanians ready to act in the Serbian interest.

But the mood among Albanian Kosovars had been changing radically. They were no longer the frightened docile nation the Serbs had got used to over the generations, but were increasingly ready to stand up for their rights. They found a leader, Azem Vllasi, around whom they could rally. Realizing Vllasi's danger as a potential Albanian national hero, Milošević was not content with forcing him out of power; he also held him responsible for the widespread disturbances in the province that were a response to Belgrade's political machinations. In doing so he made Vllasi a Kosovar hero, and a potential martyr.[20] In the end, though, the whole action against Vllasi turned out to be self-defeating. He was put on trial for subversion and incitement in October 1989, but the political nature of the whole operation was so obvious that the trial was discontinued the following April. A federal court dismissed the charges, and Vllasi's symbolic importance became stronger than ever.

His acquittal, and that of several members of the Kosovo youth parliament tried on similar charges, had been aimed at easing the tension in Kosovo. It only aggravated it, giving Albanians renewed determination and a prospect of victory in the new era Yugoslavia was entering. The previous month, in March 1989, Albanian aspirations in Kosovo were apparently shattered when the Serbian government enacted constitutional amendments killing articles in the 1974 federal constitution that had given virtual independence to Kosovo and Vojvodina. Now, with greater Serbian control over its internal security, judiciary, external relations, and social and financial planning, Kosovo began to resume the status most Serbs had always wanted for it – that of a dependent province.[21] There were widespread protests in the province, but as so often in the past, these might have lapsed into a sullen apathy but for the judicial decisions on Vllasi and the youth assembly members. This now emboldened the Kosovar Albanians to try to retrieve and then secure their rights. The Albanian language media in Kosovo, although subject to increasing persecution and harassment, became a more vigorous nationalistic force than ever before.

On 2 July 1990, a historic decision was made by the Albanian ethnic majority in the Kosovo provincial assembly, the constitutional legislative body of the province. They declared Kosovo 'an independent unit' in the Yugoslav community, equal to the other republics. In other words, Kosovo declared its sovereignty according to the principle of self-determination. In the future, this decision may become known as Kosovo's own 'declaration of independence'. It came on the very same day that the Slovenian assembly in Ljubljana declared Slovenia's sovereignty, a move that was the culmination of a long period of political and national reawakening.[22] Whether the timing of the moves in Ljubljana and Pristina, the capital of Kosovo, was orchestrated is not particularly important, but the Albanian action was of decisive importance in Yugoslav politics, attracting much sympathy throughout the federation as well as in the West.

The Kosovar decision seemed more explosive at the time than the Slovenian. The latter was part of a drawn-out process, the response to which came from the federal centre, if it came at all, and was likely to be delayed, indirect and feeble. The Kosovar action, on the other hand, was directed not against the federal centre but against the republic of Serbia, whose reaction was likely to be swift and severe. What the Kosovars essentially demanded was for Kosovo to become Yugoslavia's seventh republic. In its declaration the Pristina assembly did not specifically state this, but 'Kosovo-republic' had been the Albanians rallying cry since 1981. Republic status, however, was not the Albanians' *immediate* objective; it was independence from Serbia. Republic status would then follow. Albanians in Yugoslavia should now be recognized as a 'nation' and no longer a 'minority'. This also implied, of course, republic status.

The Serbian response was indeed swift and severe. Only three days after the Pristina assembly's announcement, the Serbian National Assembly in Belgrade ordered the dissolution of both the Kosovo government and assembly.[23] Serbia began governing the province directly from Belgrade for the first time since 1946. What followed was an attempt to stamp out all expressions of Albanian political autonomy. Kosovo became virtually an occupied province. The Albanian language media was now brought under direct Serbian control. Public buildings were tightly guarded and essential public services and industries 'protected'. Tension throughout the province increased, and many incidents reflected Albanian discontent. One such incident could at any time cause a bloodbath. Many observers had begun predicting it.

Civil Society and Nationalism in Slovenia

It was in Slovenia that dissident elements began in 1986 the agitation for sovereignty that would eventually lead to the breakup of Yugoslavia. Economically, Slovenia was clearly the most important and developed republic. From this standpoint its importance to the federation as a whole was obvious. It was, in fact, precisely on this point that Slovene nationalist grievances began to develop. Slovenes claimed that their republic was putting much into the federation, mainly to help the 'have not' republics, and getting little out of it. With Croatia it had conducted a rigorous campaign for a quarter of a century against the central government's syphoning off too much of its earnings from hard currency exports. But Slovenian nationalism, as such, had never played much of a role in Yugoslav politics either before or after the Second World War. There was none of the antipathy to the Serbs, for example, that characterized the Croats. In the pre-war kingdom, the Slovenes had supported the Yugoslav idea and had enjoyed good relations with the Serbs.

In sharp contrast to Serbian development, Slovenian politics in the second half of the 1980s developed from socialism to a democratic liberalism infused with nationalism. While Slovenian socialism was evolving in response to the progress of civil society, Serbia was still in the grip of traditional and orthodox, even dogmatic, socialism. Subsequently, as Slovene politics evolved toward the building of the constitutional state, so Slovene nationalism developed, too. But it was almost a reluctant phenomenon, partly in response to Serbian belligerence and what was beginning to look like old-fashioned Serb great-nation chauvinism. In any case Slovene nationalism has never had the brooding edge that has characterized the Croatian, or the insensitive arrogance of the Serb. Ethnically homogeneous and insulated from the passions that have rent other parts of Yugoslavia, the Slovenes were different – calmer, cooler, more materialistic, not inclined to push to extremes. To many southern Slavs they seemed non-Slavic.

The 'civil society' concept in Slovenia began as 'socialism with a human face', rather of the Prague Spring variety. Since the early 1960s the Slovene Communist Party had been reformist and open-minded. Slovenes claimed, with some justice but with little tact, that even their communist politics distinguished them from the rest of Yugoslavia. Certainly the Central European heritage played some role here. The Habsburg–Ottoman divide, with its Roman Catholic–Byzantine Orthodox parallel, is a valid enough explanation for many of the regional differences in Yugoslavia as long as it is not carried too far. What and where the divide is between Central and Eastern Europe is a complex matter easily vulgarized or corrupted. But, bearing in mind the perils, Slovenia is a distinct, 'Central European' corner of Yugoslavia. It is also more open to Western influences than any other part, except the Dalmatian coast of Croatia. It was no surprise, therefore, that its politics should become affected by liberal developments in the rest of the socialist world. Originally, what Milan Kučan and the group of reformers in the Slovene party aimed for was political democratization and the switch to a market economy. This reform concept also envisaged tolerating alternative youth movements and other political groupings under a much enlarged communist party umbrella. But like other communist reformers in the second half of the 1980s, Gorbachev chiefly, Kučan and his followers found themselves swept along by the accelerating tide of reform.[24]

By the end of 1989 Slovenia was almost abreast of Hungary in the progress toward a democratic, constitutional state and by the end of 1990 was a fully working parliamentary democracy. A democratic government had been in place since May. In the free elections held in April, Kučan's services in helping usher in democracy were rewarded when he was elected president with a clear majority over his opponent from the united democratic opposition parties (DEMOS). But the DEMOS won an overall majority in the newly elected Slovene National Assembly, and the Christian Democrat, Lojze Peterle, became prime minister.

The Revival of Croatian Nationalism

More than Kosovo, far more than Slovenia, it was the increasingly bitter interaction between Croatia and Serbia that presented the biggest danger to Yugoslavia's stability and survival. The key to Yugoslavia's very existence had always been the Serbia–Croatia nexus. Relations between the two nations had been blighted by jealousy, hatred and the most atrocious violence. But both nations had known that as long as there was a Yugoslavia, their fates were intertwined. They were hostage to Yugoslavia's survival. Both also knew that separation, however desirable it might seem to many, might be impossible without serious bloodshed.

Croatian nationalism had ruined the prospects of the Serb-dominated inter-war Yugoslavia and, as mentioned earlier, the outburst of Croatian nationalism in 1970–71 had caused communist Yugoslavia's worst domestic crisis till then. After that Croatia had retreated into hibernation. Politics became conventional and conservative, and the nation as a whole lapsed into moody introspection. But the crises in 1989 in Kosovo and Slovenia shook the Croats out of their lethargy.

Unlike in Serbia, where nationalism revived under orthodox communist rule, it was democracy that helped revive nationalism in Croatia. The Slovenes were first in the democratic race but the Croats ran them a close second. Croatia's first free general election since 1945 began in late April 1990 and completed its final round early in May. It resulted in an overall majority in the Croatian *Sabor* (parliament) for the Croatian Democratic Community coalition led by Franjo Tudjman. The former ruling Communist Party in Croatia gained only 66 seats out of a total of 356 and went into opposition for the first time since 1945. It had tried very hard to modernize itself and keep up with the new democratic times. Like communist parties elsewhere in Yugoslavia and throughout Eastern Europe, it had modified its name: it was now the League of Communists–Party of Democratic Change. But this did not impress an electorate bent on radical change. The majority of Croatian voters wanted as little to do as possible with any kind of socialism. They opted for democracy.

But they also opted for nationalism – and it was nationalism that began to consume Croatian politics. This was the big difference between Croatia and Slovenia. The Slovenes were nationalist, too, but they were 'civil-nationalists'. Croatian nationalism was more dominant, and much more bitter – and it was nationalism with a palpable anti-Serbian tinge. Franjo Tudjman, the new president, had been a young partisan general under Tito. He later moved to strongly Croatian nationalist positions and, after the Croatian crisis of 1971, was imprisoned by Tito. More recently Tudjman had attracted attention by statements smacking of the *Ustaša* type of Croat nationalism that had marred Croatia's reputation during the Second World War. Some of his attacks on Serbs were very extreme.[25] After his election he took markedly more moderate positions, but there was still a strong anti-Serb edge to his rhetoric.[26]

The turn of events in Croatia met with a powerful reaction in Serbia. For most Serbs, Tudjman's election gave a new impetus to Serbian nationalism, a second front to go with Kosovo. Even without Tudjman and the ghosts, real or imagined, of the *Ustaša,* Serbian interest in Croatia had markedly increased under Milošević because of a new and potentially disruptive principle proclaimed by the Serbian leader. He virtually assumed the patronage of *all* Serbs throughout the federation. In doing so, he swept aside what one writer has called the 'Titoist feudal principle, that had firmly tied each leadership to a particular territory, and began to speak for all Serbs'.[27] Nearly a quarter of the Serbs in Yugoslavia (two million) live outside Serbia. Nearly 12 per cent of the total Croatian population of 4 600 000 are Serb; in Bosnia-Herzegovina the percentage is about 33. Some of these now began to look to Milošević for support, protection, and even eventual reunion with Serbia. In doing so they were responding to increasingly obvious signs from Serbia that the government there now regarded them as part of the Serbian patrimony.

The Serbian minorities most responsive to Milošević's overtures were the *prečani*, the Serbs 'beyond the border' in Croatia. Most of them live in ethnically homogeneous districts on the border now with Bosnia-Herzegovina. They are Knin-Benkovac on the Dalmatian coast, Lika, the Kordun, and Banija. The dual effect of Milošević's one-nation mindset and Tudjman's electoral victory made these Serbian enclaves ripe for disruption. The first serious disruption occurred in Knin in the summer and autumn of 1990. Its details were widely reported at the time.[28] Basically it arose from demands from all the Serb communities for cultural and eventually political autonomy inside Croatia. But few doubted that many Serbs hoped for detachment from Croatia. In the late summer, disturbances spread to other Serb enclaves but soon petered out without any real bloodshed.

These disturbances in the summer of 1990 were minor compared with what was to come. But despite the general relief over this, most Yugoslavs were already aware of their serious implications. Serb–Croat distrust was as deep as ever, and the memories of a half-century ago were as clear as ever. Next time the incidents could be major ones. When civil war came to Yugoslavia it would certainly begin here. These incidents also underlined the impotence of the federal government. The main actors here were Croatia and Serbia, both in the grip of heady nationalism. The hope was that responsibility, even statesmanship, might assert itself. The fear was that a relatively minor incident would set off a train of events leading to disaster. And that was what did happen.

Bosnia the Key

The incidents in the Serbian enclaves in Croatia reminded everyone of the role Bosnia-Herzegovina might play in the future of Yugoslavia – in its reconstruction or in its dissolution. The southern Slav republic, *par excellence*, multi-ethnic and multi-religious, Bosnia-Herzegovina had played a relatively subdued role so far in Yugoslavia's history. But, as discussed in Chapter 9, some observers saw it as the key to the country's future.

The very artificiality of Bosnia-Herzegovina gave it both its significance and its weakness as a nation-state. Its ethnic composition was over 40 per cent Muslim, 33 per cent Serb, and 18 per cent Croat. This was the basic reason for its vulnerability, even more so than its overall economic and social backwardness. Serbia had historical and ethnic claims to large parts of it; Croatia had similar claims to smaller parts of it. Both claims were being aired with increasing persistence (although ostensibly unofficially) at the end of the 1980s.[29] And the claims overlapped, with Serbs and Croats sometimes claiming the same territory and ever higher numbers of ethnic kinsmen. In the crossfire of these claims were the Muslims. The descendants of converts to Islam during the Ottoman occupation, the Muslims of Bosnia-Herzegovina (though not the Muslim Albanians of Kosovo) were allowed by Tito in 1968 to become members of the new Yugoslav Muslim nation.[30]

Bosnia-Herzegovina had been created to keep Serbs and Croats apart, an essential precondition for a stable Yugoslavia, and the decision regarding Muslim nationhood was a further step towards this end. For a while it seemed to be succeeding, but as the promise of Tito's Yugoslavia faded, it was only a matter of time before the artificiality of the Bosnia-Herzegovina solution became apparent, only a matter of time before the Serb–Croat scramble for both its territory and its citizens began. Many Serbs and Croats had never really accepted the concept of Muslim nationhood. Throughout the centuries Christian Serbs had seen Bosnian Muslims as traitors to both their faith and their nation – renegade Serbs, in short.[31] And few Croats were satisfied with the official statistic of 18 per cent of the republic's population as Croat. As mentioned earlier, both Serbs and Croats also had territorial claims on Bosnia-Herzegovina. And, finally, there were those crucial Serbian enclaves in Croatia, separated from Serbia by Bosnian-Herzegovinan territory. The fact that they were thus separated might well have prevented civil war in Yugoslavia in 1989. But, as Yugoslavia disintegrated further it made Bosnia-Herzegovina more vulnerable.

In these circumstances how stable was the republic internally? How much Bosnian-Herzegovinan consciousness could survive? Such a consciousness had been seen as essential to the development of the Yugoslav consciousness. But whatever Yugoslav consciousness that had ever existed was fast disappearing in 1990. How much of a Bosnian-Herzegovinan consciousness had *ever* existed, anyway? Generally speaking, only among Muslims. It gave statehood to their religion; it legitimized their sense of nationhood; it gave them dignity and power. They had to share their power, but they still had enough to feel relatively secure for the first time since Ottoman rule. Besides, power brought place and patronage, which those Muslims who benefited had no difficulty in accepting.

For the Serbs and Croats it was different. Bosnia-Herzegovina, for all except the place-men in the bureaucracy, was a second-best solution, a political arrangement made by Tito after the Second World War. For them, it was not a nation-state as it was for the Muslims. This difference in attitude became more marked as the tensions within Yugoslavia increased. The Muslims started caring even more about Bosnia-Herzegovina; its Serbs and Croats even less.

Serbian Montenegro; Macedonian Macedonia

In Montenegro the situation was as simple as in Bosnia-Herzegovina it was complicated. Despite their own distinctive, proud and turbulent history, the Montenegrins were basically Serbs, or a strikingly similar variant thereof. Few Montenegrins had ever questioned this fact, even those cultural propagandists after the Second World War who set out to justify the establishment of a Montenegrin republic numbering less than half a million people. The Montenegrin political elite had always been divided between those wanting to preserve separation from, and those wanting a merger with, Serbia.[32] But in times of crisis Montenegrins knew where their place was, and in this new situation where both Montenegrins and Serbs felt threatened, common cause was inexorably leading to common identity.

In Macedonia, the situation was quite different. Montenegro had never been wholly subdued by the Ottomans and had been granted formal independence at the end of the eighteenth century. Macedonia had remained Turkish till the eve of the First World War. The Montenegrins were never in any doubt that, if they were not Montenegrin, they were Serbian. The Macedonian identity had always been a matter of controversy. Montenegro, though not without ethnic minorities, had not been unduly troubled by them. The very name of Macedonia had become a synonym for ethnic mixture, and even today the presence of well over 500 000 Albanians and a large number of ethnic Turks seriously complicates the domestic scene. Historically, Serbs, Greeks, and Bulgarians have claimed the Orthodox Christians of Macedonia as theirs. Most nineteenth century Western ethnographers tended to agree that they were Bulgarian, and the weight of historical and linguistic evidence seemed to confirm this.

Macedonian revolutionaries at the end of the nineteenth century were divided between pro-Bulgarians and those claiming separate Macedonian nationhood.[33] In the Serbian dominated kingdom of Yugoslavia Macedonia was called 'South Serbia', with no doubt (at least in Belgrade) about its Orthodox inhabitants being Serbs. After the Second World War Tito's Yugoslavia revived the historic concept of Macedonian nationhood and a minor industry sprang up bent on rediscovering and refurbishing it. In the republic's capital of Skopje a new Macedonian ruling elite moved into place. A Macedonian nationalism developed quickly, and for many years most inhabitants of the republic responded positively to it.

Macedonian nationalism, though, would always remain vulnerable until it received general international recognition, especially from its neighbours. But from Bulgarians, Greeks and most Serbs it never did. Bulgaria, with its intense feeling of historical deprivation, reluctantly recognized the territorial integrity of Macedonia but proceeded to gainsay this by refusing to recognize the Macedonians as a nation. The same went for Greece, in whose territory most of historic Macedonia lay. Within the Yugoslav federation itself, both Macedonia and Macedonians were officially recognized by everybody. But the vast majority of Serbs still saw Macedonia as another artificial concoction, like Bosnia-Herzegovina. For Macedonia they still read South Serbia. As for Macedonians, whatever they might claim to be, they were not entitled to nationhood at Serbia's expense. And as Slobodan Milošević strode to power on a wave of Serbian frustration, he too seemed to represent this thinking.

Most Macedonians for a long time thought their national aspirations best served by the survival of the Yugoslav framework. Federal Yugoslavia had given them a dignity they had never previously had and they wished its continuance, no matter how modified the form. The idea of a confederation attracted those who now realized that Tito's Yugoslavia was doomed. Thus the champions of confederalism in prosperous Slovenia and Croatia found supporters in impoverished Macedonia. As will be discussed in Chapter 9, a growing number of Macedonians, however, were already leaning to outright independence, and this would have international ramifications.

The Enigma of the Military

No military in any East European communist country – with the possible exception of Poland – historically enjoyed more respect and prestige than the Yugoslav. This dated from the legendary Partisan days in the Second World War. Subsequently the military was seen as one of the most important institutions unifying the Yugoslav federation. As other such institutions died (Tito) or faded into insignificance (the League of Communists of Yugoslavia), the *centripetal* property of the military increased accordingly.

It always had a privileged position and had always pursued an active role in Yugoslav politics. But this had never been an interfering one. The closest military force ever came to being used in communist Yugoslavia was when Tito threatened its use in the Croatian crisis of December 1971. And this was at Tito's behest, not theirs. The threat, plus Tito's towering prestige, brought the crisis to an end. But even in 1971, with Yugoslavia relatively strong and Tito still at the height of his powers, doubts were expressed about how effective the military would have been. Some suspected it could have led to civil war, meaning that – even then, in this most supranational of all institutions – nationalist, ethnic centrifugalism within the army would have caused an implosion that could have engulfed the country. Such suspicions had become near certainties by 1990. But many politicians and citizens continued to be wary of the army. Some still saw it as the only force now capable, not so much of preventing, but even resisting, disintegration.[34]

An increasing number of senior officers, almost exclusively Serbs, in the second half of the 1980s began to voice concern over the state of Yugoslavia, and some of them seemed prepared to take action. This coincided with a recentralization of the structure of command of the federal army (JNA – Yugoslav People's Army). In the 1960s and 1970s the command had, to a considerable extent, been decentralized along national lines. Thus, most frequently, a Croat general commanded federal units in Croatia, a Macedonian in Macedonia and so on. In the course of the 1980s, however, this trend was reversed and Serb generals tended to move back into command positions in other republics. This was to be of great significance when civil war broke out in 1991. Early in 1988 in Slovenia, when communist power was beginning to disintegrate, the Military Council in Belgrade apparently devised a contingency plan for intervention in case 'counter-revolutionary' disorder broke out in the republic.[35] Exposure of this plan was actually a boost to Slovene nationalism. It also strengthened anti-Serb feeling in the republic. The possibility of military action, therefore, stiffened rather than softened national resistance.

Tension between the military and nationalists in Slovenia continued, and as nationalism gathered strength in Croatia, civil-military tension increased there too. Disturbances in Knin in the summer of 1990 have already been discussed. In view of what was to happen the next year, the most disturbing aspect about them was the refusal of federal military units to help the Croatian police in dealing with the rebellious Serbs. (The Croats complained that their police had actually been prevented by federal units from taking necessary action.) This naturally strengthened the conviction in Zagreb that the federal military was simply the tool of Serbia. It should have been a warning to outside observers.

An even more serious incident took place in Ljubljana at the end of September 1990. An amendment to the republic constitution transferred control over Slovenian territorial defence forces from the federal state presidency to that of Slovenia. The Yugoslav federal secretariat for national defence denounced the measure as unconstitutional and promised steps to prevent it from being implemented. But the Slovene authorities announced that they were replacing the federally appointed general who commanded the republic's territorial defence forces with a Slovene officer. The dispute became centred on the control of the territorial defence force headquarters in Ljubljana. The tension was eased, at least temporarily, when the Slovenes set up their own defence force headquarters. Now, therefore, Slovenia had two such establishments – one federal, one republican. There was an *opera buffa* aspect to the whole affair, very Slovenian in its practical way out and its avoidance of bloodshed. But this first big challenge to their sovereignty aroused much emotion even among the placid Slovenes.[36] If a new incident occurred it might not be managed with such finesse. And if something like that were to occur in Zagreb it might not be handled with such maturity.

But the question remained: How credible was the military as an effective arm of the federal government at the beginning of the 1990s? Against determined republican resistance how effective would it be? The senior officer corps was still reported as being about 70 per cent Serbian, but among the junior officers and particularly among the other ranks, the Serbs were nowhere near so strong and nationalist feeling often ran high. Some 12 per cent of the enlisted men were Albanian, and in 1988 one new recruit in four was reported as being Albanian.

The truth was obvious: By the beginning of the 1990s the military was also infected by nationalism and would not be effective in any *protracted* action designed to protect the federation. As for the Serbian-dominated officer corps, their Yugoslavism was no longer that of Tito and the Partisan-inspired legend (if indeed, in the case of many it ever was that). It had now reverted to the Serbian-style Yugoslavism of the inter-war era.[37] For many officers Yugoslavia was identical with Serbia, or at least an extension of it. They were dedicated to their military profession and, of course, their careers, livelihood, and sense of purpose were bound up with the federal army. But they were incapable of any loyalty of which Serbia was not the core.

Notes

1 For pre-war Yugoslavia see Stephen Clissold (ed.), *A History of Yugoslavia from Early Times to 1966* (Cambridge, Cambridge University Press, 1966). For Tito's Yugoslavia, see Rusinow, op. cit.

2 For a fuller discussion of these 'myths' see J. F. Brown, *Surge to Freedom: The End of Communist Rule in Eastern Europe* (Durham, NC, Duke University Press, 1991), pp. 221–3.

3 Still the best biography of Tito is by Milovan Djilas, *Tito: Eine Kritische Biographie* (Vienna, Verlag Fritz Molden, 1980).

4 See Lendvai, op. cit., pp. 57–65.

5 Duncan Wilson, *Tito's Yugoslavia* (Cambridge, Cambridge University Press, 1979), p. 141, quoting Tito's remarks to delegates from the party school of political science.

6 The literature on self-management is vast. Much of it has turned out to have been too impressionable. One of the most insightful comments on it was by Dusko Doder: 'In dealing with Yugoslavs generally I could never figure out where Balkan habits let off and self-management took over', *The Yugoslavs* (London, Allen and Unwin, 1979), p. 96.

7 In conversation with well-educated and 'internationalist' Yugoslavs in 1986 in four Yugoslav cities, I heard nothing but contempt for the whole nonalignment policy and

experience. On Yugoslavia's developing relations with the European Community, see R. T., 'Engerer Kontakte zwischen Jugoslawien und der EG', *Neue Zürcher Zeitung*, 1 June 1990 (Fernausgabe, Nr. 125).

8 Quoted by Rusinow, pp. 281 and 312.

9 See Brown, *Eastern Europe and Communist Rule*, pp. 338–9. On the moves during the 1980s to *de facto* 'confederalization', see Viktor Meier, 'Jugoslawien als Konföderation', *Frankfurter Allgemeine Zeitung*, 14 May 1984.

10 See Brown, *Eastern Europe and Communist Rule*, pp. 358–61.

11 On reform attempts in the early 1980s and Mikulić's failure, see Viktor Meier, 'Yugoslavia: Worsening Economic and Nationalist Crisis', in William E. Griffith (ed.), *Central and Eastern Europe: The Opening Curtain?* (Boulder, CO, Westview Press, 1989), pp. 267–70.

12 On Marković see Viktor Meier, 'Marković will Jugoslawien mit einem Notprogramm retten', *Frankfurter Allgemeine Zeitung*, 23 December 1989.

13 For a graphic illustration of the hardships being caused, particularly by inflation, see Carl E. Buchalla, 'Das Land der notleidenden Millionäre', *Süddeutsche Zeitung*, 14 August 1989.

14 Reuters (Belgrade), 23 January 1990.

15 Brown, *Surge to Freedom*, p. 236.

16 Ibid., pp. 224–30. One of the most important books illustrating this Serb mentality was by Veselin Djuretić, *The Allies and the Yugoslav War Drama*, which was published in Belgrade in 1985 and caused a minor sensation.

17 On mounting Serb resentment, see Christopher Cviic, 'The Background and Implications of the Domestic Scene in Yugoslavia', in Shoup and Hoffman, *Problems of Balkan Security*, op. cit., pp. 89–119.

18 Brown, *Surge to Freedom*, pp. 228–30.

19 Ibid., p. 228.

20 Ibid., p. 229.

21 Ibid., pp. 226–7.

22 Milan Andrejevich, 'Kosovo and Slovenia Declare Their Sovereignty', Radio Free Europe Research Background Report, 3 July 1990.

23 Milan Andrejevich, 'Serbia Cracks Down on Kosovo', Radio Free Europe Research Background Report, 6 July 1990. See also Carl Buchalla, 'Kolonisationsversuche mit der Dampfwalze', *Süddeutsche Zeitung*, 21 August 1990.

24 For a revealing glimpse of this reform communist turned liberal democrat see Kučan's interview with *Der Spiegel* (Hamburg), 26 November 1990.

25 For examples of this type of sentiment see C. Sr., 'Wachsende Nationalismus in Zagreb', *Neue Zürcher Zeitung*, 24 March 1990 (Fernausgabe, Nr. 69).

26 See, for example, his interview with Carl Gustav Ströhm in *Die Welt*, 1 September 1990.

27 Cviic, loc. cit., p. 92.

28 See 'The Serbs Start to Play It Rough', *The Economist*, 25 August 1990; see Chuck Sudetic, 'Croatia's Serbs Declare Their Autonomy', *The New York Times*, 2 October 1990.

29 For an excellent description and analysis of the situation in Bosnia-Herzegovina in the fall of 1990 see 'Im Zeichen des Satans', in *Profil* (Vienna), 29 October 1990.

30 On the important difference between Yugoslavia's Muslims and muslims, see Brown, *Eastern Europe and Communist Rule*, pp. 417–18. On Muslim nationality generally see Sabrina P. Ramet, 'Primordial Ethnicity or Modern Nationalism? The Case of Yugoslavia's Muslims Reconsidered', *South Slav Journal*, Spring–Summer 1990.

31 Many Serbs would still agree with the sentiments of Stojan Protić, a former prime

minister of Yugoslavia and a leading member of the Serbian Radical Party. At the end of the First World War, when asked what was in store for the Bosnian Muslims, he reportedly said, 'As soon as our Army crosses the Drina (i.e., into Bosnia – ed.), it will give the Turks (i.e., Bosnian Muslims – ed.) twenty-four – perhaps forty-eight – hours to return to the faith of their forefathers (i.e., Orthodox Christianity – ed.), and then slay those who refuse, as we did in Serbia in the past.' Quoted by Ivo Banac, 'The National Question in Yugoslavia: Origins, History, Politics' (Ithaca, NY, Cornell University Press, 1984), p. 107.

32 See Banac, pp. 289–90, for this division between Montenegro's 'Whites' and 'Greens'.

33 See Elisabeth Barker, *Macedonia: Its Place in Balkan Power Politics* (London, Royal Institute of International Affairs, 1950); Stephen Palmer and Robert R. King, *Yugoslav Communism and the Macedonian Question* (Hamden, CT, Shoestring Press, 1971); Paul Shoup, *Communism and the Yugoslav National Question* (New York, Columbia University Press, 1968), pp. 111–19; Robert R. King, *Minorities under Communism: Nationalities as a Source of Tension Among Balkan Communist States* (Cambridge, MA, Harvard University Press, 1983), pp. 91–9; Duncan M. Perry, *The Politics of Terror: The Macedonian Revolutionary Movements, 1893–1903* (Durham, NC, Duke University Press, 1988).

34 See Brown, *Eastern Europe and Communist Rule*, pp. 361–2.

35 See Meier, 'Yugoslavia: Worsening Economic and Nationalist Crisis', in Griffith (ed.), *Central and Eastern Europe*, pp. 271–2.

36 For a review of this and other incidents in which the military were involved in the course of 1990, see Milan Andrejevich, 'The Military's Role in the Current Constitutional Crisis', Radio Free Europe Report on Eastern Europe, Vol. 1, No. 45, 9 November 1990.

37 See Viktor Meier, 'Weshalb der Armee Jugoslawiens das Putschen Schwerfällt: Serben beherrschen das Offizier – korps, die anderen Nationalitäten stellen die Mannschaften', *Frankfurter Allgemeine Zeitung*, 17 October 1990.

5 Albania: A Matter of Survival

The Albanians, heirs to the ancient Illyrians, were one of the last Balkan peoples to fall under Turkish domination, in the second half of the fifteenth century. Most of them converted to Islam, many fought with distinction in the Sultan's armies, and some formed part of the palace and military elite. The relatively benevolent treatment Albanians experienced at the hands of the Porte did not make them any less anxious for their freedom than most other Balkan peoples. They had their own folk hero, Skanderbeg, who resisted the Turks in the middle of the fifteenth century shortly after the Albanians were submerged in the Ottoman Empire and who personified the national myth.

But in the nineteenth century Albanians were caught between the retreating imperialism of the Ottomans and the advancing nationalism of liberated Balkan nations like the Serbs, Montenegrins, Greeks and Bulgarians. For the Albanians these newly liberated nations became the new imperialists, disputing their territory and regarding them as inferior beings in a way the Turks had never done. The Serbs and Montenegrins in particular became their most rapacious enemies. When Albania finally achieved independence in 1912 it was largely a result of the Western powers' determination to prevent Serbia, Tsarist Russia's spearhead in the Balkans, from gaining direct access to the Adriatic.[1]

The circumstances of its creation made Albania a client-state almost by definition, unable to survive without patronage. In the inter-war years its president and then king, Ahmed Zogu, first depended on Yugoslavia. Then to escape Yugoslavia he turned to Italy; hence began that fatal embrace with Mussolini that ended with Italian troops in Tirana on Good Friday, 1939. After the Second World War, the Albanian Communist Party, a minuscule formation led mostly by Western-educated sons of Moslem landowners from the southern part of the country, seized power thanks partly to the help of Yugoslav partisans and the sponsorship of the British military command in the Balkans.[2]

The Yugoslav communists had established the Albanian party in 1941 and after 1945 completely dominated both it and the country as a whole – politically, economically and militarily. There was a strong possibility that Albania might be incorporated into the Yugoslav federation as a seventh republic, including Kosovo (or the Kosovo-Metohija Region, as it was first called). Stalin in his celebrated gesture to Djilas indicated that he had no objection to this, just as he had no objection later to union between Bulgaria and Yugoslavia.[3] Some senior members of the Albanian party (most notably the interior minister, Koce Xoxe) strongly supported the union with Yugoslavia. But others, including the leader of the party, Enver Hoxha, and Mehmet Shehu, later to become prime minister, opposed it. In their internal struggle with the Xoxe faction they played the national card, and there is little doubt that they had the support of whatever Albanian public opinion existed at the time.[4]

The Tito break with Stalin in 1948 saved Albania from total Yugoslav domination. It also saved the position, and probably the life, of Enver Hoxha, whose faction declared full support for the Soviet Union. From then on began Hoxha's fantastic career. With a combination of skill, courage, ruthlessness and luck, he became master of Albania and remained so till his death in 1985. He very narrowly survived the Tito–Khrushchev rapprochement of 1955–56. Probably only the Hungarian Revolution and the renewed Moscow–Belgrade enmity saved him then. Later, at the end of the 'fifties and the early 'sixties, he was in danger again from Khrushchev's renewed attempt at rapprochement with Tito – and perhaps also from Moscow's attempts to improve relations with Greece, the country Albanians feared most after Yugoslavia. He then took advantage of the emerging Sino–Soviet dispute, denounced Khrushchev, personally and politically, and now made Albania the client state of China.[5] The further away the patron the greater the scope for manœuvre, and Chinese patronage was by no means of the dominating variety the Soviet, not to mention the Yugoslav, had been. And Chinese economic help, though sparse compared with what the Soviets had given, did enable Albania to fight serious food shortages in the early 'sixties and then proceed with a classic communist industrialization.[6] Albania has quantities of raw materials – oil, natural gas, hydroelectric power – and has derived considerable foreign income from the export of chrome and nickel. (It is the world's third largest producer of chrome.[7]) Industrial and agricultural progress, in terms of statistics that brook little auditing, was always impressive – mainly because of the base from which it all began.

While under Chinese patronage the Hoxha regime, more probably of its own free will than under any constraint, initiated some of the massive mobilization campaigns that were usually considered the hallmark of

Chairman Mao. One of the most spectacular of these was the war against religion and in 1967, after the closure of all churches and mosques, Albania was declared the first atheist state in the world. The 'only religion for an Albanian is Albania', said Hoxha, misusing one of the first slogans of his country's national movement of the nineteenth century.[8]

All in all, Albania's relationship with China brought some advantages. These were mostly economic,[9] but there was also a degree of protection involved – protection against those enemies (real or imagined) that have always haunted Albania's as well as Hoxha's, national, sensitive psyche. True, 'distant waters cannot quench fire', in Chou En-lai's phrase in 1971,[10] and Hoxha, Shehu, and their associates never dreamt they could. China could never militarily protect Albania. But still Beijing provided a political and psychological cover of value. And Albania had *its* uses for China during that brief period in the 1960s when the latter seemed to be challenging the Soviet Union for communist world hegemony. Albania, after all, *was* a ruling party, the Chinese bridgehead in Europe. At the first Albanian party congress after the break with Moscow there were four important ruling parties represented: China, Romania, North Korea and North Vietnam. There were also 31 representatives from splinter, pro-Chinese parties from various parts of the world.[11] For the Chinese leaders this must have seemed a promising muster.

But despite their temporary uses for each other, the alliance between China and Albania was a bizarre one of temporary convenience only. It began to cool in the 'seventies and eventually ended in 1978, with the kind of denunciation, if somewhat less violent, by the Albanian media, led by Hoxha personally, to which the Soviet leadership had been subjected in the early 'sixties.[12] The rift began well before Chairman Mao died and widened considerably after his death. For Mao's more pragmatic successors the importance of being Albania dwindled substantially. The question of ideological purity, of hegemony in the world movement, gave way to more practical considerations of undoing the damage caused by Mao, encouraging economic development, and formulating a practical rather than romantic foreign policy. From the Albanian view, the worse sin of all was Beijing's rapprochement with Yugoslavia.

After the final break with China in 1978 Chinese specialists soon left the country and Albania for the first time in its history as a modern state was alone, without either patron or occupier: Yugoslavia, Italy, then the occupation of the Second World War, then Yugoslavia again, the Soviet Union, and finally China. Where now? It was a question many, both inside and outside the country, were asking. In their public pronouncements, the Albanian leaders, none more determinedly than Hoxha himself, loudly maintained that Albania would ask favours of no one. This was the kind of rhetoric

Hoxha had used after the break with the Soviet Union; but then he knew he had China to fall back on. Now there was no one – or no one acceptable.

Between 1978 and his death in 1985, Hoxha made 'self-reliance' part of the Albanian national mythology. He also consecrated it in Albanian law. A new constitution in 1976 expressly forbade the raising of international loans. But reality was not as stark as Hoxha's rhetoric. What he seemed to have in mind within the framework of self-reliance was a three-cornered strategy: intensified economic relations with the third world; business (not client) relations with China; and expanding (but, again, not client) relations with the West.[13] But still no relations with the United States and the Soviet Union, the two superpowers.

Trade with the third world increased perceptibly. It resumed with China, although economic relations were never to be like what they were before 1978. The fact that there was any resumption at all puzzled some observers. But it was mutually beneficial. Albania needed parts and servicing for the Chinese equipment it had received in the past. China's interest was probably more political: to do what it could to prevent Albania from looking toward Moscow.

But it was Albania's opening to Western Europe that was to matter most. Before his death Hoxha improved relations with Greece and Italy, and economic relations with France were intensified. But the most intriguing and promising West European opening was with the Federal Republic of Germany. Franz-Josef Strauss, minister-president of Bavaria, had much to do with establishing early contacts, and in 1984 he made his first personal visit to Tirana.

The Diplomatic Revolution

But the real opening came only after Hoxha's death in April 1986. The new Albanian leader, Ramiz Alia, built on the foundation already laid. By the end of 1987 relations with Greece had improved beyond recognition. The 47-year-old state of war that still technically existed between the two countries finally ended and agreements reached on top-level exchanges of visits. With Yugoslavia, though, there was only marginal improvement. The worsening situation in Kosovo prevented anything more.

But while still remaining selective in its bilateral relations in the region Albania, after 20 years of resolute opposition to the notion, became a convert to multilateral schemes of co-operation. It was a basic change of attitude. In December 1987 Albania attended an all-Balkan conference on the Balkans and in February 1988 even took part in a regional foreign ministers' conference in Belgrade. The highpoint of this new policy of co-operation was in October 1990 when Albania itself hosted a Balkan foreign ministers' conference.

Ground-breaking though these developments were, they were provincial compared with other diplomatic initiatives by Tirana. The biggest breakthrough came with West Germany: the already promising contacts led to the establishment of diplomatic relations with West Germany in October 1987.[14] Work began on a programme of economic co-operation, and Albania looked set to benefit considerably from its new relationship. In the meantime the Albanians were busy making new openings in several Western countries. Even so, the diplomatic revolution that occurred in 1990 took most observers by surprise.

In April 1990 at a plenum of the Communist Party's Central Committee, Ramiz Alia announced that Albania was ready to establish diplomatic relations with both the Soviet Union and the United States, as well as with the European Community in Brussels. He also announced his country's intention to join the Conference on Security and Co-operation in Europe (CSCE), an organization which Hoxha had denounced. Alia also signalled a willingness to negotiate with Britain about settling the dispute about the Corfu Channel incident in 1946 when two British destroyers were sunk by Albanian mines.[15]

The Albanian regime claimed that these sensational announcements in April 1990 represented not so much an about-face in its diplomacy as an acceleration of a course already embarked upon. There was some truth in this, but these changes were more qualitative than quantitative and signified a revolution forced on Tirana by the dramatic changes in Eastern Europe. Alia himself recognized that, because of these changes, the 'political equilibrium' in Europe had been 'upset'. The question now was 'how to manœuvre in the world arena to protect the interests of the homeland'. Albanian foreign policy had been realistic in the past, he claimed, but the international situation and the national interest now demanded a reappraisal.[16]

Nationalism without Democracy

Enver Hoxha had tried, with great success, progressively to insulate his country from outside influences: first from Western Europe; then after 1948 from Yugoslavia; after the beginning of the 1960s from the Soviet Union; finally after the middle of the 1970s from communist China. After the break with China he was aware that Albania's new isolation, together with its economic need, would expose it both to the dangers of Western liberal democracy and of East European liberalized communism. He was determined to resist both.

His task seemed made easier by the fact that Albania had always been largely isolated from outside liberal influences. The northern parts of what is today's Albania were missionized by the Roman Catholic Church. More than 10 per cent of Albania's population, concentrated in the north, remained Roman Catholic. There was a large Albanian community in Italy dating from the 15th century, and this strengthened the Italian connection, by far Albania's strongest in the West. In the United States there were communities of some size in cities like Baltimore, Boston, and St Louis. Bishop Fan Noli, who had headed the most democratic government in the country's history, became leader of the Albanian community in Boston after he was exiled from his native country.

Fan Noli had led a democratic government in 1924, and his ouster ended a short period of liberal and constitutional experiment. The Albanian experience with democracy was a telescoped version of the Bulgarian and the Romanian. There were obvious differences but also a basic similarity. Romania had its liberal constitution in 1866, Bulgaria in 1879, and now at Lushnje in 1920 Albania adopted its own enlightened version. But, whereas in Romania and Bulgaria, constitutional government limped along for many years, if more honoured in the breach than the observance, in Albania liberal democracy blossomed rapidly for just three years, between 1921 and 1924. It seemed promising while it lasted, but it was essentially a hothouse plant without hope of durability. Ahmed Zogu, who was leader of the conservative grouping in Albanian politics, opposing the liberal faction led by Fan Noli, took advantage of the growing unpopularity of the liberals and assumed power, the first step on the road to making Albania a kingdom, with himself as monarch.[17]

Every condition necessary for democratic development had been lacking in Albania, more so there than in any other Balkan country. It had no international security; its borders were only finally agreed to in 1926; but after that the ambitions of other powers induced an almost constant siege mentality – the mentality that Enver Hoxha was later to exploit so well. Its economy, though with considerable natural resources, was primitive, even by Balkan standards; its living and health standards were among Europe's lowest. Nor was there the faintest sign of a liberal tradition, except among a small group of intellectuals.

It was into this vacuum that nationalism, long delayed, now began slowly to move. It was the situation that awaited Ahmed Zogu (King Zog) when he began his 15-year rule in 1924. He did nothing to build a democratic tradition in Albania, but he did begin to give Albanians a sense of identity, of nationhood. He was Albania's first nation-builder. 'Whatever his flaws', wrote Stavro Skendi, 'he made a nation and a government where there had been a people and anarchy.'[18] Zog certainly gave Albania an international profile and a degree of unity it had never known before. Albanians had always had a sense of *ethnic* identity and regarded themselves as superior, at least in character, to their neighbours. In the second half of the nineteenth century, with nationalism gradually awakening, the cult of Skanderbeg developed as more looked into history beyond the centuries of Ottoman domination. There was also an increasing pride in the nation's Illyrian origins. But compared with their Balkan neighbours – Greeks, Serbs, Bulgarians – the sense of national identity remained slight.

Hoxha's Unity

This was the insignificant and inchoate national legacy that Zog inherited, and from it he was able to forge something more definite and tangible. But completing the task would have required a longer time than the international situation gave him. In 1939 he was forced to leave the country for ever. During the wartime occupation, first by the Italians and then the Germans, there was little united resistance and considerable collaboration. But one development of great national symbolic significance did occur: unity with Kosovo in Greater Albania. After 1945 Kosovo was restored to the new Yugoslavia, but the memory of the union remained.

After the war the Albanian communists, who had emerged as the strongest resistance force, came to power. They seemed to hold the weakest credentials possible for nation-building. They were, as already mentioned, an offshoot of the Yugoslav communist resistance, and thus created by Albania's greatest historical enemies. Within Albania itself the communist leadership was also seen as a divisive rather than a uniting force. It was dominated by Tosks, a tribal formation in the southern part of the country which spoke a dialect different from, but not incomprehensible to, the Gegs living in the northern part. The first Albanian communists had been mostly Tosks, indoctrinated at West European universities. Traditionally the Gegs, who constituted the large majority of the population, despised the Tosks. Now they found themselves dominated by them.[19] Indeed, despite the cohesive effect communist rule had on Albania, many Gegs continued to regard it as a Tosk conspiracy.[20] Tribal differences, of this sort, at least at the emotional level, still persist.

Enver Hoxha could not bridge such chasms, but his rule of 44 years did give Albanians a sense of identity they never had before. He achieved this by a combination of nationalism and ruthless centralism. By responding to, perhaps partly creating, certainly dramatizing, national peril Hoxha helped develop a certain commonness of purpose. Domestically his ferocious repression broke down many of the historic local and centrifugal forces. The most important focal point in this relentless centralization was Hoxha himself. His immense personality cult, like that surrounding Stalin, was a force for unity; the state became Enver; his problems became Albania's problems.[21]

There was nothing benevolent about Hoxha's Albania. Taking his rule as a whole it was, except for Ceauşescu's later years in Romania, the most repressive in the whole of Eastern Europe's communist history. But it was precisely this interaction of isolation, independence, centralism, and despotism that helped create the new Albanian unity out of what had been, in spite of King Zog's efforts, a condition of amorphous tribalism.

Thus Communist rule, under Enver Hoxha, helped make Albania a state in the modern sense. But for that state to become viable another, post-Hoxha, revolution was now needed after his death in April 1985. Persisting in the mould set by Hoxha would now have undermined rather than strengthened the unity he created. After Enver there had to be de-Enverization. The Albania he had built could only be preserved by radically changing the way it was run.

After Hoxha's death there were bound to be changes. In this sense tiny Albania after April 1985 was similar to the huge Soviet Union after March 1953 when Stalin died. Change was inevitable: perhaps at first only in the style of rule, but changes in style usually lead to changes in substance. Moreover, the international situation was conducive to change and beginning to demand it. Mikhail Gorbachev had just succeeded Konstantin Chernenko as general secretary of the Soviet Communist Party. It would take about two years for Gorbachev to evolve into a radical reformer in both domestic and bloc policy, but it was already obvious that change was in the making, both in the Soviet Union and in Eastern Europe. East–West relations were also reverting to the spirit of *détente* after the brief return of the Cold War in the early 1980s.

Closer home, in neighbouring Yugoslavia, disintegration, both ideological and national, was beginning. In particular the resistance of sections of the Albanian community in Kosovo to Serbian efforts to restore domination began to be seen in Albania itself as both an example and a reproach. The strengthening of resistance in Kosovo and the emergence of Albanian leaders there of courage and capability were to become a strong incentive for action in Albania itself.[22] Yugoslav leaders since the Second World War had constantly been nervous about the pull Albania might have on Kosovo. Now, however, the situation was reversed: it was Kosovars that were now exerting influence over their kinsmen in Albania. Finally, it was becoming increasingly obvious, even to Albanian communist leaders of an orthodox mould, that their country's isolation was untenable. As outlined above, more and more steps were now taken to establish contacts with Western Europe and with neighbouring Balkan states. Within five years of Hoxha's death Tirana had stepped out of its shell with arms outstretched not just to Europe but to the world, including the two superpowers it had so firmly rejected for so long.

One part of Enver Hoxha's legacy – the easy part, his isolationism – was quickly overturned. His domestic legacy presented a more difficult problem. It was more solid and multifaceted; there was also a set of well-entrenched vested interests bent on its survival: the party, state and economic apparatuses, the military, and the security apparatus (*Sigurimi*). Below them was the largely inert mass of the Albanian people, terrorized when need be, but largely inured to tyranny. In any case many had been given opportunities for material, social, professional and educational advancement that largely reconciled them to their condition.

Such strong vested interests notwithstanding, it was not long before cracks began to appear in Hoxha's domestic legacy. At first these were caused not by any pressure from society but by moves coming from the communist leadership itself. At the beginning the new leader, Ramiz Alia, did not so much initiate change as allow the generation of an atmosphere conducive to change, one that encouraged some initiative from senior and middle levels of the party and stimulated, however indirectly, a certain movement in society. In this sense Albanian reform followed a course not unlike that of other reform movements in earlier East European communist history – in Hungary and Poland in 1956, and Czechoslovakia in 1968. Restless intellectuals and youth, sensing that the framework of the possibility was expanding, tried to broaden it further. The press became livelier, literature bolder, questioning old certainties and even breaking old taboos now became almost fashionable. As for the youth, their assertiveness could best be judged by the indignant criticism of their behaviour in orthodox circles – circles that continued to control all but a tiny sector of the media. But it was that tiny sector that began to make the difference and it slowly expanded. So did exposure to the West, as Albania moved out into the world. And all this took place against the background of the total rejection of communism in most of the rest of East Europe.[23]

Change was on its way in Albania, too. At first it was slow, almost imperceptible. In the drama of 1989, the year of revolutions, Albania played no role at all. But by the end of that year, with the official concessions, the growing relaxation and the swelling popular impatience, Albania was already on the revolutionary carousel. The concessions, political and economic, as well as the relaxation may have been small but they were essential ingredients in the revolutionary mix that was brewing. Already at the beginning of 1990 there were Western reports of popular disturbances in several Albanian cities and towns. Most of these were based on official Belgrade sources, defensive to the point of paranoia about Kosovo, and anxious to project a disintegrating Albania. They were largely untrue. But not totally: some disturbances did occur, notably in the northern city of Shkodër.[24] Albania was late, but it was beginning to catch up.

It was, in fact, only about one year behind the rest of Eastern Europe. Albania's year of revolution was 1990 instead of 1989. The revolutionary mix became more potent as the year went on. The regime made more and more concessions.[25] It was hard to tell which had been planned beforehand and which were in response to public pressure. Certainly, the more concessions, the greater the pressure. Ramiz Alia realized he had simply not enough fingers to put in the dyke, and by the end of the year the dyke looked in danger of collapsing. In the summer there was the extraordinary spectacle, after 40 years of virtual isolation, of thousands of young Albanians bursting into Western embassies for visas for the outside world.[26] In October Ismail Kadare, Albania's foremost cultural figure and a writer of world renown, defected to France, partly out of dissatisfaction with the pace of reforms, partly to help spur them on.[27] Then in December serious demonstrations and rioting took place in several Albanian cities, immediately after which several thousand ethnic Greeks streamed southward over the border into Greece itself.[28] At the beginning of 1991 opposition parties were legalized, a new and more democratic constitution announced, full religious freedom was being practised, and freedom of movement, and foreign travel, at least in theory, was authorized. Most significant, a new democratic opposition party, formed and legalized and attracting enthusiastic support, was on the road, not perhaps to democracy, but to its post-communist phase. It seemed that what some observers had, with reason, been fearing – a 'Romanian' outcome of the events of 1990 – had been averted, if only just.[29]

In many ways Ramiz Alia and the post-Hoxha leadership had become the victims at home of their audacity abroad. If Albania was to be accepted in the world community it had to acquire some respectability by improving its behaviour at home. This was particularly the case with human rights. But improvement in human rights implied overall relaxation and that meant political change. For joining CSCE there were standards to be met. One of these, of course, was freedom of travel: hence the permission, however grudging, to emigrate for those who could get foreign visas.

Another – one that was to prove vital – was freedom of access for foreign journalists. It was through this that Albania became part of the global revolution-media publicity syndrome. The East European revolutions in 1989 had been conducted amid the glare of publicity. They were in no sense caused by it but, to some extent, were promoted by it. The East European revolutionaries knew they were on television. Not their own – they never expected that – but on world television, often in a matter of a couple of hours. The East European communist leaders knew that they were on world television, too, which helped stay their hand in a way it would never have done earlier. Albania in 1990 never got the publicity that, say, Czechoslovakia did, but it got enough for it to be decisive. The communist regime survived the relatively free general election in February 1991, but it now had to operate in a totally new political environment: not yet democratic, but far from the Leninism it had professed, and light years away from the Stalinism it had practised.

What Albania needed by 1991, even more urgently than full political democracy, were changes in the economy that would lead to economic viability. Only through economic viability could it ever achieve real liberal democracy. The situation was even more urgent than it might at first have seemed, more so even than in any of the other East European countries. It was not just a case of a bankrupt state socialist structure, or of unsuitable heavy industries turning out unsaleable goods (this Albania shared with the rest of the countries). It was eventually a question of survival by holding off starvation. For many years the fastest growing in Europe, the Albanian population in 1991 stood at about three million; by the end of the century it would be four million. This population would be inhabiting a tiny country, only small parts of which could be cultivated. It could only sustain such a population increase if it grew (and distributed) more food. This could be achieved not by reforming the state and collectivized system of agriculture, but by largely abolishing it and introducing extensive privatization. There were already signs that Ramiz Alia and other Albanian leaders were aware of the problem. In communist terms quite extensive reforms allowing greater flexibility of management, more incentives, and increased private holding of land and livestock had been initiated. But the ultimate heresy of privatization was still being avoided.[30] This, though, was essential, a necessary concomitant to the process of change already underway in so many other spheres. If Albania was to *survive* with any degree of independence, it needed the market. And the market operates best in a free society.

What followed, though, after the elections of February 1991 reflected not so much a free society as an anarchic society. Violent demonstrations almost immediately occurred organized by people, mainly youth – and here they were following the Bulgarian–Romanian pattern – who refused to accept the results of the elections. In Shkodër several people were killed and the violence there only gave elements of the *Sigurimi* the chance they were waiting for – to overreact with deadly violence. A coalition government was then formed which included several representatives of the democratic opposition. These developments passed almost unnoticed in the outside world but what then brought Albania global publicity of the most adverse kind was the 'boat people' attempts at emigration to Italy in the summer.

Over 20 000 Albanians crossed the narrow straits separating Albania from Italy in the mostly vain search of refuge. The Italian government received much criticism during this episode, but what it revealed about Albania was the primitive chaos into which the country was falling. The rest of the year saw much of the same: lawlessness in many sections of society and political ineptitude and irresponsibility at the top. Albania had a long way to go and time was short. In March 1992 the Democratic (opposition) Party won a dramatic election victory ending nearly a half-century of communist rule. The euphoria was great but the problems were also as great as ever. Democracy was now on probation, and it would not prevail without extensive Western help.

Notes

1 See Stavro Skendi, *The Albanian National Awakening, 1878–1912* (Princeton, NJ, Princeton University Press, 1967); J. Swire, *Albania – The Rise of a Kingdom* (New York, Arno Press and *New York Times,* 1971); Paul Lendvai, *Eagles in Cobwebs,* pp. 173–205.

2 On Albanian resistance and British sponsorship see Julian Amery, *Sons of the Eagle: A Study in Guerrilla War* (London, Macmillan, 1948).

3 Vladimir Dedijer, *Tito* (New York, Simon and Schuster, 1953), p. 311.

4 See Peter R. Prifti, *Socialist Albania since 1944: Domestic and Foreign Developments* (Cambridge, MA, M.I.T. Press, 1978), pp. 168–72.

5 See Griffith, *Albania and the Sino-Soviet Rift,* especially pp. 20–60.

6 For a succinct but comprehensive discussion of Albania's development, including its association with China, see Elez Biberaj, *Albania: A Socialist Maverick* (Boulder, CO, Westview Press, 1990).

7 Ibid., p. 4.

8 The expression was first attributed to Pashko Vasa (1825–1892), one of the founders of the Albanian national movement.

9 See Louis Zanga, 'China Stops Aid to Albania', Radio Free Europe Research Background Report, 13 July 1978; Michael Kaser, 'Trade and Aid in the Albanian Economy', in *East European Economics Post-Helsinki* (Washington, DC, GPO, 1977), pp. 1327–8.

10 This memorable expression was given in an interview to the Zagreb daily, *Vjesnik,* 28 August 1975, to squash conjecture about a Chinese-led, anti-Soviet, Romanian, Yugoslav, Albanian grouping.

11 Lendvai, *Eagles in Cobwebs,* pp. 198–9. This congress was held in November 1966.

12 Louis Zanga, 'The Sino-Albania Ideological Dispute Enters a New Phase', Radio Free Europe Research Report, 15 November 1977.

13 See Brown, *Eastern Europe and Communist Rule,* pp. 378–81.

14 See Brown, *Surge to Freedom,* p. 244.

15 Albanian Telegraphic Agency (ATA), in English, 19 April 1990.

16 Ibid.

17 On the Fan Noli-Ahmed Zogu struggle, see Barbara Jelavich, *History of the Balkans*, Vol. II, pp. 179–84.
18 Quoted by Lendvai, op. cit., p. 181.
19 See R. V. Burks, *The Dynamics of Communism in Eastern Europe* (Princeton, NJ, Princeton University Press, 1964), pp. 144–9.
20 I am grateful to Louis Zanga for his advice on the persistence of the Geg-Tosk rivalry.
21 See Brown, *Eastern Europe and Communist Rule*, pp. 374–7.
22 I am grateful to Elez Biberaj for emphasizing this to me.
23 See Peter Humphrey, 'Albania Opts for Reforms with a Socialist Face', *The Independent* (London), 24 February 1990.
24 Agence France Presse (AFP), in English, 11 January 1990.
25 Among the most notable concessions were the allowing of religious practice and the easing of travel restrictions. See David Binder, 'Albania is Easing Curbs on Worship and Ban on Travel', *The New York Times*, 10 May 1990.
26 See Louis Zanga, *The Dramatic Developments in Albania*, Radio Free Europe Research Background Report, 9 July 1990.
27 Kadare's decision not to return from a visit to France caused much disappointment among the opposition movement in Albania, especially in Tirana, because many regarded him as the future Václav Havel of Albania. For a not altogether convincing explanation of his decision, see his interview with *Le Monde*, 25 October 1990. For an excellent review of Albanian reform in 1990, see Jean-Michel de Waele, 'Temps de réforme en Albanie', *Le Monde Diplomatique*, August 1990.
28 For a summary of all these events, see Louis Zanga, 'Recent Developments in Albania', Radio Free Europe Research Background Report, 3 January 1991. See also Jose-Alain Fralon, 'La révolution sans nom', *Le Monde*, 26 December 1990.
29 See, for example, Viktor Meier, 'Drohen in Albanien rumänische Verhältnisse', *Frankfurter Allgemeine Zeitung*, 9 July 1990.
30 See Laura Silber, 'Albania Opens the Door to Reforms', *Financial Times*, 7 November 1990.

6 Romania: The Nationalist Condition

Romania was the third Balkan country, after Greece and Serbia, to achieve autonomy under Turkish rule (Serbia finally achieved it in 1830, Greece finally in 1832). The two Romanian principalities of Moldavia and Wallachia achieved autonomous status, under Turkish suzerainty, in 1856. They had achieved a degree of autonomy in 1829 when, by the Treaty of Adrianople, Russia forced the Ottoman Empire to agree that the princes of the two principalities be chosen from among the Romanian nobility. This ended Greek Phanariot rule that had pillaged the principalities for well over a century and helped give Romania a civic culture (or lack of it) that has persisted to the present.

Although the change meant replacing Phanariot–Ottoman domination with Russian, it was an essential step forward toward eventual independence. Never in their history were Romanians treated by Russians in so enlightened a manner. The *règlement organique,* a set of ordinances amounting to a constitution the Russians gave them, between 1831 and 1832, provided for the same regulations to govern both principalities, making their eventual union simpler.[1]

Russian influence, therefore, was important in putting Romania on the road to independence, just as it was decisive in giving Bulgaria its independence over half a century later. It was obvious that, as nationalism developed in Eastern Europe in the course of the nineteenth century, Russia would see newly emerging states like Bulgaria and Romania in terms of both security and expansion. Romania would be the basis of Russia's Balkan ambitions while Bulgaria would be their wedge or spearhead. Thus the modern Russian–Romanian interaction – with Romania as part of Russian imperialist designs – was established in the first half of the nineteenth century.

At the same time, another international interaction was beginning to develop which was also to have a profound effect on Romania's future.

French influence began to spread in the new principalities. Though it mainly affected the intelligentsia, this influence was political as well as intellectual. Many educated Romanians had admired Napoleon and already in the early part of the nineteenth century a growing number of young Romanians were going to Paris for their education. The French revolution of 1848 had a decisive impact on educated young Romanians. There was an abortive rising in Iasi, in Moldavia, and a short-lived republican government was set up in Wallachia. They came to nothing.

Russians and Turks, the great power rivals, realized they had something in common when challenged by republican independence movements deep in South-eastern Europe, and they joined forces to destroy the Wallachian republic. Romanian nationalism in Transylvania, decisive in the future development of the nation-state, was summarily put down at the same time. In 1848, realizing their enemy was not the distant Habsburgs but the Hungarians who were oppressing them, the Romanians in Transylvania refused to support the Hungarian rebellion and sided with Vienna. When the Hungarians were defeated, Transylvania was ruled from Vienna, but the Romanians got none of the rights the Emperor had originally offered them for their loyalty.[2] After the *Ausgleich* of 1867 between Austria and Hungary, Transylvania was ruled from Budapest, and the Romanians were left to Hungarian vengeance.

This 150-year-old history is relevant today in three ways. First, it confirmed Russia as an arbiter of Romania's destiny, at the same time making it an object of Romanian fear and distrust. Second, it introduced French influence into Romania. French culture and political liberalism had a huge and beneficial effect. It exposed Romanian public life to Western thought and established civilized standards by which it should be conducted. But the French influence was so magnetic, and the Romanian reality often so wretched, that many educated Romanians gave themselves over totally to its attractions.[3] It hindered, therefore, rather than helped the development of an indigenous Romanian political culture. Bucharest became not so much the Paris of Eastern Europe but a poor Balkan derivate of Paris. Besides, the French romantic literature that so influenced Romanians tended to encourage a romantic nationalism and idealism where an injection of rationalism and pragmatism would have been of better service. Third, the developments in Transylvania between 1848 and 1867, and their consequences, profoundly affected the future course of Romanian nationalism. Transylvania was regarded as the cradle of Romanian liberties, and the half-century of repression after the *Ausgleich* instilled into many Romanians a hatred of Hungarians that has persisted.

Romanian unity (that is between the provinces of Wallachia and Moldavia) was achieved in 1859 mainly through the interaction of two of the three factors just mentioned. One of the main reasons for the Crimean War of 1854–56 was Russian aggression against the two principalities, a move designed to put pressure on Turkey. The Treaty of Paris ending the war restored the freedom of the principalities, though still under Turkish suzerainty. But Romanian nationalists now enlisted Napoleon III and his crusade for the self-determination of nations to their cause. It was agreed in 1858 that Moldavia and Wallachia should be more closely associated but should still be ruled by elected princes and separate assemblies. But the voters in the two principalities promptly elected the same prince, Alexander Cuza, and unity was achieved by a democratic and diplomatic *fait accompli.* The powers that had finally agreed to greater Romanian unity had certainly not envisioned this. But, not anticipating the possibility of it, they had not expressly forbidden it. It was the first global demonstration of Romanian international subtlety; nor was it to be the last – regardless of what kind of government ruled in Bucharest.

Diplomacy and Nationalism

At no time in its history was Romania's diplomatic prowess more evident than 50 years later, during and after the First World War. Since 1866 the country's royal house had been German – a branch of the Hohenzollerns. This had been partly responsible for the diplomatic drift toward Germany before the First World War. During the war, however, the Western Allies outbid the Central Powers in their attempts to enlist Romanian support by offering Transylvania, the Banat, and Bukovina in the event of an allied victory. Romania entered the war in 1916, fought very well but was badly beaten by Germans and had to make a humiliating peace. At the end of the war, however, the vagaries of the new international relations, as well as Romania's diplomatic tenacity and skill, brought it everything the allies had originally promised. It also brought the bonus of Bessarabia which, though peopled largely by Romanians, had been taken by Russia in 1812 but now, with the collapse of Russian power through war and revolution, united with Romania by popular acclamation.[4]

The establishment of Greater Romania through the gains after the First World War totally changed Romania's position in European affairs. Before, it had been small, insignificant but hopeful. Now it became large, important, and fearful. The comparison with Bulgaria is instructive. Both emerged into statehood with seriously unfulfilled national and territorial ambitions, though Bulgaria was the more resentful because of the disappointment after San Stefano. (San Stefano had created a large Bulgaria that was then almost halved by the Congress of Berlin in the summer of 1878.) Both allowed themselves to be manipulated by the powers in the hope of satisfying these ambitions. There the similarity ends. Romania was as skilled in diplomacy as Bulgaria was inept and as blessed by fortune as Bulgaria was deserted by it. Romania's ambitions were fulfilled, Bulgaria's thwarted.

But Romania was never permitted to enjoy or exploit its gains in peace. The new international order that was supposed to secure the results of the First World War turned out to be totally incapable of doing so. New predators soon appeared. Romania's gains became the target of Hungarian, Soviet, and Bulgarian designs. Romanian diplomacy which, during the few years of hope for collective security administered by the League of Nations, had achieved international respect, now degenerated into frantic attempts to avoid or minimize territorial dismemberment.[5] With Nazi Germany and Fascist Italy dominating the Balkans in the 1930s and openly supporting Hungarian, Bulgarian, and then Soviet demands, Romania, already seriously weakened internally, eventually collapsed. It surrendered northern Transylvania to Hungary, Bessarabia and northern Bukovina to the Soviet Union, and south Dobrudja to Bulgaria. Greater Romania had reverted to rump Romania, the old *Regat* with a few trappings.

Romania's conduct during the Second World War was remarkably similar to what it had been during the First World War although its options were now more limited. *Raison d'état,* in fact, dictated only one course of action: to support Germany to an extent that would restore Bessarabia and, if it supported Hitler better than Hungary did, might restore some, or all, of northern Transylvania. Again, the Romanians fought very well, especially at first, recovering Bessarabia and then becoming openly expansionist by occupying parts of Southern Ukraine. In August 1944, however, with the Germans facing certain defeat and the Red Army advancing, Romania changed sides, joined the allies, and then fought well in East Central Europe. It was thus able to regain northern Transylvania in the post-Second World War settlement, though obviously not Bessarabia which stayed with the victorious Soviet Union. (South Dobrudja also stayed with Bulgaria.) It was not what the Romanians had originally hoped for, but it was now all they could realistically hope to get. And what had always meant most to them they did get: Transylvania.[6]

Romanian National Communism

Otherwise, the circumstances in which Romania found itself after the Second World War were the most unenviable in its modern history. Once again it fell under Russian domination. In terms of international power both Romania and Bulgaria were once more serving Russian security concerns and imperialist designs as they had in the nineteenth century. But now, like Bulgaria, it was in the midst of domestic revolution. Romania became subject to the new ideological imperialism. After 1945 that meant ruthless Stalinization.

Soviet troops guaranteed this transformation. Soviet police and officials supervised it. But it was actually carried out by the Romanian Communist Party. Unlike in Bulgaria, where communists had a strong tradition, the Soviet Union found it hard to find enough able communists in Romania to do its work. Between the wars the Romanian Communist Party probably never had more than 1000 members.[7] Its illegal status was hardly conducive to mass recruiting drives but, in a country were nationalism was the only pervasive philosophy, it was perceived both as un-Romanian and anti-Romanian. Many of its leaders were Jewish in a country where anti-Semitism was strong; some were Hungarian, Ukrainian, or Bulgarian. Few were ethnic Romanians. Its composition was therefore against it in the eyes of the public. So was its policy. Loyal to the Soviet Union, the party supported the Comintern's directives calling for the reincorporation of Bessarabia into the Soviet Union. Economic and social conditions in inter-war Romania would have made it ripe for communism. But national communism was not yet thought of – except by the Soviet Union.

The communist-led regime, in Romania, therefore, installed and propped up by the Soviets, had probably less legitimacy than any other in Eastern Europe. For several years it presided over both the Sovietization and the economic spoliation of Romania by the Soviets. The Romanian regime was, and seemed set to remain, the most satellite of satellite regimes. It was this that made its future course so remarkable; remarkable but, in retrospect, so logical. It began to embrace what its whole history had been a negation of: Romanian nationalism.

The history of the Romanian 'nationalist deviation' has been written and rewritten many times.[8] The latest research on the subject indicates that differences between Bucharest and Moscow began earlier than previously suspected.[9] But the essential point about the 'Romanian deviation' remains the same: that it was another example, the third in Eastern Europe after Yugoslavia and Albania, of communism becoming national communism. Despite the skepticism of most experts it should not have been all that surprising in view of Romania's history, and particularly its relations with Russia. From the perspective of 1992, with world communism having collapsed, with nationalism as the prime reason for its collapse, it almost assumes the appearance of inevitability. What made observers originally so disbelieving was that it should have been a regime so weak as the Romanian that defied Moscow. The Yugoslav and Albanian cases had been rationalized as deriving from the strength of their regime, and the fact that each country had 'liberated' itself in the war. Thus their nationalism was 'self-evident'. The Romanian regime apparently could not have been more different. But it had to resort to nationalism through weakness, whereas the other countries had exploited it through strength.

In its defiance of the Soviet Union three familiar strands of Romania's nationalist history again became evident. The first, of course, was its anti-Russian mainspring. The second was its Western orientation. This time it was not so much the traditional French connection, although interaction between the Romanian leadership and President de Gaulle during most of the 1960s was close. Now it was the West in general, but particularly the Federal Republic of Germany and the United States. West Germany was the economic power the Romanians hoped primarily to tap. The United States was the Western superpower with which, as the age of détente slowly replaced that of the Cold War, it was now safer, and potentially beneficial, to dally.

Romania conducted its own version of Westpolitik with extraordinary skill, illustrating a third strand in its nationalist tradition: its diplomatic prowess. It was now safer to flirt with the West, but it still carried risks. At the beginning of 1967, for example, Romania publicly defied Soviet policy by establishing diplomatic relations with Bonn. With the United States, too, it had to move gingerly throughout the 1960s. But nowhere was Romanian diplomacy put to better effect than in its exploitation of the Sino–Soviet dispute during the 1960s. Even more delicacy was needed here than with the West, because the challenge of China and the deepening split in the socialist camp was for Moscow the most crucial external issue of the time. Again, the story of how the Romanians threaded their way through this minefield has often been told. It still makes fascinating reading. In general, Romania's disentanglement from the Soviet Union, its successful overtures to the West, and its manipulation of the Sino-Soviet dispute constitute one of the most spectacular and successful diplomatic operations of the twentieth century.[10]

Nor should this operation be seen as solely affecting Romania. The most important tangible result of its defiance of the Soviet Union was its successful opposition in the early 1960s to Nikita Khrushchev's plans for supranational planning within COMECON, the Soviet led 'Council for Mutual Economic Assistance'. If Khrushchev had succeeded, the whole character of the alliance could have changed. It would have been increasingly difficult for East European states to preserve whatever theoretical independence they had, and then to use this as a basis from which to enlarge their freedom of action. Not just their formal independence but their individual identity would eventually have been threatened and the way opened for that socialist 'internationalization' early communist theorists had advocated and even practical politicians, like Khrushchev himself, still dreamed about. The Romanian success in turning back Khrushchev's plans for COMECON meant that this great danger was averted. It changed the whole course of East European history and helped make the revolutions of 1989 and the defeat of communism possible.[11]

Against the Hungarian Minority

But Eastern Europe being what it was, Romanian nationalism was not just directed against the Russians. It was an internal, as well as an external, issue.

Romania had always had what many of its citizens considered more than a tolerable burden of ethnic minorities. But its successive governments almost always refused to recognize, in terms of definition, policy, and institutions, the consequences of its being a multinational state. In fact, they adamantly refused to recognize that Romania *was* a multinational state. Instead, Romania has pursued the goal of unitarism.

Historically the three most numerous minorities had been the Hungarians, the Germans and the Jews. (The Gypsies were never recognized historically as a minority.[12]) By 1945 the Jews had been decimated by the Holocaust and the German minority, which had numbered about 700 000 between the wars, had been about halved as a result of the Second World War and the expulsions and migrations after it. Subsequently they presented no problem to the Romanian authorities, being a valuable civic, economic and cultural asset. They were always an obstacle to the assimilation drive, but emigration to the Federal Republic of Germany was by the 1980s 'solving' any problem caused by the German minority by steadily eliminating it. By 1990 there were about 110 000 Germans left.[13]

The real problem in terms of the unitary aspiration was the Hungarian minority. By 1990 it was believed to number about two million.[14] And since Transylvania was disputed territory and the object of such deep-seated passion on both sides, the Hungarian minority had always been regarded as the most crucial issue on the national agenda. The Hungarian minority was a domestic problem, but the region in which they lived, Transylvania, was a foreign problem.

Hungary lost all the gains it had made by its association with Nazi Germany, despite an intense diplomatic campaign immediately after 1945. Romania recovered the whole of Transylvania but it was not allowed to proceed with the total incorporation and repression that many Romanians would have wished. Parts of Transylvania, containing a section of the Hungarian minority in Romania, were to be modelled on the example of so many regions of mixed nationality in the Soviet Union. It became, therefore, an extension of Soviet national minority doctrine – the only one of its kind in Eastern Europe, if one excludes the overall case of Yugoslavia. It also reflected Moscow's way of giving some satisfaction, or compensation, to Hungary. The 'Hungarian Autonomous Region' was eventually established in 1952 by a communist leadership in Bucharest, still dominated by 'Muscovites', Soviet-trained, ethnically non-Romanian for whom national considerations had never played much of a role anyway.

The Hungarian Autonomous Region remained subject to the laws of Romania, but it was intended that, along the lines of its counterparts in the Soviet Union, it would have its own administrative organs, be responsible for its own public order, the enforcement of laws, local economic and cultural activity, and a certain degree of economic and financial administration. These provisions were never completely fulfilled in the case of the Hungarian Autonomous Region, but its citizens did get a considerable degree of home rule. It should be remembered, however, that only some 600 000, or less than one-third of the total number of Hungarians in Romania, lived there.[15]

The Hungarian Revolution in 1956 was the real turning-point in the experience of the Hungarian minority in Romania during communist rule. There was much sympathy for the revolution among its members. This only increased the nervousness of the regime in Bucharest, which responded with savage reprisals and a regime of oppression afterwards. But this was only the prelude to a reconsideration of the entire principle and policy that had led to the original establishment of the autonomous region in 1952, and had taken into account the distinct existence of the Hungarian minority.

Within five years the two most important institutions guaranteeing this distinctness had been abolished. In 1959 the separate Hungarian university in Cluj was merged with its Romanian counterpart in the same city; more accurately it was submerged beneath it. This was the beginning of a drastic restriction of education in the Hungarian language at all levels. But the principal target of Romanian unitary nationalism was the Hungarian Autonomous Region. The decisive move against it was made in 1960 when its compactness was broken up by moving two heavily Hungarian-populated counties out of it and two heavily Romanian-populated counties into it. This reduced the percentage of Hungarians in the region from 77 per cent to 62 per cent.

Even more important was the political symbolism involved in changing the name of the region to Mureş-Hungarian Autonomous Region, thus modifying its Hungarian title. In 1968 the Ceauşescu leadership introduced a new territorial reorganization affecting the whole country which abolished the autonomous region altogether. In only two out of the newly formed 39 counties were the Hungarians in a majority. The principle of treating the minority as a distinct entity had now, therefore, been abolished. The path was open for a steady assimilation drive, which narrowed even further (although it did not abolish) the Hungarians' rights for education in their own language. The eventual goal was to break down the Hungarians' sense of separate identity.

As Ceauşescu's rule degenerated into tyranny, other steps were used to try to achieve this. The most notorious was the 'systematization' programme, a plan that, if it had been completed, would have condemned to destruction 7000 to 8000 of Romania's 13 000 villages. By far the majority of these villages would have been those inhabited by the Romanian population, but many would have been Hungarian. The very nucleus, therefore, of the Hungarian existence, the villages that had nurtured and protected the Hungarian way of life, would have been endangered.[16] One of the first acts of the post-communist regime in Romania was to abandon systematization.

The Dearth of Liberal Democracy

Strikingly different though Romania and Bulgaria are there have been some strong similarities in the course of their domestic political development as well as in their external relations.

As already mentioned, both adopted constitutions after liberation that were generally models of liberalism (although the Romanian was marred by anti-Semitic implications that became the subject of international controversy and later had to be abandoned). But both constitutions were manipulated or ignored with such frequency and cynicism that they became reproaches rather than guides to ongoing political behaviour. Both had German royal houses and, before the First World War, long-reigning monarchs who left deep imprints on the history of their countries.

By the end of the First World War the success of Romania's foreign policy and the failure of Bulgaria's was evident. But it was then that similarities in political development became apparent. During the 1920s, a period of economic growth, it seemed that constitutional government might take root in both countries. But the world depression seriously affected their mainly agrarian economies and brought political instability to the surface. The rise of Nazi Germany and Fascist Italy and the decline in French and British influence in the 1930s also tended to dull the appeal of democracy and sharpen that of authoritarianism. In Romania, too, the siege mentality born of hostile irredentism also strengthened this tendency. In both countries the constitutional progress previously made was lost.

Authoritarian politics took hold and royal dictatorships were established in both countries. Both countries went through political violence and terrorism. After the Second World War both countries were forced into the Soviet imperium and had communist systems imposed on them.

Had Romania been allowed to develop on its own after the Second World War in close association with the West it might well have developed a viable democracy as a constitutional monarchy under the young King Michael, a man of sincerity and courage. It had better preconditions for it than any state, except Czechoslovakia, in what became known as Eastern Europe. But after 1945, of course, the question became an irrelevancy. Hopes of Western democracy were replaced by the firm facts of Stalinist communism. Nor did Romania ever go through phases of reform communism that would have eased the burden of repressiveness, given its citizens some sustaining self-respect, and eventually made its post-communist phase after 1989 easier to negotiate. After Stalin's death, Romania never experienced any real 'thaw'. As already mentioned, the repercussions in Transylvania of 1956 in Hungary led to a hasty renewal of harsh repression.

But the 1960s were at least a decade of hope – hope that the regime's nationalist policy abroad would also be accompanied by meaningful domestic relaxation. Many Romanians were hoping for their own version of the Polish October of 1956, though with a longer duration. For a time the hope looked like it might be fulfilled. Already under the Gheorghiu-Dej leadership, dominated by 'home' communists who had taken over after 1952, there was an amnesty for many political prisoners in 1964 that had a considerable psychological effect on the country as a whole. It seemed logical that, with the regime conducting a risky foreign policy, it would try to appease the population through reform. Also, as it gained legitimacy through its embrace of nationalism, it would feel confident enough to introduce domestic liberalization. So the reasoning – and the hopes – went.

In retrospect it seems ironical that the accession to power of Nicolae Ceauşescu in March 1965 gave real hope that the relaxation would be continued and broadened. It seems even more ironical that the first five years of Ceauşescu's rule appeared to be doing precisely that. A reappraisal of some of the repressive aspects of Gheorghiu-Dej's period of power was begun, some of the victims of Romanian Stalinism were rehabilitated, and reassuring reorganizations of the security apparatus were carried out. On the cultural level there was meaningful relaxation; even the regime's policy toward the Hungarian minority appeared more enlightened. Above all it was the unity temporarily forged between regime and people by Ceauşescu's stand against the Soviet invasion of Czechoslovakia in August 1968 that seemed to promise a new beginning.[17]

It is not relevant here to discuss why Ceauşescu so abruptly changed course at the beginning of the 1970s, or just how much his famous visit to China and North Korea in 1971 affected his personality and political outlook.[18] For a few years after 1970 his repressiveness was often excused by Western observers on the grounds that, had he combined his independence policy with 'liberalism' at home, he would have risked Soviet intervention. What is relevant, though, is that the deterioration which began in the early 1970s and ended with Ceauşescu's execution in December 1989 marked the worst period of rule any East European country, except possibly Albania, had suffered since 1953. (By comparison, Zhivkov's rule in Bulgaria was positively benevolent.) Not only were there no attempts at reform, however limited (there were numerous, increasingly capricious attempts at reorganization), but there was a repressiveness that became increasingly squalid and bizarre. Whatever legitimacy nationalism had gained for the Romanian communist regime had been squandered already by the end of the 1970s. Ceauşescu remained devoted to Romanian nationalism until his death, but now his domestic tyranny simply debauched it, making it an insult to the nation it purported to serve.

The population's passivity facilitated this repression and invited more. And this passivity cannot totally be explained by Romanian history, the long years of survival through patience. It has been a source of acute embarrassment to most Romanians since the end of communist rule. There was, indeed, opposition in Romania, but it was minimal by the standards of Poland, Hungary, Czechoslovakia, and the GDR. There was probably even less opposition than in Bulgaria, where dissidence positively sprouted toward the end of the 1980s.

Within the regime itself cases of explicit opposition were very rare. Some of the veterans from the Gheorghiu-Dej era, all senior to Ceauşescu at one time, obviously nursed grievances against him. A closer reading of some of the regime's specialized journals also indicated demur. Ceauşescu himself sometimes acknowledged it publicly. A few senior officials, including Ion Iliescu, to become the first president in the post-Ceauşescu era, were demoted because of differences of opinion. Finally in March 1989, with reform already in full swing in the Soviet Union and other parts of Eastern Europe, a number of old communists wrote a letter of protest that became public. But it was all very little and amounted to nothing.[19]

It was certainly less important than worker opposition. There was a serious strike among coal-miners in the Jiu Valley in 1977 and intermittent strikes and protests in the early 1980s. There was a big anti-regime demonstration in Braşov in November 1987 which many consider to have been the prelude to December 1989. Among the ethnic minorities the main form of German protest was emigration to the Federal Republic. Among the

Hungarian minority a network of self-protective opposition burgeoned during the 1980s, with the support of semiofficial and unofficial groups in Hungary itself. But there was little evidence of *active* resistance on the part of the Hungarian minority. Among religious groups the numerous Baptists in Romania, with their good American contacts, were the target of regime vindictiveness. But the Romanian Orthodox Church, true to the Erastian tradition, actively collaborated, especially at the senior level. As for the intellectuals, with a bare handful of exceptions, they were anything but the 'conscience of the nation'. Some actively supported the regime, fed Ceauşescu's personality cult, and were rewarded accordingly. But most were content to keep their feelings to themselves, using whatever surplus energy that might accrue to fight each other instead of the regime.

How, then, could Ceauşescu do all this? How could a leader, no matter how strong-willed, terrorize a nation of 23 million people, when terror in the entire communist system, except possibly for Albania, had largely become a thing of the past? Some find the explanation in the formidable strength and efficiency of the *Securitate,* for which, at the height of the terror before the revolution, a large number of Romanians were believed to have worked, if only indirectly. But how did the *Securitate* get to a pinnacle of power which none of its counterparts had reached since the days of the Soviet NKVD? Their success presumably lies in the utter demoralization of Romanian society, pressed down by poverty, war, oppression, then Stalinist communism, and without the benefit of any supportive institution like the Church (such a buttress in a country like Poland). An important contributory factor was the sheer physical isolation of Romania, tucked away in a corner of south-eastern Europe, bordering only on other communist countries. Another was the fact that the most coherent sections of society allowed themselves to be seduced by a nationalism that became arid, bankrupt and eventually self-defeating. Romanian nationalism became a means of tyranny rather than of popular fulfilment, a debasement rather than an inspiration. Brought down to this condition, the Romanian people, with a few notable exceptions, became defenceless against a ruler who eventually perfected terror and never hesitated to use it. After a while many people simply became mesmerized by terror. And terror needed, and created, paranoia. Many visitors to Romania agreed that this was the outstanding characteristic of society there. It travelled from the top downward, and then spread out.[20]

In this situation Ceauşescu could only be removed by popular explosion. There was no prelude of reform as in Hungary, relaxation as occurred in Poland, or even partial regime moderation as in the GDR and Czechoslovakia. Even in Bulgaria, the situation inside the regime as well as society was more fluid. Albania experienced some reform before the explosions came.

In Romania it was popular explosion or continued tyranny. And, obviously, such an explosion would never have occurred had not the rest of Eastern Europe, as well as the Soviet Union, been in ferment.

It was almost inevitable that after the revolution of December 1989 counter-interpretations of it should have been advanced purporting to refute its essential spontaneity.[21] The revolution certainly left questions unanswered and loose ends waiting to be tied. The whole atmosphere of distrust in which the new Iliescu government became engulfed also invited rumours questioning its legitimacy and its own version of how it took power. But the evidence so far offered suggesting massive communist deception and Soviet manipulation has remained unconvincing to say the least. There may well have been a number of plots, hatching and unhatching over the years. There was perhaps one, in either an early formative, or moribund, stage when the uprising occurred. Certainly, the full story of the revolution remains to be told. But it was the popular uprising that brought down Ceauşescu and that was genuine.[22]

The welter of conspiracy theories regarding the revolution reflected the chaotic and destructive politics that followed Ceauşescu's downfall. The National Salvation Front that took power bore some of the characteristics of a communist regime and included many officials who had served Ceauşescu. It was unfair to call President Iliescu a former 'close collaborator' of the old dictator. His *close* collaboration with Ceauşescu had, after all, ended in 1971, when he was removed from the Central Committee Secretariat. But, however 'reformist' Iliescu became, many of his statements and actions still betrayed the familiar Marxist-Leninist mind-set. Bringing the Jiu Valley miners into Bucharest in June 1990 to quell disturbances damaged his reputation severely. He was clearly the outstanding personality in the immediate post-Ceauşescu order, and however flawed the general election in May 1990 that returned him to power with a huge majority may have been, he was the most popular among the nation at large. There was more personal freedom than could have been imagined under Ceauşescu. And a new government, led by premier Petre Roman, did try to usher in an economic reform, involving a gradual switch from state socialism to the market.[23]

The political opposition in Romania, often not so much democratic as anti-communist, was poorly led. Unless it could produce personalities of stature and responsibility, prepared to lead rather than to posture, the future of constitutional government in Romania looked bleak. Many intellectuals in Bucharest were now protesting a dedication to freedom and liberalism. But except for a few, their behaviour reflected irresponsibility and a dedication to sectional rather than the national interest. As for the numerous students who, mainly in Bucharest but in other cities also, were in almost permanent active opposition to the government, it was hard not to sympathize with their frustration over the lack of real democracy. But they seemed reluctant to accept that elections rather than street demonstrations decide the fate of governments in democracies. The democratic convictions of far too many people in both Romania and Bulgaria seemed to hinge on whether and when the democratic process went in their favour.

It would not be the students or the intellectuals who would decide the fate of Iliescu or the government; it would be the workers. As long as most of them, however disgruntled they might be, and however often they downed tools over the social consequences of economic change, saw no viable alternative, then the government would remain in power. But even by the end of 1990, even this *faute de mieux* loyalty was wavering. In the event it was the workers who intervened in the political process and dramatically undermined it. And it was the very same miners who had come down from the Jiu Valley in June 1990 who now came down to Bucharest in September the next year protesting the effects of the economic reform and leaving a trail of devastation in their wake. They succeeded in getting Premier Roman removed, but in doing so they scarcely helped themselves and they also delivered a serious blow to democratic development in Romania. They indicated that lawlessness gets results and they established a ghastly precedent. They somehow symbolized the historic weakness of Romania as a modern democratic state.[24]

But if 1991 was, all in all, a bad year for democratic development in Romania, 1992 began promisingly. First, the cumbersome, never homogeneous National Salvation Front began to split roughly into democratic liberal and more communist-nationalist groupings. Second, the democratic opposition achieved a degree of coherence. Third, the Front's stranglehold on power was broken at the local elections in February when the opposition made a good showing and took control of most of Romania's larger cities. The stage was set for the presidential and parliamentary elections scheduled for summer. There was little doubt that it would be a manifestation of democracy at work – probably the best example in the entire history of Romania. But would it lead to stable, democratic rule under which both economic and political development could proceed?

One thing was certain: nationalism would not only survive but was also likely to burgeon. Romanian politics could become hostage to it. In the post-communist period, four aspects of it were already evident: virulent anti-Semitism, propounded by a relative few, but finding an echo among many; racism toward Gypsies, manifested by very many; growing antagonism toward Hungarians; reunification sentiments regarding Moldova. (These two last are discussed in Chapter 9). Already the great danger was that nationalism would again become the great Romanian diversion – away from the democracy and prosperity the country most urgently needed.

Notes

1 See Barbara Jelavich, *Russia and the Formation of the Romanian National State, 1821–1878* (Cambridge, Cambridge University Press, 1983).
2 On the importance of Transylvania in the development of Romanian nationalism, see Keith Hitchins, *The Rumanian National Movement in Transylvania, 1780–1849* (Cambridge, MA, Harvard University Press, 1977).
3 Wolff, *The Balkans In Our Time*, p. 21.
4 For Romanian diplomacy at the end of the First World War see Sherman David Spector, *Rumania at the Paris Peace Conference: A Study of the Diplomacy of Ioan I. C. Brătianu* (New York, Bookman Associates, 1962).
5 The respect was gained by Romania's great foreign minister, Nicolae Titulescu; the frantic attempts were led by King Carol II.
6 Barbara Jelavich, *History of the Balkans*, Vol. II, pp. 250–5.
7 On the pre-war party, see Robert R. King, *History of the Romanian Communist Party* (Stanford, CA, Hoover Institution, 1980).
8 See, for example, Kenneth Jowitt, *Revolutionary Breakthroughs and National Development: The Case of Romania, 1944–1965* (Berkeley, University of California Press, 1971), and David Floyd, *Romania: Russia's Dissident Ally* (New York, Praeger, 1965).
9 See Sergiu Verona, *Military Occupation and Diplomacy: Soviet Troops in Romania, 1944–1958* (Durham, NC, Duke University Press, 1992).
10 For a fuller discussion of these points, see J. F. Brown, 'Conservatism and Nationalism in the Balkans' in Griffith (ed.), *Central and Eastern Europe*, pp. 283–313.
11 This point is argued at length in Brown, *Surge to Freedom*, especially pp. 17–21.
12 On the much neglected subject of Gypsies *throughout* Europe, see Grattan Puxon, *Roma: Europe's Gypsies* (London, The Minority Rights Group, 1987), No. 14, revised edition; on Romania, see pp. 10–11.
13 See Viktor Meier, 'Die Deutschen in Rumänien fühlen sich als etwas Besonderes', *Frankfurter Allgemeine Zeitung*, 18 July 1990.
14 For a comprehensive review of the history and structure of the Hungarian minority, see George Schöpflin and Hugh Poulton, 'Romania's Ethnic Hungarians' (London, Minority Rights Group, 1990, revised edition).
15 King, *Minorities under Communism*, pp. 154–63.
16 See Brown, *Surge to Freedom*, pp. 202–4.
17 Brown, *Eastern Europe and Communist Rule*, pp. 276–7.
18 Ibid., p. 278.
19 See Brown, *Surge to Freedom*, p. 211.
20 Ibid, p. 206.
21 By the end of 1990 no less than five books had appeared attempting to prove a conspiracy. Perhaps the most serious is Anneli Ute Gabanyi, *Die unvollendete Revolution: Rumänien zwischen Diktatur und Demokratie* (Munich, Piper Verlag, 1990). To keep all these plot theories in some kind of historical perspective it is worth

quoting two Western observers' views of the conjectures raging at the time around King Michael's *coup* against Antonescu on 23 August 1944, the move that pulled Romania out of the German alliance and on to the side of the allies: 'A careful analysis of all the evidence obtained on the spot reveals that on the night of the King's proclamation there were so many plotters plotting, conspirators conspiring, traitors committing treason and cheaters cheating – that nobody knew who was who and what was what. We traced nine separate plots all striving for the same goal', Robert Bishop and E. S. Crayfield, *Russia Astride the Balkans* (New York, Robert M. McBride & Company, 1948), p. 34. I am grateful to Larry L. Watts for drawing my attention to this.

22 The best review of the various plot theories is by Michael Shafir, 'Preparing for the Future by Revising the Past', Radio Free Europe Report on Eastern Europe, Vol. I, No. 41, 12 October 1990.

23 Western media reporting on Romania was largely unfavourable to Iliescu and the National Salvation Front government. Some of it was exaggerated and tendentious, obviously influenced by opposition circles. Viktor Meier, the East Europe correspondent for *Frankfurter Allgemeine Zeitung,* tried to see Romanian developments more in the context of Romanian and Balkan history. See especially his 'Rumänien braucht Verständnis', *Frankfurter Allgemeine Zeitung*, 26 November 1990. For the view, sober and fair, of another experienced expert, see Harry Schleicher's two articles in the 22 December and 27 December 1990, editions of *Frankfurter Rundschau.* For the view of a prominent and responsible leader of the Romanian opposition, see Radu Campeanu's interview in *Neue Zürcher Zeitung,* 5 December 1990. Campeanu was for a time an advocate of the formation of a coalition government.

24 For a most perceptive overview of post-Ceauşescu Romania, see Gail Kligman, 'Reclaiming the Public: A Reflection on Creating Civil Society in Romania', *East European Politics and Societies,* Vol. 4, No. 3, Fall 1990.

7 Bulgaria: Shaking Off the Nationalist Heritage?

The communist period in Bulgarian history lasted almost exactly 45 years. It began on 9 September 1944, the officially proclaimed day of 'liberation' by the victorious Soviet armies, and ended on 10 November 1989, when President Todor Zhivkov, also General Secretary of the Bulgarian Communist Party, was ousted from power.

The installation of communist rule after the Second World War delayed Bulgaria's introduction to a viable liberal democracy by a further half-century. It had never known one throughout its pre-communist history. A very liberal constitution – the 'Tirnovo Constitution', promulgated in 1879 one year after liberation by Russia from the Ottoman Empire, was little more than a neglected ornament. Democratic forms were rarely backed by democratic substance,[1] and the cynicism with which they were so often manipulated led to widespread cynicism about their very worth. They were openly suspended several times between 1878 and 1940 because of emergencies – real, contrived, or imagined.

Many Bulgarians are sensitive about their country's lack of democratic tradition. But there is nothing uniquely Bulgarian about the lack of a liberal political culture. No Eastern, or East–Central European, country except Czechoslovakia had a viable democracy before the Second World War. In the 1930s all the Balkan countries discussed in this book fell under dictatorships, royal or military. So did some major West European countries. And, though Bulgaria lacked in political refinements, it had more social egalitarianism and less racial intolerance than most countries in any part of Europe.

Nor need Bulgarians blame themselves for their lack of liberal culture. Their newly independent country after 1878 lacked the three essentials for the development of liberal democracy: a political tradition; a sound economic basis; and a sense of national fulfilment or satisfaction. Five hundred years of Ottoman rule were hardly conducive to either good politics or sound economics. Bulgaria was not without some agricultural assets, but its fledgling agrarian economy proved totally unable to withstand the rigours of twentieth century international capitalism. Between the two world wars it was the victim, first of economic depression and then of shrewd economic imperialism by Nazi Germany. Together, they reduced it to an almost colonial-type dependence.

But overshadowing Bulgaria's political and economic inadequacies was a national obsession, often fed by the faltering political and economic development, and often used by Bulgarian rulers to distract attention from their own inadequacies. This national obsession arose from what successive generations of Bulgarians have regarded as the monumental injustice perpetrated by 'the powers' when Bulgaria became independent in 1878. Russia, the liberator, forced Turkey at the Treaty of San Stefano in March 1878 to agree to the creation of a Greater Bulgaria, including not only most of today's Bulgaria but also parts of Macedonia that are now included in Greece and Yugoslavia. In Europe generally there was considerable sympathy for the idea of Greater Bulgaria on ethnic, cultural and historical grounds. But the issue immediately became embroiled in the 'Eastern Question' and the complexities of the balance of power. The new Bulgaria was seen by Western powers as a Russian wedge in the Balkans. Turkey, the sick man of Europe, could not be allowed to expire.

The Greater Bulgaria of San Stefano, therefore, immediately became the rump Bulgaria of the Congress of Berlin. Bulgarians have never got over it. The frontiers of San Stefano, with the historical birthright of Macedonia, became the grail of national fulfilment,[2] which led Bulgaria into the disastrous second Balkan War in 1913, into the First World War and then into the Second World War, both on the side of Germany. Bulgaria suffered enormous human casualties and economic losses. It also lost its international good name, being seen by many Europeans and Americans as a brutal Balkan destabilizer – and as a loser. 'Caitiff Bulgaria' was a term used in the Second World War by Winston Churchill. He was always prone to invest states with human virtues or failings. But many Westerners thought they knew what he meant.

The National Inferiority Complex

The sense of thwarted destiny, continual defeat, and international opprobrium unquestionably had its effect on the Bulgarian national psyche. It produced both an inferiority complex and a victimization psychosis. Bulgarians have wistfully compared their record and reputation with those of Greece and Serbia, neighbours and traditional enemies, two neighbours to whom the twentieth century has been kind, as much respected – at least, in Serbia's case, up to the present – as Bulgaria has been despised.

These judgements have been harsh and unfair, however much Bulgarian policy and behaviour may have lent them some credence. It was the luck of the first half of the twentieth century that kept Serbia and Greece in Western favour and Bulgaria in disgrace. But Bulgaria's history in the second half of the century has done little to redress the balance in its favour. The ferocious behaviour of its communist regime in the Stalinist period only strengthened international prejudice.[3] So did the long post-Stalinist political drought that only ended in November 1989.[4] And in its foreign policy Bulgaria again found itself in unenviable company. The old regime that had tied it to Germany now gave way to one that tied it to the Soviet Union. It was, though, not so much the Soviet alliance as the manner of its observance that lowered Bulgaria's reputation. After all, most East European countries remained tied to the Soviet Union. What distinguished Bulgaria was the demonstrative servility of its relationship. Bulgaria's subordination – in addition to its military, ideological, political, and economic character – was now endowed by Bulgaria's communist leaders with given historical, ethnic, and cultural dimensions as well. Russia, the 'liberator' in 1878 *and* 1944, was now venerated as the shrine of the Slav mystique, genius, and implicit superiority. True, there was a perceptible element of self-interested calculation about all this servility,[5] as will be discussed later, but what most of the world saw was the servility, not the self-interest. Nor did the suspicions (whether justified or not) that the Sofia government was implicated in the assassination attempt against the Pope in 1981, and various murders and other crimes abroad, do anything to raise its reputation.[6]

Many Westerners put this multifaceted abasement down to traditional Bulgarian Russophilia. It unquestionably existed and played a role. Some Bulgarians have denied this. Many middle-class Bulgarians were traditionally pro-German, it is true, strongly influenced by German culture. Some of these Bulgarians found themselves in exile after the Second World War and sought to dispel the Russophile myth. They were subsequently joined by a trickle of their compatriots who, while not sharing this pro-German background, were surpassingly anti-communist, anti-Soviet, and hence often anti-Russian.

Eventually, as communism in Bulgaria lost whatever viability and legitimacy it ever had, many Bulgarians who remained, especially of the younger generation, sought to dissociate themselves from the traditional pro-Russian sentiment. This was despite the emergence of Gorbachev, *perestroika* and *glasnost*. The Soviet mending of ways came too late. It was to the West, particularly to America, that the young now turned. Rejection of communism was now meaning rejection, not just of the Soviet Union, but of Russia, and everything associated with it.

What Bulgarians were now rejecting was best personified by Todor Zhivkov. Born in 1911, Zhivkov became leader of the Bulgarian Communist Party in March 1954, and remained 35½ years at the helm. His development remained basically limited. He began as a colourless young apparatchik and ended as a colourful old apparatchik. In between there was little to celebrate, much to regret and condemn. But what is relevant here is not Zhivkov's entire record but Bulgarian political development during his long period of rule in terms of the liberal–nationalist interaction.

Communism had been relatively strong in Bulgaria before the Second World War. Although the Bulgarian Communist Party (BCP) had made many errors, it had produced some outstanding leaders – most notably Georgi Dimitrov – and, despite persecution, had maintained a fairly numerous following.[7] But on achieving power there was no constructive interaction between rulers and ruled that could have led to even the glimmerings of public life. Pre-communist Bulgaria, with all its defects, did contain some promise. Constitutional government did at least remain a professed goal, however distant, or however hypocritical the professions.

Bulgaria's communist history is also dismal compared with that of most of the rest of Eastern Europe, as well as the Soviet Union itself. There was nothing like the Polish October, the Prague Spring, or even the drawn-out, and eventually unsuccessful, reform programme of János Kádár in Hungary. Nor were there any of the Khrushchevian lurches that made the Soviet Union so stimulating between 1956 and 1964. By way of reform Bulgaria had the April plenum of 1956, a faint echo of the 20th Communist Party of the Soviet Union (CPSU) Congress that Zhivkov used more to strengthen his power than to change political course. After that there was little reform but much reorganization – party, governmental, economic, territorial, educational, social. No walk of public life seemed to escape the meaningless change that characterized the Zhivkov years. But there was no *systemic* change.[8] Whereas, after 1989, the aspiring democracies in other countries in Eastern Europe, with the obvious exception of Romania, could pick up something of value from the rubble, to go with whatever liberal, precommunist history they had, Bulgaria could salvage very little. Coming into the post-communist era, therefore, its entire liberal heritage was meagre.

The Nationalist Impulse

But, paradoxically, there was a considerable heritage of nationalism. Zhivkov was ostentatiously pro-Soviet and was often accused of 'betraying' Bulgarian interests to those of the Soviet Union. Petûr Mladenov, who temporarily succeeded him as Bulgarian president and party leader, charged him with wanting to make Bulgaria the sixteenth republic of the Soviet Union.[9] Certainly, Bulgaria was for many years the model satellite. But, as already mentioned, it was not an uncalculating, or an unrewarded, model. It derived economic advantages not granted to Moscow's other satellites. Strategically located next to two exposed and unstable Western allies, Greece and Turkey, it was valuable to the Soviet Union as an ideological, strategic, and diplomatic outpost. On this account, too, Bulgaria did not go unrewarded.[10] The economic favouritism shown Bulgaria was sometimes the subject of grumbling by some of its allies. It did bring considerable apparent advantage, although in the long run Bulgaria's status as preferred client could prove to have been a serious liability. Its economy, especially its industry, became so closely tied to that of the Soviet Union – more than any other East European economy – that the collapse of the Soviet economy and the whole COMECON system was bound to affect it in an almost catastrophic way.[11] Once considered one of the most stable of the East European economies, it was now seen as one of the weakest.

Despite these ties to Moscow, Bulgaria occasionally showed some independence on international issues which the Soviets obviously considered important. The best examples were in relations with the Federal Republic of Germany.[12] On other issues, most notably in the Balkans, where the Bulgarians acted as the Soviets' spokesmen, there were elements of the Bulgarian national interest involved. Moscow's and Sofia's state interests, therefore, coincided.[13]

But, compared with all other East European states, Bulgarian nationalism *vis-à-vis* Moscow was muted to the point of silence. Where it did show was in relation to its own minorities and its neighbours, its assertiveness in this sphere often appearing as a form of compensation for its docility toward the Soviet Union, a form of 'surrogate nationalism'. The Bulgarian communist regime, an example of 'socialist internationalism', was also heir to the nationalism of its bourgeois predecessors. Its nationalism was muzzled by ideology, by constraints imposed by the Soviet alliance and the general international setting. But as international communism became transmuted into a diversity of national communisms, nationalism became increasingly discernible, and familiar.

It was inevitable that it should be directed toward Macedonia. It was the 'San Stefano' complex in a new setting. And Yugoslavia, since Tito's break with Stalin in 1948, had been an obvious and, within limits, a permissible target. After Stalin, Soviet policy was aimed at coaxing Yugoslavia back into, or toward, the Soviet alliance. It could not, therefore, allow any unbridled Bulgarian irredentism. Besides, to connive at one *irredenta* would mean taking the lid off all of them, including some against the Soviet Union itself. Bulgaria had to recognize the integrity of Yugoslavia, denying at the same time that it had any territorial claims regarding Macedonia. But it refused, after the early 1950s, to recognize the existence of a separate Macedonian *nation,* thus rejecting the entire *raison d'être* of the Macedonian republic within the Yugoslav federation set up by Tito after the Second World War. This was that the Macedonians were a distinct nation entitled to their own statehood. Historically, Bulgarians had always disputed this. Their case that Macedonians were Bulgarians and had been an integral part of the united Bulgarian medieval kingdom was the basis of their claim to Macedonia itself. And by maintaining this argument they were nursing their claim, regardless of their denial of territorial ambitions.[14]

Awakening Nationalism

The Bulgarian–Yugoslav dispute over Macedonia (in which the Yugoslav government's case was most strenuously proclaimed by the republic of Macedonia's government in Skopje) simmered for almost 40 years. It was once possible to see a pattern to it that made sense in terms of the vicissitudes of Soviet–Yugoslav relations and of Bulgaria's role as a model Soviet satellite: When relations between Moscow and Belgrade deteriorated, polemics between Sofia and Belgrade over Macedonia flared up, only to cool down when Soviet–Yugoslav relations improved. Thus Macedonia became the weathervane. Indeed the first sign of renewed Soviet–Yugoslav tension was often a war of words between Sofia and Skopje. Bulgaria's muzzle was loosened, its leash was extended – and history was revived.

The pattern made sense, but it was too schematically applied by those who discounted the possibility that any East European satellite, especially Bulgaria, would show any spontaneous nationalism. After the second half of the 1960s the Macedonian factor ceased being a useful gauge for measuring the state of Yugoslav–Soviet–Bulgarian relations; it became, if anything, misleading. This factor in Bulgarian domestic and foreign policy acquired a momentum of its own, independent of Soviet–Yugoslav relations. There was even circumstantial evidence suggesting occasional Soviet efforts to restrain the Bulgarian government on the issue.

By the middle of the 1960s the spirit of nationalism was very much abroad in the entire socialist camp. The Sino–Soviet split had shattered the myth of internationalism in the world communist movement, a process that had actually begun in 1948 with the Stalin–Tito break. In Eastern Europe, Albania and then, partly, Romania had also broken with Soviet hegemony. At the national level, in the individual East European countries communism was no longer reshaping national identities; it was being reshaped by them. Brezhnev's conservative and integrationist counter-reformation after the crushing of the Prague Spring was designed to slow, even reverse, this trend. But its early successes were illusory. Beneath the reimposed internationalist forms and style of the early 1970s, the nationalization of communism proceeded apace. And as global distractions, complacency, and inertia diverted Moscow's attention from Eastern Europe, the pace quickened, carrying away the socialist superstructure imposed on Eastern Europe 30 years before.

Bulgaria was part of this rehistoricization process. To avoid being engulfed by it its communist leaders had to respond to it and move along with it. In the Balkans, short on political culture, long on nationalism, the latter inevitably dominated the rehistoricization process. It was no coincidence that communist Romania, with neighbouring Russia as its great historical enemy, should concentrate its rediscovered nationalism on turning back Soviet influence. With Bulgaria the goal was different. Russia had been the traditional friend and protector. The enemies had been Turkey, Yugoslavia (Serbia), and Greece (Romania to a much lesser degree). And the nub of national concern was Macedonia.

During the 1970s Bulgarian nationalism received an impetus from a quite unexpected quarter, from a member of Zhivkov's own family. Lyudmila Zhivkov, daughter of Todor, put the nepotism from which she benefited to uncommonly good account. As Minister of Culture and member of the ruling party Politburo, with an apparently unlimited budget and paternal backing, Lyudmila Zhivkov pursued a policy of unashamed cultural nationalism, based not on any Russian model but rather on the French. Her object was to overcome Bulgarian 'national nihilism' by publicizing the high degree of civilization that had flourished on Bulgarian soil in ancient and medieval times. Bulgarians should be aware, and hence be proud, of their cultural heritage, which made them part of European civilization. Zhivkova, of course, was a communist, but a Bulgarian communist. She made a considerable impact both in her own country and, through the exhibitions of Bulgarian culture she organized, in Western Europe as well. Not surprisingly, she was no favourite in Moscow. For the Soviets she was an element of national spontaneity in a country where they had least suspected it.[15]

The Turkish Minority

Nationalism's domestic manifestation is in the treatment of ethnic minorities. Historically the Bulgarian record has been good in this regard. Often a menacing threat to its neighbours it had treated its own minorities with more tolerance than most. By far its biggest minority, and its biggest problem, was presented by the Turkish minority, a massive reminder of the 500-year Ottoman 'yoke'. After independence in 1878 several hundred thousand Turks emigrated to Turkey. The Turks that remained and multiplied were tolerated, but their rights were grudgingly given, inconsistently applied, and often arbitrarily withdrawn. Their exact number was impossible to ascertain, but by the beginning of the 1980s they probably numbered more than a million, a tenth of Bulgaria's total population. They had always resisted assimilation, and there had been periodic disturbances in Turkish-populated areas. Turkish cultural and educational privileges were steadily eroded during the 1960s and 1970s. It was a process punctuated by occasional violence but never a general organized resistance.

Specialists on minority questions in the Balkans had been watching this erosion of Turkish rights with concern. But few expected the massive acceleration at the end of 1984 and the beginning of 1985 in what became known as the 'name-change operation'. All members of the Turkish minority were suddenly forced to abandon their Turkish names and to adopt Bulgarian ones. They were also forbidden to speak Turkish in public. Their historical Turkish identity was even denied, a fact that Zhivkov himself had previously conceded. They were now pronounced to be descendants of Bulgarians who had been 'Turkicized'. In essence, therefore, they were now considered no different from the Pomaks, the some 200 000 strong Bulgarian Muslim minority whose ancestors had been converted to Islam during the Ottoman period. Now it was time to 'Bulgarize' them back again! There appears to have been widespread Turkish resistance to the government's repression which was put down mercilessly, with many casualties.[16] At that time, it should be noted, no Turks were allowed to emigrate to Turkey. The official contention in 1985 was that they had no right to do so because they were not, and never had been, Turks.[17]

There was much speculation at the time about the reasons for the Bulgarian government's action. On closer examination it appeared that, unexpected though it was, it was not something new and uncharacteristic, but rather the massive culmination of a policy in operation for some time – that of whittling away the compactness and the distinctiveness of Bulgaria's biggest minority. But the sheer scale of the name-changing operation made it qualitatively different from anything that had gone on before.

Why? Why was Bulgaria prepared to risk internal disruption and international ignominy by resorting to this? The best single reason can be found in a comparison of birthrates: the Turkish population in the country was growing quickly; the Bulgarian birthrate was stagnating.[18] Bulgarians were getting nervous and, whether regime supporters or not, had a vague feeling that something should be done. The fact that the minority involved was

Turkish, descendants of the old master race, was also not irrelevant. Any move against the Turks, therefore, would not be unpopular. It would be *actively* supported in those parts of north-east and south-central Bulgaria where Turkish and Bulgarian communities had regular contact.

The timing of the regime move was also significant. By the end of 1984 the most successful period in Bulgaria's communist history had come to an end. The end of the 1970s and the early part of the 1980s were marked by economic progress, general political and cultural relaxation, a confidence on the part of the ruling elite, and a degree of hope among many sections of the population that the situation would continue to improve. By about the middle of 1984 the situation was quite different. Bulgaria was in a serious economic downturn and the population knew it. Hence the need, it was calculated in Sofia, for a nationalist diversion, gratifying and appeasing.

The regime's move should also be seen in a historical and regional perspective. It was part of the nationalist drive toward the unitary state. In terms of Bulgarian history it was seen as settling the last account with the Ottoman Empire. Similar policies had been pursued in other parts of the Balkans as well. In Greek Thrace, the Athens government resolutely refused to allow over 100 000 citizens of Turkish nationality, another residual of the Ottoman Empire, to call themselves Turks.[19] They were Greek Muslims. (Bulgarian policy, therefore, sought to catch up on the Greek example.)

In Romania the regime's assimilationist policy was being applied to the Hungarian minority, although even Ceauşescu dared not contemplate such a drastic move as Zhivkov carried out. The international uproar would have been deafening. In parts of Yugoslavia, too, policies of ethnic discrimination were in force – most notably by Serbs and Macedonians against Albanians. In Turkey itself the long-standing policy against the Kurds[20] had much in common with what the Bulgarian regime was attempting. And with regard to Turkey many Bulgarians not only nursed their historical grudge but also a current fear. Turkey was growing in population and power. By the end of the century its population would be seven times the Bulgarian. The Bulgarian Turks, therefore, could, it was feared, become the fifth column for an aggressive Turkey in the future. For Bulgarians who thought in such terms, Zhivkov's action in 1984–5, therefore, was more pre-emptive than repressive – and by no means unique.

Once the name change had been completed, most Bulgarians simply wished the problem would go away. For a few years it seemed to have done exactly that. International criticism soon evaporated and Bulgaria resumed its international backwater status. But the matter continued to simmer, and it boiled over again in the summer of 1989. At this time Bulgaria still hardly seemed to be in a pre-revolutionary situation, but the growing ferment was unmistakable and throughout Eastern Europe the Gorbachev phenomenon was giving discomfort to the rulers and hope to the ruled. Human rights, including those of minorities, were actively on the agenda of East–West relations, most notably at the CSCE conference in Vienna. Zhivkov was obviously losing his political touch. His policies became contradictory and self-defeating. At home he was becoming more tyrannical; abroad he craved respect and status. He was, after all, the dean of Warsaw Pact leaders by a considerable margin!

The Bulgarian Turks gradually became aware of the significance of the changing international situation. Their resistance to the continuing assimilation campaign increased, and towards the end of May 1989 mass demonstrations were organized in some of the Turkish-populated areas. There were clashes with the police, and casualties. The Bulgarian authorities immediately began expelling from the country those it considered ringleaders of the discontent. International opinion was quick to respond to these acts of repression. It became thoroughly aroused in June when Zhivkov announced that a law already passed giving all Bulgarians the right of free travel abroad as from the following September would now apply immediately to the Bulgarian Turks ('Bulgarians of the Muslim religion', as they continued to be called). This was primitive cunning on Zhivkov's part and it proceeded to backfire. The free travel enactment was a concession to CSCE, Helsinki and human rights. What, therefore, could be the objection to letting dissatisfied citizens be the first to take advantage of it? There was, in the event, plenty of objection and Bulgaria received much unusual and unwelcome publicity.[21] For many Bulgarians, too, whatever they felt about the Turks, it was a cause for shame, especially when it became clear that many Turks were being 'encouraged' to emigrate and many more simply fled out of fear or uncertainty. On the other hand, many Bulgarians welcomed the move, especially those living in the regions inhabited by Turks. For them it was not only a chance to get rid of Turks but also to get their hands on their property. (Czechs moving into German property during the post-Second World War expulsions in Czechoslovakia provide a historical parallel.)

Over 300 000 Turks crossed the border into Turkey, whose government closed the border toward the end of August, unable to cope with the influx. Because of hardships in Turkey over 100 000 of the emigrants subsequently returned to Bulgaria. They were far from welcome. Many found it impossible to recover their property. And, when, after the fall of Zhivkov in November 1989, they could officially resume their Turkish names, the legal formalities involved were made deliberately complicated.[22] The Turkish question in Bulgaria was far from settled. It could complicate the development of democracy there.

In Zhivkov's Bulgaria, therefore, beneath – or alongside – all the internationalism, there was nationalism in abundance. To many, even those prepared to concede its validity, it seemed to be residual nationalism, based on past grievances rather than present reality. But it was precisely the past that was to outlive and supersede the present reality of Soviet power and domination.

Dissent and the Democratic Attempt

But if Bulgarian nationalism was alive and kicking, Bulgarian reform communism continued either moribund or stillborn. In response to Gorbachev there was much movement, but little purpose, enormous verbiage, but little substance. In July 1987 Zhivkov himself outlined a reform proposal parts of which, taken at face value, involved real systemic change, so much so that even Gorbachev was startled over them. But, in the end the 'July Concept', as it became known, proved to be more sloppy window dressing than an earnest of intention. Zhivkov then relapsed into political conservatism, claiming that the April plenum of 1956 had been the real turning-point of reform and that there was no real need for another one. Some 18 months later, in January 1989, new gestures were made towards economic reform. But apart from its presumed insincerity what was most noteworthy about this decree, too, was the same primitive thought processes and pretentious provincialism that had characterized Zhivkov's rule. And by the end of the 1980s that rule was one of desperation with the end not far away.

But feeble though this Bulgarian version of *perestroika* was, it was at least a response. Of the new Soviet spirit of *glasnost,* however, there was little trace. Freedom of expression was certainly growing in Bulgaria. But compared with the Soviet Union and any other East European country (Romania and Albania always excepted), Bulgaria lagged far behind the spirit of the times. And the freedom that was growing was due more to the beginnings of pressure from below than to any concessions from above. It was still difficult, though, for opposition to express itself effectively and to coalesce. But helped by their own determination, encouraged by changes inside the socialist alliance, and protected, to some extent, by Zhivkov's own craving for international respectability, democratic groups of different types began to emerge and to acquire some coherence.

The year of 1989 was the 'take-off' year for dissidence in Bulgaria, the regime, however grudgingly, acknowledged its presence and the likelihood that it would persist. The first important dissident group was not ostensibly political, but rather social: *Eco-glasnost,* an ecological pressure group that originated in the heavily polluted city of Ruse and was backed by influential establishment figures.[23] Zhivkov tried to suppress it, but it survived.

During the course of the year many other groups sprang up and by the time Zhivkov fell in November there were believed to have been over 40 of them.[24] After years of suppression and acquiescence many Bulgarians showed themselves as eager for freedom as any other East Europeans.

But it was not *popular* opposition that was responsible for the fall of Zhivkov in November 1989 – at least not directly. It was a palace coup that toppled him, a cabal within the top leadership. Its aim was not to destroy communism but to enable it to survive the rigours of a totally new situation. Zhivkov had become expendable as well as a distinct liability. But this was a new situation in Bulgaria's communist history. It was not simply a matter of changing the leader. In the prevailing international context – with communist rule collapsing throughout Eastern Europe, with the Berlin Wall opened just one day before – the removal of a leader, especially an institution like Zhivkov, simply opened the floodgates. Forty-five years of communist government were swept unknowingly aside by that anti-Zhivkov cabal. What emerged under Petûr Mladenov and then under Andrei Lukanov was a post-communist regime, not democratic by choice, but becoming less authoritarian through circumstance and pressure. Many communists, including many in the governing bureaucracy, particularly at the local level, could not even attempt this transition. But many, with varying degrees of conviction, could. Bulgaria's fledgling democracy would do itself a disservice if it failed to recognize this.

Post-Communist Bulgaria

After Zhivkov, what? A deluge or a transition? Either was possible: a transition to constitutional democracy based on a recovering economy or a deluge of political anarchy compounded by destitution. In June 1990 the reform Communist Party (discreetly renamed Socialist Party) won the general election against the Union of Democratic Forces (UDF), an opposition grouping composed of many of the leading dissidents of the last Zhivkov years.[25] It was a clear victory in what was, despite the irregularities, one of the fairest elections in Bulgaria's entire history.

But what emerged after the election was not the slow but steady progress toward democracy, with a stable government and a vigorous but responsible opposition, that at first seemed possible. The election had revealed the polarization of Bulgarian society along social, educational and generational lines – the towns against the countryside, the young against the old, and intellectuals against the workers, particularly the peasants. Such a polarization is also known in Western democracies. But what was dangerous about it in post-communist Bulgaria, as in neighbouring Romania, was that factors that might have contained and then reduced it were either too weak or totally absent. Again, the lack of liberal political culture in pre-communist Bulgaria, the repressive orthodoxy of the communist period, and then the indecisive way in which Bulgarian communism was ended sharpened the polarization.

The socialist government, led by Andrei Lukanov, was partly to blame for the failure to narrow this polarization. Lukanov himself, the scion of a communist dynasty, was both an intellectual and an impressive politician who, however, was unsuccessful in office both in communist and post-communist Bulgaria. He was clearly the object of great suspicion because he had served in senior positions under Zhivkov. But he was never in the old dictator's ruling circle. Zhivkov did not trust him. Like Ion Iliescu in Romania, Lukanov was often spoken of as a potential successor to, and huge potential improvement on, the ruling incumbent. A more substantial criticism of Lukanov was that, as minister in charge of foreign trade during the 1980s, he pursued a policy that landed Bulgaria with a $10 billion debt by the end of the decade.[26] It was not an impressive calling card, but even Lukanov's enemies had to recognize his personality.

Confirmed as prime minister after the general election, Lukanov was expected to show his leadership through measures designed to slow the accelerating economic downturn, to make a comprehensive break with the state socialist system, and to move toward a market economy. It was also demanded that he dispel doubts about his real intentions by clearing the government stables of unrepentant adherents to the old order. But he showed himself hesitant and ineffective. At first he advocated a slow-tempo approach to the market so as not to avoid destructive social consequences. There was nothing uniquely Bulgarian about this kind of caution: it was still official policy in democratic Hungary, for example. But even some relatively detached observers explained Lukanov's policy, like Iliescu's in Romania, as being partly due to the old communist mind-set.[27] He later changed his policy and introduced a programme of economic reform not dissimilar to the 'shock therapy' in Poland. It was a measure of the increasing desperateness of the situation, aggravated mainly by the virtual collapse of Soviet and COMECON trade, and to some extent by the Persian Gulf crisis.[28] As for changing the substance, composition and image of his party and government, he did make considerable strides in that direction. He claimed that in prevailing circumstances he could not have done more. But many people thought he should have identified more closely with reform groups inside the Bulgarian Socialist Party who were trying to make it a social democratic party. He might have split the party in doing so, but in the long run he would have helped it survive. He would also have helped something more important: the growth of Bulgarian democracy.

But Lukanov and his socialist colleagues were not the only ones to blame for Bulgaria's faltering start to the post-communist era. The democratic opposition, parliamentary and extra-parliamentary, played a role that betrayed its immaturity and irresponsibility. At the end of November 1990 the Lukanov government was actually forced out of office, not by any democratic or parliamentary methods, but through parliamentary boycotts, street demonstrations and workers strikes – in fact, it was rather like Prague 1948 in reverse. It was replaced by a coalition government composed of socialists, independents, and members of the opposition parties. It was good for Bulgaria that it had a president during this period who, though lacking in charisma, combined sincerity, dedication, and restraint. Zhelyu Zhelev, who took over after the forced retirement of Mladenov in July 1990, managed to project a dignity which gave Bulgaria a respect abroad that could be beneficial for its future.

Zhelev undoubtedly saw that public opinion was turning against the socialists, but he had the good sense to see that it was the ballot box alone, and not public opinion polls, demonstrations and strikes that should decide. He helped hold public life in Bulgaria together during the critical months of 1991 when the coalition government, under Dimitûr Popov, struggled to keep parliamentary government intact and set economic reform in motion. The economic situation deteriorated, but Bulgaria did give the impression of sincerity in implementing tough economic measures and won the respect of the international financial community. In October 1991 new parliamentary elections were held. They were orderly and fair and the UDF (Union of Democratic Forces), an uneasy grouping of democratic forces, won a narrow majority and Bulgaria had its first democratic government in over half a century.

In fact by the end of 1991 Bulgaria, after its unpromising start, looked like something of an oasis in a Balkan desert when compared with Yugoslavia, Romania, and Albania. Parliamentary government was proceeding, as was economic reform. But the dangers were far from being overcome. The socialists, though beaten, had made a very good showing at the elections and were now strongly playing the nationalist, anti-Turkish card. The Turkish Rights and Freedoms Party actually held the balance in the new parliament. And unemployment was rising dangerously. Something of an oasis, certainly! But could it turn out to be a mirage?

Notes

1 C. E. Black, *The Establishment of Constitutional Government in Bulgaria* (Princeton, NJ, Princeton University Press, 1943).
2 See Richard J. Crampton, *Bulgaria 1878–1918: A History* (Boulder, CO, East European Monographs, 1983); Benjamin Constant, *Foxy Ferdinand: Tsar of Bulgaria* (London, Sidgwick and Jackson, 1979).
3 See Nissan Oren, *Revolution Administered: Agrarianism and Communism in Bulgaria* (Baltimore, Johns Hopkins University Press, 1973); Brown, *Bulgaria under Communist Rule*, pp. 3–38.
4 Brown, *Bulgaria under Communist Rule*, passim.
5 See Brown, *Eastern Europe and Communist Rule*, pp. 329–32.
6 Brown, 'Conservatism and Nationalism in the Balkans', in Griffith (ed.), *Central and Eastern Europe*, pp. 303–5.
7 On the history of the BCP see the following two excellent books: Joseph Rothschild, *The Communist Party of Bulgaria: Origins and Development, 1883–1936* (New York, Columbia University Press, 1959), and Nissan Oren, *Bulgarian Communism: The Road to Power, 1933–1944* (New York, Columbia University Press, 1971).
8 See Brown, *Surge to Freedom*, pp. 185–8, 192–3.
9 Interview with *La Vanguardia* (Barcelona), 1 April 1990, FBIS-EEU-90-072, 13 April 1990. Mladenov was asked whether Zhivkov had offered 'to make Bulgaria the sixteenth republic of the USSR'. He replied, 'Yes. The first time, the proposal was made at the end of 1962 and in 1963, but there are no documents. In 1973 Zhivkov offered again an integration that Gromyko did not accept.' BTA, in English, had reported this charge as early as 29 December 1989, quoting that day's edition of *Narodna Kultura*.
10 Brown, *Eastern Europe and Communist Rule*, pp. 319–20.
11 Joseph Rothschild stresses the eventual complementarity of Bulgarian economic development with that of the Soviet Union. After Stalin, concessions were granted to Bulgaria enabling it to concentrate on its marginal advantages – light industry, agricultural industry, electronics, and tourism. 'This neatly dovetailed its economic interests with Soviet needs and lubricated its political loyalty, in return for which it received extensive and sustained Soviet capital assistance', *Return to Diversity: A Political History of East-Central Europe Since Second World War II* (New York, Oxford University Press, 1989), p. 212.
12 Brown, *Eastern Europe and Communist Rule*, pp. 67–9.
13 Brown, *Bulgaria under Communist Rule*, pp. 269–83.
14 Lendvai, *Eagles in Cobwebs*, pp. 31–7, 246–8.
15 On Zhivkova, see Brown, *Eastern Europe and Communist Rule*, pp. 321-3.
16 This forced assimilation of the Turks drew widespread Western media coverage. For an excellent historical summary of the erosion of Turkish rights in Bulgaria, see Hugh Poulton and MLIHRC (pseudonym), *Minorities in the Balkans* (London, The Minority Rights Group, October 1989), pp. 3–22.
17 'Officials Say There Are No Turks in Bulgaria', Radio Free Europe Research Bulgarian Situation Report, 28 March 1985.
18 The Turkish minority had been growing by some 2 per cent a year while the Bulgarian population was slightly diminishing.
19 See Chapter 9.
20 See Chapter 2.

21 For a discussion of the 1989 moves against the Turks, see Brown, *Surge to Freedom*, pp. 194–5.
22 See Sylvie Kauffmann's report from Kurdzhali, a centre of Turkish settlement, in *Le Monde*, 7 June 1990.
23 See Richard Crampton, 'The Intelligentsia, Ecology and the Opposition in Bulgaria', *The World Today*, February 1990.
24 Brown, *Surge to Freedom*, pp. 190–1.
25 See Judy Dempsey, 'The Anatomy of a Rare Communist Victory', *Financial Times*, 15 June 1990.
26 Dr Dimitûr Ivanov, an economic expert, writing in *Trud* after the fall of Zhivkov, said between one-third and one-half of Bulgaria's earnings from exports to nonsocialist countries went to service the country's hard currency debt. The annual debt service payment was $1 billion which was 40 per cent more than the value of Bulgarian exports to the industrialized West; BTA, in English, 1 December 1989.
27 For a revealing glimpse of Lukanov, see Berthold Kohler, 'Ein Gespräch mit den bulgarischen Minister – präsidenten Lukanow', *Frankfurter Allgemeine Zeitung*, 14 May 1990.
28 The Gulf crisis appears to have been particularly severe on Bulgaria; see Laura Colby, 'Crisis in the Gulf Grinds Down Bulgaria's Economic Shift', *International Herald Tribune*, 5 September 1990.

Part II
Conflicts – Actual and Potential

8 The Greek–Turkish Confrontation

In January 1985 the Greek government officially announced a 'New Defence Doctrine' involving a 'reorientation' in its primary threat perception. This was because, though the Warsaw Pact remained the potential enemy, Turkey was considered Greece's only bellicose neighbour. What this meant in effect was that Turkey, its nominal ally in the North Atlantic Treaty Organization, was now considered by Greece to be its main enemy.[1]

The announcement caused much international comment but no great surprise. The Turkish invasion of Cyprus in August 1974 had sealed Greek–Turkish enmity. Cyprus added a crucially emotional issue to the deteriorating relationship between the two countries.[2] Many Greeks and Turks had already been killed on Cyprus since the unrest began in the middle 1950s. The Turkish invasion in 1974 not only killed more: it also made tens of thousands of them into refugees who lost everything. In this sense the Cyprus dispute, though less immediately threatening to the security of the two countries, had more impact on the two nations than the other disputes dividing them: the four interacting sets of issues that became known collectively as the Aegean dispute:[3]

(1) *Delineation of airspace*. Many of the Greek islands in the Aegean, and the Dodecanese Islands which Greece gained from Italy after the Second World War are within a few minutes flying distance of the Turkish coast. Greece maintains that the division between Greek and Turkish airspace should extend ten miles. Turkey has rejected this, arguing that it should correspond to the territorial waters limit of six miles. It maintains that the very close proximity of so many foreign islands to its shoreline is unique and should call for new procedures. The existing situation is such that Turkish airplanes often fly over Greek airspace, as defined by Greece, in order to publicize Turkish claims. Greece has periodically protested and carried out interception manœuvres.

This issue has not been just a bilateral one. Turkey has wished to link it with the issue of control over Aegean air traffic. The ensuing complications have been serious. According to international convention civil air traffic up to the six-mile limit of Turkish airspace has been controlled by Greek air traffic control. This meant that important international air flights to the Greek islands were Greek controlled. Turkey always accepted this, but as a result of the 1974 Cyprus crisis demanded that all flights to Turkey from the West must now be controlled by Turkish air traffic control once they reached the *middle of the Aegean*. To the Greeks this looked like Turkish expansionism, since it was similar to Turkish claims regarding the continental shelf (see below). They refused to accept the demand and declared Turkish airspace unsafe – an obvious attempt to force the issue. For six years international air travel across the Aegean was suspended until in 1980 Turkey withdrew its claims but reserved the right to bring them up again in the future.

The question also affected NATO air surveillance and operational control in the Aegean Sea. Until the Cyprus crisis in 1974 a Greek officer at NATO's 6th Tactical Air Force (ATAF) base at Izmir in Turkey was in charge of air surveillance in the Aegean. He reported to an American general. The military and civilian areas of air traffic control were then identical. But in 1974 Greece withdrew from the NATO military integrated structure, because of dissatisfaction with its allies over Cyprus, and in 1978 a Turkish general became commander of ATAF at Izmir. Greece refused to participate in NATO's Aegean command structure and objected to the construction of a new Tactical Air Force centre in northern Greece, at Larissa, as long as the Aegean situation was not clarified to its satisfaction. The situation was aggravated in 1985 by Greece's revision of its military doctrine, mentioned above, making Turkey, at least by inference, its principal enemy.

(2) *The continental shelf*. This dispute centres on what actually constitutes a continental shelf. Turkey contends that only a mainland, or continental land mass, can have a continental shelf and has proposed a median line halfway into the Aegean Sea as the delimitation between the continental shelf of the two countries. Greece argues that each of its Aegean and Dodecanese Islands has its own continental shelf and insists on exclusive control over the numerous shelves and their resources. International law, as interpreted by the Geneva Law of the Sea Convention of 1958, favours the Greek contention. But the issue has become more than one of legal interpretation. Oil deposits are believed to lie below certain parts of the shelf (though few traces of them have been found so far). In March 1987 a war between the two countries seemed imminent when the Turks sent a research ship into one of the disputed parts of the Aegean and it looked as if

the Greek government might order it to be attacked. The danger was averted. But if oil, in substantial quantities, were ever discovered, the dispute could degenerate into hostilities.

(3) *'Remilitarization' of the Greek Islands.* This is a historical issue affecting all Greek Aegean and Dodecanese Islands. But it has become concentrated on the two north-eastern Aegean Islands of Lemnos and Samothrace which lie just a few miles from the entrance to the Turkish Dardanelles. Again the issue is tied up in international treaties and their interpretation. Turkey argues that the Treaty of Lausanne of 1923, which finally regulated its relations with Greece after the First World War, stipulated the full demilitarization of those two islands. The Greeks argue that the Montreux Convention of 1936, which restored to Turkey control over the Turkish Straits and regulated the transit of foreign shipping through them, replaced the Lausanne Treaty in several important respects and, since the new treaty did not mention the demilitarization of the islands, then this part of the Lausanne Treaty was now null and void. This interpretation was strengthened by several statements by Turkish officials at the time. After the hostilities over Cyprus in 1974 Turkey began vigorously to dispute this contention, arguing that the Greek fortification of the islands – Lemnos in particular – constituted another direct threat to its security.

(4) *Territorial water limits.* Greece has confined itself to claiming a six-mile territorial limit around both its mainland and islands, but has reserved the right to follow much contemporary international practice and extend it to 12 miles. Obviously this is an issue having a direct bearing on the questions of both airspace and the continental shelf. Turkey has said it would regard such a move as amounting to a *casus belli* and Greece has not yet tried to implement the 12 mile limit.

These four issues were so interconnected and were such a reflection of the overall mutual hostility between Greece and Turkey that it would be difficult to distinguish the most serious. On the face of it, Turkey's threat to declare war if Greece were to extend the territorial water limits is obviously the most serious. But only the most irresponsible government in Athens would be likely to do this. As for the airspace dispute this lost some of its more immediate seriousness with the demise of the Cold War after 1990. The 'remilitarization' of Lemnos and Samothrace will always be as serious (or unserious) as the general climate of Greek–Turkish relations. It could never become a cause for war except in the case of a Turkish strike against the islands – again rather hard to imagine except in the case of general hostilities. As for the continental shelf, if ever large deposits of oil are found there this certainly could lead to more serious incidents. If moderation prevails in both Athens and Ankara it could lead to nothing more serious than interminable international judicial deliberations.

Cyprus and the Embrace of History

As one observer has remarked, 'Cyprus presents one of those intractable problems in which bitter memory has superseded the desire of its peoples for a harmonious future'.[4] Cyprus has had a huge impact on the Greek and Turkish nations. It is where they have confronted and killed one another. It is where a mistrust so deep has arisen that it can never be healed. (In this respect it is now strikingly similar to the situation in Yugoslavia.) The Cyprus dispute has also, like the Aegean disputes, had important international ramifications. Cyprus lies about 40 miles from the south coast of Turkey and about 55 miles west of the Syrian coast. It sits astride three major sea routes: the Black Sea to the eastern Mediterranean via the Dardanelles and the Aegean; the western Mediterranean to the Red Sea via the Suez Canal; and the Mediterranean to the Persian Gulf overland via the Tigris and Euphrates valley. In 1991 its strategic value was once again underlined by the war in the Persian Gulf provoked by Iraq's aggression against Kuwait.

Cyprus has been largely populated by Greeks for about 3000 years. Ownership of the island has changed hands many times. Assyrians, Persians, Macedonians, Egyptians, Romans, Byzantine Greeks, Franks and Venetians have all occupied it. From 1511 to 1878 it was under Ottoman control. They garrisoned and colonized it and the nearly 20 per cent of the Cypriot population who are Turkish are the descendants of the Ottoman colonizers. In 1878 Great Britain occupied the island (or officially 'leased' it from Turkey); it was valuable protection for its sea route to India. In the First World War Great Britain annexed Cyprus, and in 1923 made it a crown colony. In the Second World War, Cyprus, without playing a significant role, was a valuable supply and staging point.

Although Greece as well as Turkey recognized British ownership of Cyprus by the Treaty of Lausanne in 1923, Greek opinion, both in Greece and on Cyprus itself, hardened during the course of this century in favour of incorporating the island into Greece. *Enosis* (union) became an aspiration inseparable from Greek patriotism and it received a considerable boost as a result of the Second World War. Great Britain was declining and 'salt water' imperialism was very much *passé*. Greece, as a member of the wartime alliance and a country that had suffered both a German occupation and a civil war against communism, was in a favourable international position. Besides this, traditional Western phil-Hellenism had by no means disappeared. A tangible result of this Western favour was the surrender in 1947 to Greece of the Dodecanese Islands by Italy, as compensation for Italy's role in the Second World War. Turkey, though its strategic, military, and political importance was obvious, enjoyed nowhere near the sympathy that Greece did.

But Greek ambitions over Cyprus brought it into confrontation with both Great Britain and Turkey. Though they were gradually closing down their empire, the British were still not resigned to shedding their major power status, and for this they needed the kind of strategic base that Cyprus provided. Hence, they determined to keep the island. Turkey worried over the prospect of having yet another Greek island (this time a large one) so close to its shores. As Robert McDonald says:

> Greece already controlled islands covering the sea routes to all of Turkey's Black and Aegean Sea ports. Cyprus lies across the shipping lanes from Mersin and Iskenderun, ports vital for the supply of central Anatolia and the eastern frontier. Although the two states were members of NATO, traditional enmities lay close beneath the surface of the relationship. In any event, some Turks agreed, alliances are impermanent and NATO eventually might be dissolved.[5]

The traditional enmities McDonald refers to were the result of the close intertwining of Greek and Turkish history over five centuries, so close that the process of separation was bound to be very painful. The second half of the twentieth century has, in fact, shown that total separation is impossible. This has made what remains of the relationship all the more bitter and uncompromising.

During Ottoman domination, which began in the fourteenth century and lasted till the early nineteenth, the Greeks as a nation were subjugated. The Byzantine Empire gradually shrank and disappeared for ever after 1453. But as individuals and in separate communities, many Greeks flourished under Ottoman rule. Culturally, through the Greek Orthodox Church, they dominated Ottoman territories in Europe. They also dominated Ottoman commerce and many other aspects of the economic life of the empire. The large Greek communities in and around Constantinople, on the Black Sea, in the Aegean and in Western Anatolia were the most affluent in the Empire. Retrospectively, Greeks now consider Ottoman domination as a period of servitude and humiliation. But throughout five centuries it unquestionably had its material compensations for millions of them. Even after the Greek mainland attained independence in the early nineteenth century, tens of thousands of Greeks emigrated from liberated Greece and settled in Greek communities still subject to the Turks. And throughout Ottoman rule many Greeks, as Orthodox Christians, preferred a generally tolerant Islam to the dogmatic Catholicism of Western Europe.[6]

But as independent Greece became consolidated in the nineteenth century and gradually enlarged at the expense of the declining Ottoman Empire, a major Greek ambition was not so much to separate from the Ottoman Empire as to replace it, to restore the former Byzantine Empire, with its capital at Constantinople, on the ruins of the power that had usurped and destroyed it four centuries before. This dream (the *Megali Idea – see* Chapter 3), which became an obsession and the distraction of Greek politics for almost a century, ended with the staggering defeat in Anatolia in 1922. This defeat was the first, the biggest, and the bitterest part of the Graeco–Turkish process of disentanglement. Subsequently there have been several smaller aspects of the same process. The most poignant has been the steady diminution of the Greek community in Istanbul. At its height this once numbered about 250 000 and, by the Treaty of Lausanne in 1923, 120 000 Greeks were allowed to continue living there.[7] Since then the number of Greeks in Istanbul has dwindled to a few thousand. The Greek Orthodox Patriarchate still remains there, a pathetic reminder of past glory and frustrated ambition.

Cyprus: The Deadlock

In its own interests Turkey first supported the *status quo* in Cyprus, the continuation of British ownership. Apart from the danger itself of Greece acquiring it, Turkey also feared for some years after the Second World War that mainland Greece and the islands could possibly fall under Soviet control. Subsequently, as the Soviet threat in south-eastern Europe diminished while the Greek pressure for *enosis* continued to mount, the Turks embraced the notion of *taksim* (partition). They sometimes coupled *taksim* with the idea of 'double *enosis*', that is partition and then incorporation of the partitioned parts into Turkey and Greece respectively.

The campaign for *enosis* mounted in the 1950s and became an underground war against the British occupiers. The British eventually concluded that holding the island was impossible. If they could maintain military bases on it, it would be better for them if they relinquished control. The result was the settlement package agreed on by Britain, Turkey and Greece in Zurich and London in 1959, by which Cyprus became an independent state in August 1960. The British got the two large military bases over which they exercised sovereign rights. They were, therefore, satisfied, but the Greeks and Turks, for opposing reasons, were not.

The treaty unravelled almost as soon as it came into effect. In November 1963 Archbishop Makarios, the president of the new republic, proposed constitutional amendments that would have taken away some of the Turkish Cypriots' safeguards and reduced them to the status of a subjugated minority.[8] In the widespread violence that followed hundreds died and thousands were injured. This resulted in a *de facto* partitioning since about 25 000 Turks fled from their homes in Greek areas into Turkish enclaves in the north and east of the island. This violence prompted the United Nations to send a small peacekeeping force to the island in March 1964.

Despite international concern the situation deteriorated to the point where Turkey looked likely to send troops to the island, presumably to establish a military bridgehead that would strengthen its position in any forthcoming talks. But the Turks were dissuaded by President Johnson, who in a note that was to have a profound effect on Turkish–American relations (see Chapter 2) warned that, if they did invade, the Turks could not count on NATO support if the Soviets took advantage of the situation and invaded Turkey. After this crisis had passed a protracted stalemate ensued, punctuated by unsuccessful international efforts to end the crisis and continued bloodshed in incidents involving the two Cypriot communities.

In April 1967 the 'Greek colonels' seized power in Athens. *Enosis* was one of their main declared aims, but opinion was divided on how to achieve it. A minority favoured the recovery of Cyprus at all costs, even if that meant war with Turkey. But Colonel George Papadopoulos, the junta's leader, together with the majority faction, feared alienating NATO and the United States. In the meantime, Archbishop Makarios, once a strong advocate of *enosis,* had obviously begun to relish his role as president of an independent state, however torn and fragile, and now appeared to be the main obstacle of a peace settlement that might possibly be achieved through direct negotiations with Turkey. Papadopoulos seemed to favour such negotiations for a time. But it soon became evident to both Ankara and the Turkish-Cypriot leaders that, however moderate he might wish to appear, Papadopoulos still wanted *enosis*. The Turkish-Cypriot answer was to take the first concrete steps leading to *taksim* (partition) in December 1967 by declaring their leadership on the island to be the 'autonomous' Provisional Cyprus Turkish Administration.[9] This was the first real step on the road that led to the forming of the Turkish Republic of Northern Cyprus in 1983.

Makarios, now set on considering Cypriot independence as a permanent status rather than a stepping-stone to *enosis,* began talks with Turkish leaders on the island aimed at securing a stable order. The Turks, though distrustful of Makarios, were prepared to negotiate and talks went on intermittently for the next six years (1968–74). They were mostly in secret between Glafkos Clerides, for the Greek side, and Rauf Denktash, the Turkish leader. But violence was never far below the surface. There were now in fact three parties to the dispute: the Turkish side, which generally remained united; the Makarios 'moderate' Greek faction; and a Greek *enosis* faction, which now regarded Makarios as an enemy and which received much 'unofficial' support from the mainland. This last group was responsible for much of the sporadic violence including several assassination attempts on Makarios himself.

In May 1971 after the military *coup* in Ankara, the Greek and Turkish governments were able to agree to a joint proposal for settlement, involving not partition for the Cypriot Turks but a substantial degree of self-government for them. Both sides reaffirmed the independence of Cyprus, and Turkey undertook not to invade Cyprus without prior notice to the Greek government in Athens. Makarios rejected these proposals ostensibly because they could lead to autonomy for the Turkish-Cypriots. But he also disliked the principle of Athens and Ankara taking the fate of Cyprus into their own hands. He can hardly have been reassured on this score by the return to Cyprus of the former hero of the *enosis* movement, General George Grivas (he had officially 'escaped' from the house arrest he had been under in Athens since 1967). Grivas began regrouping his old terrorist units (EOKA) to commit acts of terrorism against supporters of independence.

Grivas's 'escape' was believed to have been facilitated not by Papadopoulos himself but by Greek hard-liners who saw the prospect of *enosis* receding.[10] In November 1973 these hard-liners, under Brigadier Dimitrios Ioannides, chief of the Military Police, unseated Papadopoulos and began an eight-month period of rule that made the past six and a half years of repression in Greece look mild by comparison. As for Cyprus, Ioannides was known for a strong personal loathing of both Makarios and Turkish-Cypriots in general. This was also a time of Greek–Turkish confrontation over continental shelf rights and territorial waters in the Aegean. Many of those concerned felt that something decisive would happen on Cyprus soon.

It came in the form of a *coup* against Makarios's government in July 1974. It was probably Ioannides's brainchild, but it was approved by the Greek general staff and executed by the Cypriot National Guard under its (mainland) Greek commanders. The Greek general staff apparently believed that the *coup* would not only achieve *enosis* but, with the threat of hostilities with Turkey in both Thrace and on the Aegean islands, it would open up a third 'diversionary' front. This is a good example of how the Cyprus issue interacted with other contentious issues between the two countries. It is questionable whether the Greek general staff would have approved the Cyprus venture, a hairbrained scheme when taken by itself, had other Greek–Turkish issues not been perceived as having reached a critical point.

Makarios narrowly escaped the murder for which he was targeted during the *coup* and escaped abroad via one of the sovereign British bases. But the *coup* succeeded in overthrowing his administration, and Nikos Sampson, one of Grivas's erstwhile gunmen, was made president. Sampson's first televised interview before foreign journalists was enough to convince the world of the barbarous character of the whole operation.

The *coup* produced the only possible response from Turkey in the circumstances: the decision to invade. The Turkish invasion of Cyprus was, historically, another step in the Turkish–Greek separation process. As one observer wrote:

> The dynamics of history and geography – and of prejudice and fear – had dangerously coalesced around religion, language and race; in this space of five days Cyprus had been attacked by one NATO member country and invaded by another.[11]

The Greek junta, remembering 1964, had evidently gambled on the United States and NATO not allowing Turkey to invade.[12] But the situation was different from that of 1964: there had now been Greek aggression to overthrow the legal government of Cyprus; Turkish impatience and determination, especially on the part of the military, was much greater now than then; and with the resignation of President Nixon over Watergate the United States was more domestically preoccupied than at any time since it became a global power at the end of the Second World War.

Cyprus: After the Invasion

The Greek junta itself was the first victim of its own miscalculation. It was deposed by the Greek chiefs of staff just nine days after the Cyprus *coup*. A civilian government under the former premier, Konstantin Karamanlis, took over and Greece was returned to constitutional rule (see Chapter 3). The *coup*, therefore, redounded to the benefit of Greek democracy, but its results elsewhere were less fortunate. The Turkish invasion made a negotiated settlement for Cyprus practically impossible. It led to the permanent *de facto* partition of Cyprus. This was made possible by what became the permanent stationing of Turkish troops on the island and the mass migration (first in flight and later in a more orderly manner) of Greek-Cypriots away from the Turkish controlled area – now about 40 per cent of the island as a result of the invasion.

Cyprus, in fact, underwent a demographic revolution as a result of population transfers. Before 1974 there had been nearly 200 000 Greeks in the northern territory, which became occupied by Turkish forces. By 1989 there were only a few hundred. The number of Turks in Greek-Cypriot territory was slightly larger but only a fraction of what it had been previously. This demographic revolution, furthered by colonization from mainland Turkey, certainly increased the Turkish percentage on the island as a whole – by how much is yet another matter of dispute between the two communities. There were about 530 000 Greeks on the island and perhaps about 160 000 Turks of whom perhaps 35 000 were immigrants from the mainland.[13]

Partition, regardless of what the Greek side, both in Nicosia and Athens, continued to argue, thus became a military and demographic reality. The Turks lost no time in acting on the assumption. Immediately after the invasion the Turkish-Cypriot provisional administration began calling itself the Autonomous Cypriot-Turkish Administration. Early in 1975 the Turkish occupied northern territory became the Turkish Federated State of Cyprus (TFSC). This title could already have implied independence, but some Turkish-Cypriots denied this. It was meant to convey the idea of the Turkish part of a federated Cyprus. The Turkish-Cypriot position was based on three demands: political equality for Turkish-Cypriots; a bi-zonal 'federation' (actually a confederation was what they really meant) in which the two communities would live apart; and guarantees from Ankara, plus Turkey's right to intervene. The Turks began, after 1974, to create all the institutions that went with partition and 'confederation': a constitution, judiciary, executive, legislative, bank, police and army. These institutions laid the groundwork not just for a confederation but for complete sovereignty and independence. And since after 1974, most Turks in Cyprus and in Turkey itself were convinced that this was the only solution, it gave subsequent negotiations on the future of the island a somewhat academic character.

The negotiations that continued intermittently after 1974, mainly every year at the UN General Assembly meeting in New York, occasionally encouraged hopes of success. But their failure to produce any real progress enabled Rauf Denktash, the Turkish-Cypriot leader, to do what he had long before come to regard as inevitable: make a unilateral declaration of independence.[14] This he did in November 1983 when the former Turkish Federated State of Cyprus (TFSC) became the Turkish Republic of Northern Cyprus (TRNC). Although the authorities in Ankara publicly expressed surprise at the move, they must have been aware of it. At any rate, Turkey became the only country in the world to recognize the new government. All other governments, as well as the UN, continued to recognize the Cypriot government, beleaguered though it was, that had been originally established in 1960 by the Zurich and London agreements.

The UN, in particular, stepped up its efforts to achieve a new general agreement for the island before the new Turkish republic became an accepted, if still formally unrecognized, fact of life. The new UN Secretary General, Xavier Perez de Cuellar, organized several meetings between Greek and Turkish representatives. In March 1986 there was considerable optimism that a settlement could be reached within the framework of a

Draft Framework Agreement worked out by Perez de Cuellar after extensive consultations with Greek- and Turkish-Cypriot representatives. The draft Framework was a synthesis of points to which the two sides had agreed separately in previous negotiations. It was based on the principle of federation and gave extensive protection to the Turkish community. The governing institutions of the new state were to allow for adequate, even generous, Turkish representation. There should be some population resettlements and territorial readjustments. Turkish troops should be withdrawn by stages. On some aspects of these and other questions there were differences between the two sides, but to disinterested observers none looked serious enough to block agreement.

But in the whole history of negotiations in Cyprus, it was precisely when agreement looked close that the basic suspicions between the two sides always came to the fore. The Greek Cypriots said they were making extensive concessions on constitutional and institutional matters but getting very little back on matters of security and territory which had been so transformed by the Turkish invasion of 1974. They were reluctant to give up the existing Cypriot government's internationally recognized status for a leap in the dark which might not land safely. The Turkish-Cypriots, for their part, knew that the situation that had arisen since the Turkish invasion in 1974 had made their position a very strong one. The Ankara government's guarantee of the *status quo* was their ultimate reassurance.

The 1986 Draft Agreement, therefore, remained stillborn. There was renewed hope in February 1988 when the (Greek) Cypriot president, Spyros Kyprianou, who had succeeded Makarios on the latter's death in 1977, was voted out of office in the island's presidential elections and succeeded by George Vassiliou. Vassiliou agreed to meet Denktash, the Turkish leader, personally under UN auspices. But their subsequent talks indicated that, beneath the apparent agreement on most aspects and details of a settlement, there were basic questions of principle and attitude that vitiated hopes of final agreement. Above all there was a mutual distrust based on violence and warfare going back over 30 years. And in the course of these 30 years a new generation of Greek and Turkish Cypriots had come of age that had never had contact with each other. Nor did they want to make contact.

Finally, while the Greek position had been seriously eroded since the achievement of Cypriot independence in 1960, that of the Turks had been strengthened since the Turkish invasion of 1974. Why, therefore, make concessions? In the Turkish Republic of Northern Cyprus a new governing elite had begun to take shape, with all the power, privilege and patronage that goes with the process. Denktash, for one, revelled in his 'presidency'. The Turkish Cypriots' pride in themselves also increased considerably. Throughout Cypriot history the Greeks had regarded them as inferior. Now, they were on their own, backed by power. And their contact with their relatively backward Turkish kith and kin from the mainland who settled in Cyprus gave *them* a sense of superiority. The only Cypriot settlement most of them would now even consider would be a very loose confederation leaving them virtually as they are, in charge of their own political, foreign and, to a large extent their own defence and economic policy. But they would also want the external guarantee from Ankara. Even if the Greek-Cypriots were to accept such a confederative arrangement, they would balk at a Turkish guarantee, without a similar guarantee from Athens for them. But that would confirm Cyprus's dependent status and precarious existence. Two hostile outside powers would be protecting two hostile communities – a recipe for disaster.

Cyprus: The International Ramifications

What has become the permanent Cypriot crisis has had serious international ramifications. First it both reflected Greek–Turkish tensions and exacerbated them. It reopened the old wounds of the Graeco–Turkish war of 1922. These wounds had been healing after 1922. But Cyprus killed this process. The agreement on independence was precarious enough, but relations took an irreversible turn for the worse after the crisis and the carnage of 1964. When the Turks did invade ten years later each nation already regarded the other as its principal enemy. It is true that the Aegean disputes between the two countries had become serious before 1974 but Cyprus greatly reduced any chance of their being settled. In 1975 Turkey, in response to the reinforcement by Greece of several of its eastern Aegean islands, established a Fourth Army (the 'Army of the Aegean') outside NATO control. This was another dimension to the Aegean crisis, and was further evidence of how this crisis was coupled with that of Cyprus. In January 1988 there was considerable hope when Greek premier Andreas Papandreou held talks with his Turkish counterpart Turgut Özal during a conference in Davos, Switzerland.[15] Özal subsequently visited Athens but Papandreou later cancelled a reform visit to Ankara and hope subsided. The suspicions were too great and, besides, mutual enmity was a valuable electoral asset in both countries.[16]

Cyprus also seriously affected Greek and Turkish relations with the United States. American interest in the region was clearly to maintain co-operative or at least stable relations between two strategically important and exposed NATO allies.[17] In doing so the United States incurred the wrath of both countries, while each – especially Greece – came to regard the Soviet Union as the least of its worries. The American role has been unenviable. It has been impossible to please or even placate both countries.[18] But both the substance and the style of American policy has often been inconsistent, wrongly based, and clumsy. Careful initiatives for peace and mediation efforts by Dean Acheson in the 1960s and then by Cyrus Vance in the 1970s have contrasted with the type of insensitivity shown by President Johnson's warning note to Ankara in 1964, mentioned above. This warning changed Turkey from a virtual client to a wary ally. Later, the American arms embargo against Turkey, dictated by Congress in 1974 in response to the Turkish invasion of Cyprus and lasting for three years, deepened Turkish resentment. Turkey imposed restrictions on US military installations and put NATO installations under Turkish command. Turkish resentment continued, fed by suspicions that Washington, responding to instinctive preference for Greece, as well as to the active Greek-American lobby in Congress, would always favour Greece against them. For instance, the Greeks always succeeded in getting a 7 to 10 ratio in military help to the two countries (that is, Greece got seventh-tenths the value of any military aid that was agreed for Turkey). The American administration, of course, could claim that it opposed the 7 to 10 ratio but was forced into it by Congress. But these distinctions were often too nice for the Turkish government; much too nice for large sections of the Turkish population.

American policy toward Greece in the context of the Cyprus dispute has also come in for substantial criticism. The co-operative American attitude toward the Greek military dictatorship between 1967 and 1974, based on the Kissingerian notion that the junta brought stability to an otherwise volatile situation, produced a profound anti-American reaction among many Greeks (see Chapter 3). As for Cyprus, there was some evidence suggesting, not only that Washington knew about the Ioannides-planned *coup* against Makarios, but actually connived at it in the hope that this would force a settlement to the problem.[19] Not that many Greeks, whatever their view of the colonels, would have objected to such alleged collusion, had it not had such disastrous consequences for Cyprus itself and for the Greek reputation. On the other hand, the suspicion only intensified Turkish resentment toward the United States.

Washington therefore, despite its good intentions, has often succeeded only in offending both sides. It continued to offend the Turks by the arms embargo, already mentioned, of 1975. As for the Greeks, the new democratically elected Karamanlis government did what Turkey had done ten years before: it moved Greece finally out of its client-status relationship with the United States. Karamanlis began a policy of *rapprochement* with the Soviet Union and its Balkan allies. Even more, he took Greece out of the military structure of NATO to which it only returned in 1980. In 1980 the avowedly socialist PASOK (Pan-Hellenic Socialist Movement) government was voted into power in Greece. It was anti-American almost by definition. During the 1980s both Greece and Turkey realized they could not do without the United States, and the passions of the previous decade cooled. But Cyprus had changed the relationships for ever. In the summer of 1991 President Bush, fresh from the Gulf War success and with the new prestige deriving from sole superpower status, visited both Athens and Ankara and seemed to have managed to get both parties to agree to talks on Cyprus in September. Some observers rather hastily saw it as an initial success in the crusade for a 'new world order'. But the initiative fizzled out. Disagreement between the two sides was still too basic for serious talks to start. The *status quo* looked too entrenched.

Notes

1 For excellent brief discussions of the Greek–Turkish confrontation, see Jonathan Alford (ed.), *Greece and Turkey: Adversity in Alliance* (Aldershot, UK, Gower, for The International Institute for Strategic Studies, 1984); 'Alliance Problems in the Eastern Mediterranean – Greece, Turkey, and Cyprus: Part 1', by Richard Haass; and 'Alliance Problems in the Eastern Mediterranean – Greece, Turkey, and Cyprus: Part II', by Robert McDonald, Adelphi Papers, No. 229 (London, International Institute for Strategic Studies, Spring 1988). For an earlier Greek view see Thanos Veremis, 'Greek Security Issues and Politics', Adelphi Papers, No. 179 (London, International Institute for Strategic Studies, Winter 1982).

2 On Cyprus, see Robert McDonald, 'The Problem of Cyprus', Adelphi Papers, No. 234 (London, International Institute for Strategic Studies, Winter 1988–1989); Mary Anne Weaver, 'Report from Cyprus', *The New Yorker*, 6 August 1990.

3 For a comprehensive discussion of these issues, see Andrew Wilson, 'The Aegean Dispute', Adelphi Papers, No. 155 (London, International Institute for Strategic Studies, Winter 1979–1980).

4 McDonald, 'The Problem of Cyprus', loc. cit., p. 3.

5 Ibid., p. 8.

6 See Richard Clogg's excellent and fair discussion of the Greek–Turkish relationship in his chapter, 'Troubled Alliance: Greece and Turkey', in Clogg (ed.), *Greece in the 1980s* (London, Macmillan, 1983), pp. 123–49.

7 *Neue Zürcher Zeitung*, 7 June 1989 (Fernausgabe, Nr. 128).

8 McDonald, *The Problem of Cyprus*, p. 11.

9 Ibid., p. 15.

10 Ibid., p. 17.

11 Mary Anne Weaver, loc. cit.

12 On the *coup*, see C. M. Woodhouse, *The Rise and Fall of the Greek Colonels* (London, Granada, 1985).

13 These figures are for the mid-1980s and are taken from the *Encyclopedia Americana* (1987 edition), Vol. 8, p. 377. The Greek-Cypriots claim there have been about

65 000. McDonald reports (footnote 6, p. 86) that Western embassies put the figure at 30 000–35 000.

14 For a good depiction of Denktash, see Mary Anne Weaver, loc. cit.

15 There was much hopeful expectation about this meeting in the Western press. For a sober estimate see P. S., 'Die griechisch-türkische Annäherung', *Neue Zürcher Zeitung*, 3 February 1988 (Fernausgabe, Nr. 26).

16 Özal's visit to Athens only boosted hopes arising from the 'spirit of Davos' but it was obvious that, however cordial the discussion between him and Papandreou, there was no agreement on concrete issues; see Carl E. Buchalla's report from Athens in *Süddeutsche Zeitung*, 16 June 1988.

17 See Richard N. Haass, 'Managing NATO's Weakest Flank: The United States, Greece, and Turkey', *Orbis,* Fall 1986; Bruce R. Kuniholm, 'Rhetoric and Reality in the Aegean: U.S. Policy Options Toward Greece and Turkey', SAIS Review, Vol. 6, No. 1, Winter–Spring, 1986; Yorgos A. Kourvetaris, 'The Southern Flank of NATO: Political Dimensions of the Greco–Turkish Conflict Since 1974', *East European Quarterly,* No. 4, January 1988.

18 See Kuniholm, loc. cit., for an excellent review of US policy, the thinking behind it, its difficulties, and the conflicting Greek and Turkish claims on it.

19 McDonald, *The Problem of Cyprus,* p. 56.

9 Conflicts in the 'Nineties

When this book was being completed in early 1992 there had already been two wars in Yugoslavia and a third was waging out of control. The possibility of conflict breaking out in other parts of the collapsed federation was being considered very seriously. The first war was between Slovenia, which had declared its independence in June 1991, and the Yugoslav federal army (JNA). The Slovenes surprised and humiliated the small federal units deployed against them in a series of mini-battles early in July. After these defeats the decision was made in Belgrade to let Slovenia go. It had well-defined borders and did not, in any case, share a border with Serbia. Nor was there any Serb minority to speak of in this largely ethnically homogeneous republic. The federal army, therefore, limped away from Slovenia.

With Croatia the situation was entirely different. With the declaration of independence by the Zagreb government – on the very same day as the Slovenes, an obviously concerted move – a war began between Croatian forces and the federal army, which as the conflict went on, was clearly acting in the interests of Serbia. Increasing numbers of Serbian irregulars were also participating. By the end of 1991 about one-third of Croatia's territory had been occupied by the federal troops and their allies, about 20 000 people had been killed and over a half a million made homeless. Yugoslavia, like the Soviet Union of which it had often been considered a microcosm, no longer existed.

Actually, before the war in Yugoslavia began, the post-communist experience of Albania, Bulgaria, Romania and the three most southerly, or 'Balkan', states of Yugoslavia – Serbia, Montenegro and Macedonia – had been similar enough to suggest a general pattern of development. In free elections the former Balkan communist parties were initially returned to power with large, or sizable, majorities (in Macedonia they came in second and, but for a specifically Macedonian 'scare' – see below – would have won there too). They won the elections through a mixture of better organization, some intimidation and fraud, and rural and gerontocratic conservatism; but they won clearly. Subsequently, their real ability to govern was never fairly tested because of the refusal of many, mostly young, residents of the large cities to accept their authority. This is true for Romania, Bulgaria and Albania, and partly true in Serbia. In Bulgaria and Albania, extra-parliamentary tactics by the opposition forced the former communist governments out and brought in coalition governments. This nearly happened in Romania also in the summer of 1990. In Serbia it was also attempted in the spring of 1991. All the governments concerned contained leaders of real personality; but all four – Iliescu, Lukanov, Ramiz Alia, and Milošević – could not shed their old communist mind-set. One of them, Milošević, was already resorting to nationalism; the other three, as well as the Macedonian and Montenegrin leaders, were doing the same, if only to try to keep their positions and even acquire a certain legitimacy. Nationalism was being embraced by the former communists as a means of both survival and success.

The two Western allied Balkan countries, Greece and Turkey, were developing differently. But neither was stable and both could be caught up in the nationalist disputes affecting the region as a whole. In addition, neither was stable in anything like the West European sense of the word. They could also become part of the conflicts of the 'nineties.

But national conflict had already begun in Yugoslavia in the summer of 1991 and it is worth tracing in some detail the path which led to it.[1]

War in Slovenia and Croatia

In December 1990 an overwhelming majority of Slovenes voted for the independence of Slovenia in a plebiscite. Almost immediately before that the Croatian Sabor (parliament) had approved a sovereign constitution for Croatia. Both republics had already formulated proposals for the dissolution of the Yugoslav federation and its reestablishment as a confederation or an even looser arrangement, 'on the model of the European Community'.[2]

The Slovenian plebiscite was, at the time, a political *coup* attracting worldwide attention. It was certainly the most dramatic constitutional step up till then in the dissolution of Yugoslavia. But, as suggested in Chapter 4, it tended to distract attention from the much more serious danger threatening Yugoslavia: escalating violence between Croats and Serbs. In every sense except economic, Slovenia had been peripheral to Yugoslavia. And as the economic viability of the federation had become deluged by national and political issues, so the economic factor, crucial in more stable times, became peripheral, too. The Yugoslav situation had simply deteriorated to the point where economics became irrelevant.[3]

The big danger for Yugoslavia continued to be in the Serb–Croat relationship. With many Croats wanting to follow the Slovene example and formally declare independence as well as sovereignty, the response from many Serbs had become even shriller. The free multiparty elections that both republics held for the first time in half a century in 1990 – Croatia in spring and Serbia in December – were preceded by outpourings of emotion, mutual antipathy, and historical claims and counterclaims. The very fact of these free elections was a victory for liberal democracy, but it was not the liberal spirit, but national emotion that dominated them. Serbia officially stood by its proposals for a federal system, somewhat looser than before, but with strong powers remaining at the centre. The Serbian proposals were based on three principles: (1) the organs of the federation, as well as those of the republics, still had a role; (2) the Yugoslav citizens, federation-wide, and not just the republics, should be consulted on the country's future, hence the call for a federation-wide referendum similar to that Gorbachev was demanding in the Soviet Union; and (3) all Serbs should live in one state, that is, if not in a Yugoslav federation, then in a Serbian state.[4] The chance of compromise on this issue was always meagre, but the emotion-laden atmosphere made it impossible. It was this third point, the 'Serbian corollary' – that in case the present federation dissolved, the present borders would also no longer be valid – that portended the most serious danger. In any new Yugoslavia, Serbs, formerly in other republics, must now be reincorporated into Serbia. Obviously it would not just be Croatia that was affected here, but even more, the republic of Bosnia-Herzegovina. What Serbia seemed prepared to risk therefore was not just conflict with Croatia, but also with the Muslims of Bosnia-Herzegovina. This republic, always a no-man's-land between Croatia and Serbia, could now become a battlefield. Besides the more than 30 per cent of the population that declared itself Serb, old arguments about most of the Muslims being Serbs would be revived. If only a relatively small number of Muslims were to do this the Serbs could soon become the majority nation in the whole republic. Croats, on the other hand, numbering about 18 per cent of the total population, have sometimes claimed the Muslims for themselves. Tudjman, himself, had made quite extreme statements on this.[5] The potential for conflict, especially with a Muslim community much more self-confident than it had been since Ottoman times, would be very great.

It must be stressed that the danger from Serbia was not solely the result of Milošević's obduracy and that of the communist leadership under him. Nationalism by 1990 was transcending and dominating politics in Serbia, as well as in the rest of Yugoslavia. In fact Milošević, though the symbol of revived Serbian nationalism, sometimes seemed restrained, at least in public, compared with some leaders of the Serbian opposition. His most notable opponent was the writer Vuk Drašković, leader of the Serbian Movement for Renewal. This was the most important democratic party in opposition to the communists, and Drašković had been Milošević's main opponent in the presidential election, also in December 1991. It had a considerable following among Serbs in Yugoslavia and very strong support in the Serbian global diaspora. Even if the Yugoslav federation were to survive, Drašković and his followers argued that at least two autonomous districts should be carved out of the Serbian majority areas in Croatia. In Bosnia-Herzegovina more Serbian autonomous districts should be created. Furthermore, the city of Dubrovnik, originally part of Serbia but now in Croatia (and with only about a 10 per cent Serb population), should have a 'special status'. Here the claims were vague but somehow Serbia's historical ownership should be recognized.[6] Later, though Drašković was to change his course radically and, though remaining a Serb nationalist, strongly opposed 'Milošević's War'. The Serbian Chetnik Party (later renamed Radical Party) leader, Vojislav Šešelj, was far cruder than Drašković, deliberately invoking the past in stirring up anti-Croat passions. And it was no coincidence that in the course of 1991 it was Šešelj who was drawing the bigger crowds.

A Second Serbia?

Those were just a few alterations even if the *status quo* were to survive! If it did not, either through confederation or the total breakup of Yugoslavia, then the revisions, according to these Serb nationalists, should be much more drastic. Serbia should regain the boundaries of 1 December 1918, the day Yugoslavia was first officially created. This would mean the inclusion, not only of most of Bosnia-Herzegovina, but also the whole of Macedonia and Montenegro. As for Kosovo, this should not just revert to being an integral part of Serbia but all remaining elements of Albanian autonomy should be abolished. If necessary, recalcitrant Albanians should be deported. Drašković's old-fashioned nationalism was fuelled by a traditional Orthodox religiosity, and he was demonstratively supported by the Orthodox hierarchy, which had played a major role in the revival of Serb nationalism, showing no hesitation in allying with communist nationalists on this issue.[7] Drašković had promised that, in the event of victory for his party, he would arrange for a Serbian Orthodox priest to bless the assembly, thereby exorcizing the 'devil of bolshevism'. He also promised a referendum on the return of the monarchy.[8]

Unrealistic as these sentiments seemed, they were gaining increased resonance amongst Serbs at the beginning of 1991, even after Drašković and his party had decisively lost the elections in December 1990 to Milošević and the communists. Some observers argued that they were harmlessly romantic, even Utopian. But the resonance they contained made them dangerous. More immediately dangerous, though, were some practical suggestions coming from some Serbs outside Serbia proper, in those districts most closely affected by the danger of a Serb–Croat collision. Typical of these were those presented by Jovan Rašković, leader of the minority Serbian Democratic Party in Croatia. Rejecting the new 'ethnocratic' Croatian constitution that 'imposed the Croatian people's sovereignty on the Serbian people', Rašković repeated that Serbs would never accept Yugoslavia as a confederation. If this were forced on them, then the republican borders must be revised: a second Serbian state should be established in the west of what had been Yugoslavia. About two weeks before the promulgation of the new Croatian constitution in December 1990, Serbs in ten southern Croatian areas in which they were in a majority had already founded the 'autonomous region of Krajina'. This, said Rašković, should now be joined with Serbian regions in Bosnia-Herzegovina to become the new state of West Serbia. This new Serbian state would be twice as big as Slovenia and would have a population of about three million to Slovenia's two million. It would, in fact, become the third biggest part, after Serbia and Croatia, of what had been the old Yugoslavia.[9]

Most of this new West Serbian state would be taken from Bosnia-Herzegovina, not Croatia. The idea had the tacit support of some of the Serbian leaders in Bosnia-Herzegovina itself. It was a proposal totally unattainable without the use of force. And if force on a considerable scale were used the outcome of the bloodshed would involve even more drastic changes than those being suggested now. It was not clear how much ideas like Rašković's were being inspired by the Milošević leadership in Belgrade and how much was inspired locally. Many Serbs in both Croatia and Bosnia-Herzegovina had previously been highly alarmed over speculation about a 'West Yugoslav Confederation', composed of Slovenia, Croatia and Bosnia-Herzegovina, gravitating toward 'Europe'. Their own proposals could have been a form of defence against these. But such proposals and counterproposals were symptomatic of a condition that could easily lead to violence.

All these proposals again reflected the crucial importance of Bosnia-Herzegovina. In itself a microcosm of Yugoslavia with its mixture of religions and nationalities – yet with no nationality strong enough to become the nation of state – its original *raison d'être* had been to contain national rivalries. More recently the Muslim character of the republic had become more evident, first culturally but then also politically. The November 1990 elections in the republic had given it a Muslim head of state – the first such in Europe.[10] This could become a determining factor in the future course of developments not only in Yugoslavia but also in the entire Balkan region. Although the situation would be different, Bosnia was on the way to becoming a catalyst as it had been prior to the First World War.

A Deceptive Pause

Relations, then, between Serbia on the one side, and Slovenia and Croatia on the other had by the beginning of 1991 reached a breaking point that seemed set for violence. But the growing danger of civil war seemed for a time to have something of a sobering effect on the leaderships in Belgrade and Zagreb. On the subject of Serbia's own 'Manifest Destiny' Milošević, as already mentioned, had during the presidential election and parliamentary campaign seemed milder than Drašković. After he and the Serbian Communists (now Socialists) had won the elections quite decisively in December 1990, and now that, according to the new Serbian constitution, complete domination had been restored over Kosovo, it seemed possible that a more secure and satisfied Milošević would exercise some flexibility even toward the Croats and Slovenes in the interests of at least some future for Yugoslavia. That remained to be seen. But Milošević was undoubtedly the key player in Yugoslavia's future and on the question of civil war.

Franjo Tudjman, the Croatian president, would also play a decisive role. Since his own political triumph in the elections in the spring of 1990, he had surprised many observers by his relative restraint on the subject of relations with Serbia. He was obviously aware of the delicacy and dangers of Croatia's situation. Speaking at the ceremony marking the adoption of the new constitution in December 1990 he reportedly explained Croatia's decision not to hold a plebiscite on independence at this time, as Slovenia had done, by saying that such a move 'could exacerbate the misunderstanding and resistance in some other republics and among a considerable number of Serbs in Croatia and the Yugoslav People's Army, which might provide a pretext for those who want to invite bloodshed and civil war'. Tudjman went on to note that there were Croats living in Bosnia-Herzegovina, Serbia and Montenegro, implying that they would be at considerable risk if tension increased. He noted, too, the international dimension of the crisis, the fact that 'the international democratic public does not accept the programme of Yugoslavia's disintegration and the changing of the borders in Europe'.[11]

The fact was that any dissolution of Yugoslavia would affect Croatia much more than Slovenia. This was a measure of Croatia's importance in the creation, the history, and the political interaction of Yugoslavia. Slovenia was in Yugoslavia; Croatia was of it. Such was Yugoslav history that the best measure of this was that the Croats had far more grudges against Yugoslavia than Slovenes (see Chapter 4). Croats resented Serbs much more than Slovenes did, because they were tied to them much more closely. But much as they resented them they could never get rid of them.

In view of the fears, real and manipulated, of the Serb minority in Croatia over independence and the echo the issue had in Serbia itself, it was noteworthy that Tudjman did little at first to attempt to placate that minority. The new Croatian constitution of December 1990 was strongly nationalist, giving the Serbs no collective rights as a minority and containing no hint of political autonomy in areas where Serbs are the majority. Moreover the adoption of the traditional Croatian flag, which carried bitter memories for Serbs as the emblem of the fascist *Ustaša* republic of the Second World War, as well as the toleration, even quiet encouragement, of other *Ustaša* symbols, reflected at best an insensitivity toward the Serbian minority, at worst a deliberate attempt to humiliate it.[12] The truth was that Tudjman emotionally was strongly anti-Serb despite the moderation he had introduced into some of his public statements. To the right of him in the Croat political spectrum were some virulent and unabashed nationalists, the Croat counterpart to the elements just described in Serbia. And the extremists in Croatia, as in Serbia, were loudly (and, in many cases, financially) supported by their fellow-nationals in the West in exile. The truth probably was that concessions at the outset to the Serbian minority would not have reconciled it to Croatian independence, but they would have made the Croatian case that much stronger.

In the early spring of 1991, despite bilateral talks between the Croatian and Serbian leaders, collective meetings of the obviously weakening Yugoslav collective presidency, appeals for caution by, and attempts to mediate from, the United States, Western Europe, and the Soviet Union, it seemed that it would only take one serious incident for the civil war between Serbia and Croatia to begin. In January 1991 Croatia and the now increasingly Serb-orientated federal army were twice on the brink of bloodshed. During the spring there were several incidents on Croatian territory involving local Serbian irregulars and Croatian security forces that, in retrospect, formed the prelude to war. But what probably made the war inevitable was both the attempt by the federal army to stifle Slovenian independence in June–July and its subsequent failure. The attempt itself showed the army was prepared to use force; the failure stiffened the resolve of its almost exclusively Serbian high command to overcome the humiliation by a real show of strength in Croatia. And, as already mentioned, while Slovenia was, in a pinch, considered expendable, Croatia with its huge Serbian minority was not. Serbian pride and passions, the memories of the *Ustaša* horrors in the

Second World War inflicted on the Serbian minority the feeling that, at a time of Yugoslav break-up as well as that of the whole political order in Eastern Europe and the Soviet Union, firmness might bring advantage, a feeling too held by every Serb that justice was on their side – all these, carefully manipulated by the nationalist propaganda machine in Belgrade, produced the Serbian war mentality.

What finally made the war inevitable was the Serbian high command's decision to send major detachments of troops and armour into Croatia in early July 1991. Ostensibly, this was still done on behalf of the civilian Yugoslav presidency, but it was very clear by now that it was the military that was in charge and their policy was Serbian.[13] Just what the division of competence was between the federal generals and the Milošević civilian leadership was difficult to say. In the early weeks of the conflict some observers could distinguish between the two. But whatever distinction could once have been made soon became academic. General Vejlko Kadijević, Minister of Defence in the disintegrating federal government and himself a Serb from Croatia, and Slobodan Milošević, President of Serbia, ran the war against Croatia – a war involving not just military operations, but also diplomacy, particularly *vis à vis* the West, as well as political and economic management.

The course of the war to the end of 1991 need not be described in detail. It was characterized by an inhumanity on the part of many participants, on both sides, that shocked the civilized world. Militarily, despite incompetent leadership, bad organization and often poor quality, the federal troops and the Serbian irregulars achieved a number of successes against outnumbered Croatian forces. The most substantial success was the capture of Vukovar in November. To most neutral observers the destruction wrought by the federal and Serbian troops, most notably at Dubrovnik, was quite unnecessary and led to a swing of sympathy in favour of Croatia. The truth was that neither side deserved much sympathy. In Zagreb Tudjman had shown little respect for constitutional procedures and his late attempts to grant concessions to the Serbs came much too late and smacked of desperation.[14] In Belgrade the primitive chauvinism coming from the top infected large numbers of Serbs. The main hope for a moderating Serbian attitude lay in the differences, at least in emphasis, in their enthusiasm for the war between the 'two Serbias'. One consisted of those Serbians who lived outside the Serbian republic itself and who were deeply nationalistic. They were mainly the ones who felt threatened by the collapse of Yugoslavia. The other consisted of Serbs within Serbia proper, less self-conscious and aggressive about their Serbianism and obviously feeling less threatened by the present situation. Many of these were less enthusiastic about the war – among the younger ones there was much draft-dodging – and the way it was being conducted. As the fighting got bogged down and casualties mounted, opposition to the war in Serbia proper only increased. In the meantime tens of thousands of both Croats and Serbs in Croatia were suffering – they were the ones who deserved the world's undivided sympathy as despite 14 cease-fires the fighting and the destruction continued.

Finally a lasting cease-fire was successfully arranged in early 1992 through the efforts of Cyrus Vance, who had been made special UN envoy and who finally persuaded the two sides to accept a UN peace-keeping force. Some of the terms of the cease-fire were vague and unsatisfactory to the Croatian government. But it was forced to comply and at least some breathing space was gained.

The Bosnian Catastrophe

The hope now was that hostilities would not spread to Bosnia-Herzegovina. (The importance and vulnerability of this republic has been discussed in Chapter 4). They were perilously close to doing so even as the Vance-brokered cease-fire in Croatia was being signed. The Bosnian Serbs had already established several, 'autonomous regions' in the republic in parts where they were numerically preponderant – a clear breach of the republic's sovereignty. Many Serbs *and* Croats had for months made no bones about their conviction that Bosnia-Herzegovina should be partitioned, mainly between Serbia and Croats, and several secret meetings between the two republics' negotiators had taken place. Caught in the middle of this Serb-Croat intrigue were the unconsulted Muslims, the only people to whom Bosnia-Herzegovina had ever really meant something. Any Serb-Croat agreement would certainly be at their expense, leaving them a rump successor republic in place of the old. The Croats would side with them against the Serbs only if they could not make a satisfactory deal with the Serbs. In retrospect, therefore, the hopes that the fighting would not spread to Bosnia-Herzegovina seem very naive. There was too much hate, fear, ambition, sense of now or never, and sheer excitement. As in Croatia, too, there were also memories – of the indescribable slaughter, mainly of Serbs by Muslims, in World War II. There were also scores of local national militias, armed and, mainly in the Serb case, itching to fight.

When the United States and the European Community finally recognized Bosnia-Herzegovina's independence in early April 1992 (see Chapter 10), the Serbs went fully into action and their plan unfolded. Fighting had actually begun in March but, in the appropriate words of one Balkan specialist, the Bosnia recognition 'really pushed it over the cliff'. Many Serb fighters from Croatia moved into Eastern Bosnia and linked up with local militias. The federal army, always strong in Bosnia, was now backed up by units coming in from Croatia, Slovenia, and Serbia proper. These two together, army and militias, simply drove the hapless Muslims out of their way, out of the towns and villages they needed to occupy. They needed to occupy them so as to create an exclusive Serb belt in Bosnia and join this up to Serbia proper. They also aimed to link Serbian gains in Croatia with Serbia proper through a northern Bosnian corridor. But, not only this: Sarajevo, the Bosnian capital, was, according to the Serbs, to be divided into three ethnic zones – Serb, Croat, and Muslim. For centuries many members of all three communities had lived cheek by jowl in the city. It was this fact, plus the whipped-up blood-lust on all sides, that was leading to Sarajevo's destruction. Obviously, the Serbs had to take the main blame for the barbarism. But the Croatian government was pursuing a calculating, aggrandizing, policy, backed by many Croats in Bosnia-Herzegovina itself, aimed at annexing at least the western, strongly Croat, part of Herzegovina.

There was much speculation at the time as to whether the federal army or the Serbian government under Milošević was ultimately responsible for Europe's worst slaughter since the end of World War II. Whom controlled whom? Was the army totally independent? And what about the Serb militias in Bosnia-Herzegovina: who controlled them? All three elements here were acting in the 'historic' interests of Serbia. But despite this overall mutuality of purpose most observers agreed that there was sometimes little coordination between army and militias and that, if the Milošević government, for tactical reasons, wanted to stay the hand of either, it would have serious difficulties.

It was hard to predict the future. As in Croatia the fighting would probably go on till a certain tiredness set in, in spite of Western efforts. By mid-1992 partition, or attempts at it, by Serbs and Croats looked possible. A Croat-Bosnian confederation (minus Serbs) was also mooted. One thing was certain: it would be unwise over the longer term to ignore the 'Muslim factor'. The Muslims of Bosnia-Herzegovina would not tolerate now what they had had to previously in their history. They were more self-confident and knew they had strong Islamic world-wide backing. Though shattered by the trauma of 1992 they should not be written off. They would fight a (well-supported) guerrilla campaign, particularly against the Serbian 'occupiers', for as long as need be. And this could be a long and bloody time.

Kosovo the Next?

It was neither Croatia nor Bosnia but, as discussed in Chapter 4, Kosovo that had originally brought Serbian nationalism to the boil as a result of the new federal constitution of 1974 that raised the province's status. Kosovo did not become independent, but, in many important respects, virtually so.

Adding to the Serbs' rancour had been the assertiveness with which many Albanians, particularly the younger generation and the intellectuals, responded to the situation. One of the main features of Yugoslavia in the 1980s was the frailty of its political structure; one of its most volatile elements was the rise of the formerly downtrodden peoples – the Kosovars, the Muslims of Bosnia-Herzegovina, the Macedonians. Only 20 years before the Kosovars had still been subject to heavy Serbian repression. In 1966 Alexander Ranković, the Serb who as former federal minister of the interior had been the personification of that repression, was purged by Tito – for reasons, it should be said, quite other than his record in Kosovo. This was the first big step toward Albanian emancipation in Kosovo and led to some violent demonstrations that shook the Serbian authorities as well as Tito himself. Making major concessions in the 1974 constitution was Tito's way of trying to placate Albanian feeling, although Serbs construed it as another effort to keep Serbia in its place. While Tito lived, the ferment, the hostility between Albanians and Serbs could be contained. But a year after he died the violent instability had begun.

It was Kosovo that had done much to bring Milošević to power in Serbia in 1987, and it was Kosovo that had the biggest influence on the new Serbian constitution of September 1990. This constitution paid lip service to democracy, but its *leitmotiv* was nationalism. It legalized the multiparty system, and free elections with opposition participation, the separation of powers, and the market economy. All this was important enough but the constitution's real importance would only be demonstrated in the future. The constitution's immediate thrust was nationalistic and anti-Albania, centred on Kosovo.

The new constitution made Serbia a unitary, sovereign republic. Neither the province of Kosovo nor Vojvodina disappeared as such, but their former constitutions were abrogated and replaced by statutes granting them an undefined degree of autonomy. It was not clear whether this included the restoration to Kosovo of its own parliament and self-governing organs, which Serbia had suspended after Kosovo tried to proclaim republic status the previous summer. The new constitution also reflected the Serbian determination not to give the Albanians in Kosovo any specific minority rights. It guaranteed *all* citizens of Serbia the same rights whatever their nationality. (Here the Serbian stand was similar to that of the Romanian government, which was not willing to treat its Hungarian minority as a specific, distinct, community enjoying a special legal status.) Thus, while the Kosovars were demanding a sovereign republic, the Serbs were refusing to recognize their legal existence.[15]

The new Serbian constitution reflected a nationalist victory, but it brought still another defeat for Serbia's reputation and international prestige. Serbia was now seen to be treating Kosovo as an occupied territory. Some Albanian legislators had already been imprisoned, many more had taken refuge in Croatia and Slovenia. Some members of the Kosovo government had also been arrested and, in the many factories in which a Serbian administration had been installed, thousands of Albanian workers had been dismissed.[16] The Serbian authorities in Belgrade also refused to register legally the Kosovo Democratic Union that had been established in the summer, considering it a subversive, national organization, although the Union had been accepted and registered at the federal level. The vast majority of Albanians therefore boycotted the December 1991 elections in Serbia and this certainly increased the margin of Milošević's victory.

What was now happening in Kosovo was new in its entire history, whether under Ottoman or Serb domination: its people were resisting and organizing. Under a weight of Serbian oppression that became increasingly heavy during 1991 and 1992, many Kosovars – not just intellectuals, this time, but also many workers – organized resistance and became nationally self-conscious in an active way. In September 1991 a referendum on Kosovar independence was held despite strenuous Serb attempts to prevent it, and an overwhelming majority voted in favour. But, as the Croatian situation drifted toward war and then war broke out in Bosnia-Herzegovina too, something of a lull descended in Kosovo; at least foreign attention was diverted from it. After March 1992, however, with the big democratic victory in Albania itself and the increasingly open concern being expressed there about Kosovo, developments in the two parts of the Albanian-speaking world began to interact and, obviously, the chaos in other parts of the old Yugoslav federation had its influence. Kosovo boldness increased along with Serbian nervousness. At the end of May 1992 the Kosovars held an 'illegal' election for a secret independent parliament. The situation was getting very close to breaking-point.

Albania and Kosovo

So much for Kosovo in Yugoslavia. But after 1990 Albania itself became a factor in the Kosovo situation. In that year the whole Titoist policy of ensuring that the question of an Albanian–Kosovar reunion would become irrelevant became seriously endangered. For many years it had looked like succeeding: progress in Kosovo was set against Stalinism in Albania. As the national and individual dignity of Kosovars increased, along with their standard of living, the backward, repressive Albania of Enver Hoxha would repel rather than attract. The Albanian regime, in any case, was circumspect about claims to Kosovo – more circumspect than some Yugoslavs in their claims to Albania.[17]

But the remarkable democratization of Albanian life during 1990, and the promise of much more, looked set to change all that. Internationally Albania was becoming respectable, while Kosovo was progressively deteriorating. Indeed, the outlook for all Albanians in Yugoslavia looked grim. Serbia would never willingly ease its grip on Kosovo. And the more nationally assertive Macedonia became, the worse the repression against the Albanians there would get. Albania, therefore, if the progress made could be broadened and stabilized, might become a viable alternative.

Greater Albania was back on the agenda. Reunion was being openly advocated in 1991 in Albania itself as the multiparty system took hold. A 'democratic, peaceful reunion' with Kosovo was at first being urged by the opposition forces.[18] The different political parties soon found it to be a valuable issue. It was an irresponsible line to adopt in the sense that it would alarm the Serbs even more and increase repression in Kosovo. It was, therefore, subsequently modified.[19] But the new Albania, after the Democratic Party victory in 1992, was more nationalistic that ever.

It was difficult to predict the future. But one thing was certain. Greater Albania could only emerge out of a Serbian collapse and this would not happen without war. But in the meantime, however much Serbia tried to prevent this, the interaction between Albania and Kosovo would increase. The Kosovar resistance against Serbian repression in 1989 and 1990 had helped give Albanians across the border the spirit to open their own struggle. Now the victory for freedom in Albania could inspire the Kosovars. The chaos in Albania might discourage but not permanently deter.

In the long run, Serbia's position in Kosovo looked unsustainable. However great Milošević's military triumphs pressure from below was bound to increase, now probably reinforced by pressure from inside Albania. This could even lead not just to a repressive Serbian state of emergency in Kosovo but to a military pre-emptive strike against Albania itself, beginning with Shkodër but moving south as hostilities escalated. When it came to Kosovo, Serbs would strike first and only then count the international consequences. And in a situation of Balkan chaos, there would be even fewer constraints on a militant Serbia. War between Serbia and Albania, in the current Balkan lunacy, was not an unlikely proposition.

The Serb Superiority Mind-set

The whole Serbian problem in relation to Yugoslavia, ever since the foundation of the state in 1918, was their superiority complex. History had entitled Serbia to a dominant role.[20] This Serbian view of their superiority had them making decisions the inconsistencies of which they seemed either to be blissfully unaware or which they considered history entitled them to make. They justified, for example, the removal of many attributes of autonomy to Vojvodina in 1990 on the grounds that over half its population were Serbian. In Kosovo, however, which had its autonomy stripped at the same time, only a bare 10 per cent were Serb. Shklezen Maliqi, a Kosovar intellectual, made the same point regarding Kosovo:

> If Yugoslavia breaks up into national states, in which all nations strive for the unification of ethnic territories, Albanians could hardly be deprived of the right to consider themselves a divided nation which has the right to unification. Especially if one takes into account the extent of repression against Albanians and the obvious gap which will separate them from Serbia for several generations. If Milošević is considered president of all Serbs, and is striving for the unification of all 'Serbian territories', why would others not have the same right? The theories according to which the Serbs have more of a right to set up their own state than others, and according to which one set of rules applies to Serbs in Vojvodina, Croatia, and Bosnia-Herzegovina another to Kosovo and Albanians, are in fact strange and racist.[21]

The purloining of $1.4 billion from the Yugoslav federal bank at the end of December 1990 to pay Serbian wages and pensioner bills was an egregious case of such Serb self-centredness. Westerners derived considerable humour from the episode.[22] But for other Yugoslavs it was no laughing matter.

It was when Serbs ceased to dominate that they began to reinterpret Yugoslav history since 1945 as an anti-Serb conspiracy. Now, in post-Tito Yugoslavia one of the most serious consequences of this superiority complex – and it must have increased once the war with Croatia had begun – was that Serbs were not prepared to accept minority status anywhere. As long as Yugoslavia was organized federally with a strong centre under strong Serbian influence, then the condition of Serbs in Croatia, Bosnia-Herzegovina, and even Kosovo might be tolerable, however distasteful. But if these three were to become sovereign states, in a confederal Yugoslavia or with no Yugoslavia at all, then their situation was unacceptable. Serbs never saw themselves as either a subject or a minority nation, but at minimum a 'nation of state', a superior nation – even better, if circumstances allowed, a *Herrenvolk*.[23]

In this respect their historic similarity with the Hungarians after the loss of territory caused by the treaty of Trianon is striking. In a sense Transylvania was Hungary's Kosovo. For over a quarter of a century Hungary was unable to come to terms with the losses suffered at Trianon in 1920 (many Hungarians still have not), and it disgraced itself in the Second World War in trying to rectify its wrongs. Serbia, which, ironically, was one of the beneficiaries of Hungary's dismemberment, was now suffering the same sort of disgrace. Its leaders should have considered not only Serbia's resentments but also its weaknesses. At the end of 1990 the Serbian economy, in terms of all the major indices, was already close to disaster.[24] During the next year the deterioration gathered speed. But Milošević stoked nationalist emotions even more to divert public attention from the domestic crisis and disarm opposition. This course would eventually be disastrous, but it could also be immediately risky. There were not only Serbian minorities in the rest of Yugoslavia, there were also other Yugoslav minorities in Serbia itself, and they were becoming restive, even hostile.

Apart from nearly two million Kosovars, there were a quarter of a million Muslims in the Sandjak of Novi Pazar bordering on Bosnia. With the Muslims being hounded and slaughtered in Bosnia-Herzegovina the Sandjak could be a real source of weakness for Serbia. They were already demanding the kind of autonomy the Serbs were demanding in Croatia.[25] There were also nearly half a million Hungarians in Vojvodina. In Tito's Yugoslavia they had been the best treated of all the Hungarian minorities in Eastern Europe. But they were now upset by Milošević's *Gleichschaltung* policy and were trying to organize themselves against it. Even amongst the Serbian majority in Vojvodina there were differences between the descendants of the early wave of settlers there, who supported the province's autonomous status, and the newer migrants who tended to be more Belgrade centrist.[26] Serbia had enough potential enemies inside its gates without trying to make more outside them.

Macedonia: Nationalism and Transnationalism

Macedonia and Albania were the last two big remnants of the Ottoman Empire. As the empire collapsed both were the prey of its successor states who refused to recognize the right of Albanians and Macedonians to the same national expression for which they themselves had fought earlier. Both suffered as a consequence, the Macedonians more than the Albanians in one crucial respect: whereas the Albanians were at least recognized as a distinct nation, however despised, the Macedonians were not – and their own sense of nationality was dim and undeveloped anyway. While Albanians, whatever their religion – Muslim, Catholic or Orthodox – had been generally regarded as Albanians, Macedonians were not accorded a separate nationality at all. Most of them were considered Greek or Bulgarian depending on which national branch of the Eastern Orthodox Church to which they belonged. Inhabitants of the same village had often been thus divided.

In 1893 the Internal Macedonian Revolutionary Organization (IMRO) was established, designed to rekindle the ancient idea of nationhood and fight for an independent Macedonia.[27] It suffered a serious defeat in 1903, split into two, and became a byword for gangsterism and international terrorism. After operating freely in Bulgaria for many years it was abolished in 1936. But its ideal of independence was never wholly lost sight of.

After their oppressive treatment by Serbia in pre-war Yugoslavia, Macedonians blossomed in the dignity Tito offered them. But Macedonia continued to be the object rather than the subject of Balkan relations. Its existence was accepted, but Greeks, Bulgarians and most Serbians viewed it as artificial. And many Macedonians seemed content with a status that was tolerated rather than fully recognized.

This Macedonian passivity lasted about 40 years. But as Yugoslav unity began to crumble in the 1980s, a more positive, assertive and politicized Macedonian nationalism began to develop. Several factors inspired it: the Slovene and Croat examples; the growing threat of Serbian nationalism; the realization that not only Yugoslavia but the whole international order was changing and that Macedonia faced both dangers and opportunities. But there was also another reason, within Macedonia itself: the proliferation of the Albanian minority and the dangers of its interacting with developments in Kosovo. The whole situation was changing, and many young Macedonians, in particular, were eager to board the Balkan nationalist carousel that was already quickly spinning. Alexander the Great and IMRO were their sources of inspiration.

In 1989 Macedonian nationalism became an important transnational factor, too. An amendment to its constitution made a significant change in the definition of the republic of Macedonia. From being 'a state of the Macedonian people and the Albanian and Turkish minorities', Macedonia now became 'the national state of the Macedonian nation'.[28] The change is self-explanatory. Macedonia was to be a unitary state, too. This amendment was subsequently withdrawn under Western pressure, but it reflected the real and abiding Macedonian nationalism.

But as well as having constitutional aspects, Macedonia's nationalism also assumed forms of direct action. A series of five major and well-organized Macedonian demonstrations took place in 1989 (the first actually began in November 1988) demanding that both Greece and Bulgaria recognize the republic of Macedonia as a sovereign state and the existence of Macedonian minorities inside their own territories.[29] This last demand was nothing new. The republic's government in Skopje had demanded this many times over the years and had regular polemics with Sofia about the significance, and even the existence, of Macedonian history. But now in the twilight of the Yugoslav federation, the polemics over Macedonia acquired a new seriousness and urgency. Greece protested strongly about these demonstrations and the attempts by thousands of Macedonians to block the frontier posts between the two states. There were already strong hints of violence in the air.

But, still, the spread of Macedonian nationalism had not yet become a surge. There was still some sympathy for the Yugoslav idea, and the reformed Communist Party in the republic still enjoyed considerable support. Now rather laboriously styling itself 'League of Communists of Macedonia – Party of Democratic Transformation', it had been expected to come in first in the republic's first democratic elections in November 1990. The Alliance of Reform Forces, the local branch of federal premier Ante Marković's all-Yugoslav party, was also expected to do well. In fact, Macedonia was expected to complete, along with Serbia and Montenegro, southern Yugoslavia's conservative triangle. The nationalist parties were expected to make a respectable showing, but nothing more. The Movement for All-Macedonian Action (MAAK), which included some prominent intellectuals, called for the unity of all Macedonians but remained vague about Yugoslavia's future and Macedonia's place in it. The second nationalist grouping was the reincarnated IMRO, legalized in the summer and already a focal point of rising nationalist sentiment. It was drawing support away from MAAK because it was more radical and provincial.

In the first round of the elections, general expectations were fulfilled: the communists and the Yugoslav federalists did appreciably better than the nationalists. But the party unofficially representing the Albanians in the republic did surprisingly well. What followed in the second round reflected the power of nationalism and race prejudice. On the strength of anti-Albanian feeling, IMRO now topped the poll and finished with more seats in the new assembly than any other party. It was far from having a majority but it was back – with a bang.[30]

It caused much alarm everywhere in Greece and Bulgaria.[31] When Macedonia finally declared its independence at the end of 1991 Greece refused to recognize it, contending that the very name 'Macedonia' implied territorial designs on Greek Macedonia. It insisted on calling the new state the 'Republic of Skopje'. Bulgaria, nervous though it was, took a more enlightened course. It was the first to recognize the new state and urged others to do likewise. But there was resentment among many Bulgarians over the emergence of an independent Macedonia.

What was the future for Macedonian nationalism? It looked set for a struggle on several fronts. Two of them would be defensive: First of all against Serbian revisionism. With the federal system in Yugoslavia collapsing, a now unconstrained Serbia might try to reassert its historic control over Macedonia. Some Serbs were already demanding this. The second defensive front would be inside Macedonia itself, against the Albanian threat, real and imagined. The strong Albanian community was becoming more self-conscious, too, and would not be content for long with its demeaned status.

The Macedonian fronts against Bulgaria and Greece would be of a very offensive nature. An independent Macedonia would be putting constant pressure on both countries to recognize their Macedonian minorities. For the present even IMRO would not go further and make territorial demands on Bulgaria or Greece in the interests of 'Greater Macedonia'. But if regional disintegration continued, such demands would begin to be voiced, at least unofficially. In the meantime, in an increasingly volatile situation, violence could become widespread, and terrorism, once endemic in the Balkans, could be revived.

Greek–Albanian Relations

It is worth mentioning that Greek–Albanian relations seriously deteriorated at the end of 1991. Though they have been officially set aside, Greece has historically had claims to parts of Southern Albania (in Greek, Northern Epirus). Successive Greek governments, backed by public opinion, the military and the Orthodox Church, have been increasingly concerned about the fate of the Greek minority there (60 000, according to the Albanians; 300 000 to 400 000 according to some Greeks; probably about 100 000). The breakdown of order in Albania in 1991, together with the deteriorating economic situation, causing an influx of thousands of Greek–Albanian refugees, created alarm in Greece. The Albanians, in their flush of freedom, began, for their part, to refer to the condition of their own 'Cham' minority in parts of Northern Greece – 'Chameria' as some Albanians were now beginning to call it.

Turks in the Balkans

The Ottoman Empire left many traces in the Balkans, none more conspicuous than the large number of Turkish settlers. As the empire began to contract their future in the newly emerging states became a controversial issue. Many became part of population transfers, solutions that often caused very serious hardship but were probably the best in the long run.

Between 1912 and the beginning of the Second World War, for example, about 340 000 Turks had left Bulgaria for Turkey. Immediately after the Second World War about a further 150 000 were expelled amid threats that the entire Turkish population in Bulgaria, the living reminder of the Ottoman yoke, would be expelled. This threat was averted, and a steady Turkish emigration was resumed after 1964. This still left a large Turkish community in Bulgaria, officially numbered at over 800 000, but perhaps half again as large as that. In northern Greece there had also been a large number of Turks settled in Ottoman times (see Chapter 3). In 1990 these numbered about 140 000, not recognized as a Turkish minority, but simply described as Greeks of 'the Muslim religion' in the same sense as the Macedonians are 'Slavic speaking' Greeks.[32]

There are Turkish communities in both Romania and Albania. (Romania had had a large Turkish community in south Dobrudja which it lost in 1940 when it ceded this province to Bulgaria.) The other large settlement was to be found in what became first South Serbia and then Macedonia in Yugoslavia. There were almost 200 000 Turks in Macedonia after the Second World War. This number dwindled through migration and assimilation, but there were still estimated to be nearly 70 000 in 1990.[33]

The Balkan Turks were never an aggressively unassimilable minority, as the Hungarians and the Germans historically were. Nor after the establishment of the Turkish republic were they ever an irredentist spearhead, since Kemalist Turkey abjured irredentism. They were mainly farmers and small artisans wanting to keep, and be left, to themselves. But for many people in the Balkans they were both a humiliating historical reminder and an obstacle to the unitary state, the concept of which has revived strongly since the end of communist rule. The Turks would become its victims in Bulgaria, Macedonia and Greece.

Any threat, therefore, that might be presented by the Turkish minorities in the Balkans still seemed, in mid-1992, distant rather than looming. But it was only a matter of time before it could become serious. For one thing increased pressure could soon be put on some of the Turkish minorities. In Macedonia the victory of the nationalists in the November 1990 elections would seem to ensure this. In Greece growing prejudice against the Turkish community was both a reflection of Greek–Turkish relations generally and also of what was perceived as a growing 'aggressiveness' on the part of the Thracian Turks. But the main danger lay in Bulgaria.

Despite the repudiation of Zhivkov and the rescinding of discriminatory measures against Turks, much tension still remained under the calm surface. The legal and administrative problems encountered by Turks in recovering their Turkish names, after the repressions of 1984–85, and the economic and social difficulties of those returning in 1990, were often compounded by a hostile Bulgarian attitude (see Chapter 7). Despite the official liberalism shown by all the political parties in the new post-communist order (less and less though by the erstwhile communists), much prejudice remained. It was even reflected in the attitude of the first 'post-socialist' prime minister, Dimitûr Popov, appointed in December 1990 to lead a temporary coalition government, which included members of the democratic opposition. Just a few days before becoming premier, Popov, in an interview published in a provincial newspaper, said that, in the Turkish-populated regions of the country, Slavic Bulgarians were being 'threatened by outrages and even physical death'. (This charge echoed, though without – for the moment – the lurid descriptions, Serbian charges over Kosovo.) Bulgarian children, he said, were forced to leave some schools because they were Christians. He then turned his attention to the alleged danger from Turkey itself. He charged that the Turkish defence minister was an 'Islamic fundamentalist' who advocated 'Anschluss', an evocative expression intended to mean annexationist designs on parts of Bulgaria by Ankara. In an apparent indirect reference to the controversy over the returning Turks getting back their land, he appeared to suggest that legislation was needed prohibiting the sale of real estate to foreigners to prevent wealthy Turks from buying up chunks of Bulgarian real estate. Finally he stressed again the broader 'Muslim threat'. In some way this threat 'must be blocked so that it does not invade Europe. Bulgaria has the unhappy historical fate of being the barrier to the Muslims in Europe'.[34] Popov was here evidently referring to a common fear that Turkey might eventually 'do a Cyprus' on Bulgaria, that is, take over the Turkish parts and thereby split the country. Subsequently, Popov tried to undo the damage of these indiscretions by stressing his belief in equal treatment of all nationalities in Bulgaria. Actually his indiscretions attracted little attention in the country as a whole. No one tried to make political capital out of them. But this reflected not so much restraint as the fact that there was little capital to be made out of them.

Nationalist anti-Turkish feeling was likely to grow in the Balkans. That was dangerous enough. But the danger could be immeasurably increased by the growth of nationalism, in the sense of Turkic mission, in Turkey itself (see Chapter 2). The ramifications of this extended far beyond the

Balkans and well into the future. But the Balkans could become a region on which the new Turkish nationalism, galvanized by a revived Islam, could be projected. Antagonistic nationalisms could, therefore, collide.

Looking to the end of the century it was possible to see a new dimension being added to the dangers of nationalism. Two broad, opposing coalitions could develop in the Balkans: a Slavic coalition against a Muslim. The coalitions would be based not just on national but also religious lines: Orthodox Christianity against Islam. In a bizarre way, therefore, history could indeed repeat itself. The key to the issue is, of course, Turkey: how far it would feel inclined to become involved again in the region it had ruled for 500 years but on which Atatürk had turned his back. In mid-1991 there were already indications of a more active Turkish interest. Alija Iszetbegović, the Bosnian president, visited Ankara and was warmly welcomed. The Turkish press suggested that Turkey might have to help Bosnia-Herzegovina.[35]

Transylvania: Romania in Central Europe

The history and the character of the Regat, the old Romania of Wallachia and Moldavia, is south-east European. Transylvania, on the other hand, is central European by virtue of its geography, but especially by virtue of its Hungarian and German links stretching over centuries. Transylvania, therefore, is Romania's link with Central Europe. German influence is dying through emigration and atrophy. Hungarian influence has been heavily diluted by repression, assimilation, and a large influx of Romanians from the Regat. Transylvania is increasingly becoming more Romanian. But, still, the Hungarian and German influence remains, and Transylvania is still radically different from the rest of Romania.

Transylvania is also central European through 'problem linkage'. The fate of the Hungarian minority there will also affect not only domestic politics in neighbouring Hungary itself but could also influence the fate of Hungarian minorities in the rest of Central and Eastern Europe, in Slovakia (600 000); in Vojvodina (500 000) and in Sub-Carpathian Ukraine in the former Soviet Union (150 000). Transylvania, therefore, could have an important bearing on the whole Hungarian future stretching across several borders.

There was serious rioting, with some deaths, in March 1990, in Tîrgu Mureş, the old capital of the former Hungarian Autonomous Region. It should not have come as quite the shock it did to many Westerners. What was surprising was that, by early 1991, there had been so little ethnic violence in Romania (at least as reported). The universal dismay over the

Tîrgu Mureş incidents was partly a reaction to the original hope that the fall of a tyrant like Ceauşescu would replace tension with racial harmony. The truth was that there was more ethnic harmony in Romania in the last years of Ceauşescu than there was ever likely to be again. It was, though, a 'negative' harmony, predicated on a common hatred of Ceauşescu. It had its culmination in the 'spirit of Timişoara' uniting Romanians, Hungarians, and other national groups in the opening of the December 1989 uprising. But once Ceauşescu had gone, the harmony evaporated in the freedom and chaos of the new era. The historic tensions returned in all their ugliness in the first half of the 1990s.

The new National Salvation Front government in Romania had begun with liberal intentions toward the Hungarian minority. But it soon found it was far ahead of its constituency. And in this context its constituency was not only the numerous former Ceauşescu-loyal officials who switched their allegiance to the Front, but also the mass of the Romanian people. What the Front leaders balked at – but what they had first seemed to promise – were special rights to Hungarians by virtue of their recognized minority status. They were soon insisting on the classic nationalist unitary concept that debarred special minority treatment.

But in the excitement of their liberation from Ceauşescu, the Hungarians in Romania had been expecting more.[36] It was this clash of Romanian determination and Hungarian frustrated hope that produced the violence of March 1990 and could result in much more. In Transylvania there was the same feeling as in other parts of Eastern Europe: that the end of an era, even of a whole century of history, had arrived. Therefore, if Yalta was *passé* why not Trianon? It might be now or never for this historical injustice to be rectified, especially with the Soviet Union having disintegrated in the East. Such yearnings may never have been publicly articulated – spokesmen for the Hungarian minority energetically rejected them – but it formed part of the public mood and affected people's emotions and reactions. (15 March, the day the Tîrgu Mureş incidents occurred, was a Hungarian national holiday marking the revolution of 1848.)

Revisionist notions about Trianon were never articulated by responsible politicians in Hungary either. All were publicly resigned to its irreversibility. But, unquestionably, preoccupations about Transylvania became much more evident in Hungary than they had been since before the Second World War. Invoking both the spirit and the letter of CSCE, all political groups in Hungary were demanding *de jure* recognition for the minority in Romania.[37] All considered a Hungarian concern for the minority to be entirely appropriate and fully legitimate. But this concern was often ambiguously expressed, conveying the idea, perhaps deliberately, that more was intended. Premier József Antall, for example, described himself as the 'spiritual prime minister' of all Hungarians,[38] and some of his colleagues made statements similar in spirit, but occasionally even more tactless. In this context it is worth comparing the official Hungarian stand on Transylvania with that of Bulgaria on Macedonia. Both formally accepted the loss of the provinces, renounced irredentism, and denied territorial claims. But each in different ways maintained its involvement: Bulgaria denied the existence of a Macedonian nation; Hungary was indirectly hinting at a *droit de regard* in Transylvania (rather in the same way as the Republic of Ireland had in Ulster). The circumstances, hence the language, were different. The ultimate intention was the same.

But if Hungarian political leaders were limiting themselves to a tacit *droit de regard,* many Hungarians were insisting on a good deal more. The rioting in Tîrgu Mureş only increased the Hungarian public's anger. Only a few hot-heads were demanding direct intervention, but some urged action in more indirect ways, including the infiltrating of irregulars into Romania to 'protect' their compatriots. Much Hungarian feeling was also expressed in symbols and historic reminders. In the summer of 1990 some passion was expended on a proposal by a nationalist fringe group, in collusion with some exiled Hungarian groups in the West, to restore a series of statues in Budapest; these monuments dated from the inter-war period and were dedicated to Hungary's 'lost provinces'. The proposal never got far. It was the target for much sophisticated satire and ridicule. But the publicity it aroused was not without significance.[39]

The Romanian reaction to the Hungarian demands reflected their historic defensiveness, even paranoia, about Transylvania. But there was more to it than that: there was the historic Romanian dislike, fear of, and inferiority complex toward Hungarians stemming from the centuries of oppression in Transylvania. Many Hungarians despised Romanians almost as much as Serbs despised Albanians, and they were never diffident about showing it. Even the most moderate expressions of concern about Transylvania in Budapest, therefore, or of hope by members of the Hungarian minority in Romania, were greeted with serious suspicion by most Romanians. It was this that sparked so much of the virulent nationalism that reappeared in 1990. The *Vatra Romaneasca* (Romanian Cradle) movement quickly gathered considerable support and thrived on the atmosphere of ethnic suspicion. While professing friendship for the Hungarian nation as well as every other nation, *Vatra* had the capacity to poison, not only relations between the nations, but many other aspects of Romanian public life as well.

The question of how far the anti-Hungarian mood was condoned by the new Romanian government was difficult to answer. The democratic opposition charged Iliescu and company with stimulating it. But it had its own share of chauvinists and, in any case, it knew that fairness toward Hungarians was not a great vote-catcher (however useful it might be with an international audience). The government's attitude toward *Vatra* was ambiguous at times; it seemed unwilling to risk offending it too much. At the local level there appears to have been much collusion between the National Salvation Front and *Vatra*. The proliferation of magazines like *România Mare* must also have needed some official support. Amidst a widespread famine of newsprint, the neo-fascist, chauvinistic press seemed to be doing quite well – suspiciously so.[40]

Just how divisive Transylvania was in Romanian–Hungarian relations was illustrated by the ceremony at Alba Julia on 1 December 1990, commemorating the meeting in this Transylvanian city on the same date in 1918 when, by popular acclaim, the province was declared part of Romania. The new government in Bucharest declared this anniversary to be the new Romanian national holiday, replacing 23 August, the anniversary of the Soviet Union's 'liberation' of Romania in 1944. This selection was understandable and was supported by all sections of Romanian public opinion. To Hungary, however, it was an affront and to most members of the Hungarian minority a humiliation. Furthermore, the first celebration, at Alba Julia on 1 December 1990, was marred by people in the assembled crowd who tried to prevent leaders of the Hungarian minority from speaking. Some of the disturbance was obviously organized. Part of it may have been spontaneous, nationalistic hooliganism. Whatever it was, it made a tense situation even worse.[41]

All in all, then, it was surprising that violence had been so limited. Compared with many parts of the Soviet Union and some parts of Yugoslavia, Transylvania had been tranquil up to the middle of 1992. But there was no reason for complacency. It was the weakness of the Romanian government, its partial kow-towing to nationalist elements, the threat of anarchy and economic collapse, that could result in much more serious violence, probably touched off by a single incident or a wild rumour, perhaps deliberately spread. An already unstable situation could plunge into anarchy. The worst incidents might occur not in the cities of Transylvania, where publicity could be a deterrent, but in smaller towns of mixed population. The cumulative effects of a series of small incidents could result in an atmosphere of violent uncertainty amounting to terror.

But when all the immediate reasons for the tension between Hungarians and Romanians had been analysed, for the basic reasons it is worth quoting from the findings of the official Romanian inquiry into the March disturbances in Tîrgu Mureş. The findings may be open to criticism, but the following summation can hardly be faulted:

> The large gap between the previous stifling of people's aspirations and the suddenly won freedom as well as certain shortcomings in democratic culture and in adequate civic behavior of all socioprofessional categories (another aftermath of the totalitarian communist inheritance) are causes of the chain of extremist manifestations in the last few months.[42]

It was as timely for the rest of the Balkan flashpoints as it was for Transylvania: too much historical nationalism, too little civic culture.

Moldova: Romania on the Fringe of Europe

If Transylvania brought Romania into Central Europe, Moldova brought it to Europe's outer edges.

Bessarabia, which now forms a part of the Republic of Moldova, had been for centuries part of the Romanian province of Moldavia. Since the fourteenth century it had been part of the frontline in the rivalry between Tsarist Russia and the Ottoman Empire, which held suzerainty over the two principalities of Wallachia and Moldavia. Russia annexed Bessarabia in 1812, but after the First World War it was restored to Romania, which was also awarded the Bukovina, previously administered by Austria. In 1940, under the terms of the Ribbentrop–Molotov agreement, the Soviet Union recovered Bessarabia and took Northern Bukovina, the majority of whose population was Ukrainian. During the war these territories were overrun by German and Romanian troops, but after the war they reverted to the Soviet Union.

Stalin then set about creating a new Moldavian nation in the territories he had recovered, using all the historical, linguistic, cultural, anthropological – and coercive – means at his disposal. His aim was to separate, once and for all, the Romanians on the east bank of the River Pruth from those on its west bank – that is, those in Romania – to preclude forever the possibility of reunion. Whatever success he achieved was almost entirely through force, and his success, therefore, was artificial and fragile. He was much less successful than Tito was in Macedonia. But Tito was working with much more promising material. Macedonian history made Tito's Yugoslavia an attractive proposition. Soviet Russia was a decidedly less attractive proposition for the Romanians in Bessarabia. Socialist Romania, of course, hardly generated enthusiasm, but at least the Romanians would have suffered with their own kith and kin.

The number of Romanians, or Romanian-speaking citizens in Moldova, varies, like all population statistics in disputed areas, according to which side is giving the information. The most reliable observers put the number at about three million out of a total population of about five million. Some Bucharest sources claim there are five million Romanians alone.[43]

Up to the beginning of 1990 the prospect that Bessarabia might ever be restored to Romania, or even that Romanians on both sides of the Pruth would be able to conduct relatively normal relations with each other, seemed so remote as to exclude consideration. The Romanian regime, under Gheorghiu-Dej and then Ceauşescu, despite all its anti-Soviet nationalism, was always circumspect with regard to Bessarabia. Though rejecting the notion of a separate Moldavian nation, it did so quietly. At the same time it openly abjured irredentism and accepted the post-war frontiers.

Romania had no choice, of course. And apart from anything else, any hint at not accepting the *status quo* could have stoked Hungarian ambitions regarding Transylvania. But accepting the *status quo* was one thing; accepting the justice of it was another. And the Romanians sometimes subtly indicated that they did not. Gheorghiu-Dej, for example, allowed the publication of a pamphlet by Karl Marx in which Bessarabia was clearly identified as Romanian.[44] Ceauşescu castigated the pre-war Romanian Communist Party for urging the return of Bessarabia to the Soviet Union.[45] But, even so, Bessarabia was never much on the Romanian mind. Holding on to Transylvania was far more important than agitating over Bessarabia. And as Ceauşescu's rule degenerated into tyranny, it was domestic misery, rather than even the dream of foreign adventure, that preoccupied almost all Romanians.

But, then, developments, first in the Soviet Union and then in Romania itself, changed the whole picture. Gorbachev's introduction of *perestroika* and *glasnost* and its transformation of political life led to the revival of nationalism in Moldavia and demands for greater political and cultural autonomy. It led also to a discussion in 1989 of the Ribbentrop–Molotov pact. The impact of this, though greatest in the Baltic republics, was also felt strongly in Moldavia. Open resentment about the incorporation of Bessarabia into the Soviet Union began to mount. In short there was a resurgence of Moldavian nationalism which could not be ignored for long in Romania itself.

There, the fall of Ceauşescu in December 1989, while not leading to the open, democratic society most of its citizens wished, did lead to a great freedom of discussion – and this discussion included Moldavia. There was an enormous wave of sympathy for the Romanian-dominated Popular Front, established in Moldavia in the spring of 1989, and which for several months became the dominant force in Moldavian politics. The Front not only pressed for more freedom for the republic of Moldavia from Moscow but it also organized demonstrations repudiating the Nazi–Soviet treaty leading to the incorporation of Bessarabia into the Soviet Union. Already by the end of 1990 Moldavia was demanding independence from Moscow and declaring its right to secede. In August 1991 it declared independence and later its right of secession from the collapsing Soviet Union.

As aspirations of the Romanian majority in Moldavia evolved toward independence from the Soviet Union, so the links with Romania grew stronger. Cultural ties multiplied and, with them, so did Romanian concern generally about the situation in Moldavia, which could now be visited with little difficulty. A spirit of indivisibility began to develop between Romanian Moldavians and Soviet Moldavians. Iaşi, the capital of Romanian Moldavia, and Chisinau (Kishinev), the capital of the Republic of Moldova, were becoming virtually twin cities.[46]

It was only a matter of time before many Romanians became caught up in a tide of irredentism. With the Soviet Union disintegrating now was the undreamt-of opportunity. Irredentist societies cropped up in several parts of the country, and their activities were widely reported. Many of the same chauvinists who rejected rights for the Hungarian minority in Transylvania were now demanding them for their kinsmen in Moldavia. A big demonstration was held in Bucharest in early November 1990 demanding the return of Bessarabia to Romania, and indignantly rejecting the demands of the many non-Romanians in the Moldavian republic for their own independence.

There was much sincerity in these Romanian demands. But they also had a domestic political dimension: they were used by many as another stick with which to beat Iliescu and the Salvation Front government. Rumours were even spread about a 'secret agreement' between Gorbachev and Iliescu, by which the latter would refrain from reopening the Moldavian question. Iliescu, therefore, the ex-communist, alleged friend of Gorbachev, was allegedly doing what came naturally: putting Soviet interests above Romanian. At one demonstration in Bucharest there were shouts of 'Down with the Molotov–Gorbachev–Iliescu Pact'.[47]

Such accusations were more a reflection on the Romanian mood than on Iliescu. But the situation must have been embarrassing for the Romanian leader. He and Premier Roman had openly condemned the illegal incorporation of Bessarabia into the Soviet Union and supported the Popular Front in Chisinau and its demands for sovereignty. In the course of 1990 both had implied, however gingerly, that the eventual reunion of Romanians would be in the 'natural course of things'.[48] But no responsible Romanian government in early 1991 could demand the return of the territory to Romania, just as no responsible government in Chisinau could demand it either. (It was becoming all too dangerous for the Moldavian Popular Front to demand sovereignty at all.) It was not only that the Soviet Union, whatever state it was in, could retaliate against any official Romanian irredentism.

But there was the danger, now greater than ever, that if borders on Europe began to be questioned, Hungary might not hesitate to bring up Transylvania. Many of Iliescu's opponents realized this, of course, but this would not have deterred some of them.

During the course of 1991, however, the question of reunification with Romania was shelved, at least for the time being. The Moldavian president, Mircea Snegur, who headed a grouping of democratic forces opposed to the Popular Front, clearly preferred to consolidate Moldavian independence rather than to hurry into any reunion with Romania. His slogans were 'one people, two states' and 'two independent Romanian states co-operating with each other'. The Romanian government officially subscribed to this policy, too, looking forward, though, to eventual reunion. It was an issue which – just like that of reunion between Albania and Kosovo – would not go away and would certainly become more acute. But, in the meantime, it was being pushed aside by a Moldavian issue that had nothing *directly* to do with Romania: the revolt of the Russian majority in the small part of the republic of Moldavia situated on the left (east) bank of the Dniester river. Supported by Russian army units long stationed there, leaders of the Russian majority, most of them unreconstructed communists, refused to accept Moldavian independence and proclaimed their own 'Dniester Republic'. This led to serious hostilities in the course of 1992 between Moldova's Russian minority and the central government in Chisinau (Kishinev) which sent troops into the self-proclaimed republic. The result was some of the worst fighting the old Soviet Union had so far experienced, except for Nagorno-Karabakh. Again the Romanian government was caught in a difficult situation in terms of its relations with Russia and its own people. It supported Moldova but did not want to offend Russia, which obviously sympathized with the 'Dniester Republic' and suspected the Romanians were helping the Moldavians. The Romanian population, for its part, egged on by the numerous nationalists elements in its midst, wanted a more militant stand by Bucharest. Romanian–Ukrainian relations also suffered strain stemming from the Moldova issue. Romania had, in the context of the denunciation of the Soviet-Nazi pact giving Bessarabia to the Soviet Union in 1940, formally asked Ukraine for the return of surrendered territory that had been incorporated into the then Ukrainian Soviet republic. Kiev sharply rejected the request. Thus the independent republic of Moldavia not only had serious trouble of its own; it was also radiating trouble in several directions.[49]

A Typology of Crisis

The common thread running through all these crisis points just discussed is *nationalism*. In this context Ernest Gellner's definition of nationalism is the most apt:

> Nationalism is primarily a political principle, which holds that the political and national unit should be congruent.
>
> Nationalism as a sentiment, or as a movement, can best be described in terms of this principle. Nationalist sentiment is the feeling of anger aroused by the violation of the principle, or the feeling of satisfaction aroused by its fulfillment. A nationalist *movement is* one activated by a sentiment of this kind.[50]

Gellner then refers to a situation that has particular relevance to the Balkans:

> But there is one particular form of the violation of the nationalist principle to which nationalist sentiment is quite particularly sensitive: if the rulers of the particular unit belong to a nation other than that of the majority of the ruled, this, for nationalists, constitutes a quite outstandingly intolerable breech of political propriety. This can occur either through the incorporation of the national territory in a larger empire, or by the local domination of an alien group.[51]

Isaiah Berlin discussed the same subject with rather more style and directness:

> ... a wounded Volksgeist ... is like a bent twig, forced down so severely that, when released, it lashes back with fury. Nationalism, at least in the West, is created by wounds inflicted by stress. As for Eastern Europe and the former Soviet Empire, they seem today to be one vast open wound. After years of oppression and humiliation, there is liable to occur a violent counterreaction, an outburst of national pride, often aggressive self-assertion, by liberated nations and their leaders.[52]

In the Balkans this overriding theme of nationalism has several different but interacting aspects. They can be categorized as follows:

(1) *Aggressive/territorial/irredentist:* Present Serbian nationalism *vis-à-vis* Croatia is the most obvious case in point. Serb designs on parts of Bosnia-Herzegovina should also be included. So should: possible Hungarian efforts to regain some or all of the territory lost at the Treaty of Trianon after the First World War; possible Bulgarian designs on Macedonia. These are the main simmering or latent *irredenta* but there are also smaller *irredenta* that could, in given circumstances, be revived, like Greece's historical claims to Northern Epirus. Bulgarians and Greeks fear possible Turkish irredentism.

(2) Aggressive nationalism – actual or potential – is sometimes, though not always, linked with questions of ethnic or *national minorities*. The current example relates to Serbs in Croatia and Bosnia; Hungarians in Romania, Vojvodina, Slovakia, even Subcarpathian Ukraine are a potential example; so are Greeks in Albania and Turks in Bulgaria and Thrace.
(3) Ethnic minorities give rise to *protective* nationalism, concern of the 'parent' or metropolitan nation for its nationals beyond its borders. Present Hungarian policy is the best example of this. Serb policy in Croatia is ostensibly based on this. Turkish concerns in Bulgaria and Greek Thrace derive from it.
(4) *Reunification of divided nations*. The two potential cases here are Albania with Kosovo and Romania with Moldova. Possible Bulgarian ambitions toward Macedonia could be included here. All three recognize the territorial integrity of the states in which their kith and kin (actual or claimed) live but refuse to recognize their distinctiveness as a nation. Tirana, Bucharest and Sofia recognize these countries as *states* but not as *nation-states*. In the case of Bulgaria with Macedonia this could eventually be a crucial distinction.
(5) *Defensive nationalism* – wholly or mainly. Bosnian Muslims are a clear example of this, fearing the carve-up of their republic between Serbia and Croatia. Macedonian nationalism is also at present largely defensive – against Serbia and, potentially, Bulgaria. So is that aspect of Bulgarian nationalism based on fear of Turkey. Albanian nationalism in Kosovo is partly defensive against the oppression of a small minority Serb *Staatsvolk*.
(6) *Emotive nationalism*. In the case of the Balkans, this deserves special consideration. Emotion is a factor in all nationalism, but in the case of Serbia in Kosovo it is virtually all-consuming. A Serbian Orthodox bishop described Kosovo as 'our Jerusalem'. Bulgaria's (frustrated) nationalism also has a strong emotive content but it plays no role in shaping current official policy.
(7) *Religious nationalism,* or an amalgam of religion and nationalism, could play a big role in Balkan developments. In the case of the Muslims of Bosnia and Herzegovina it already is. It has also affected Muslims in the Sanjak of Novi Pazar, in Serbia proper, in Macedonia and in Bulgaria, where Turkish–Muslim nationalism is strongly affected by the proximity of Turkey. To a lesser degree this is also the case with Greek Thrace. Religious nationalism, affecting both Muslims and Christians, could become a decisive factor in the Balkans in even the short-term future. It is in this context that Turkey could assume a major role.

It will be noted that, except possibly in the Romanian case, the *economic factor* plays little direct role. The economic destitution which covers practically the entire region has undoubtedly exacerbated the different aspects of nationalism that are present there. But it has not caused them. Nor would economic prosperity have removed them. It would only have mitigated them. Nor would a general economic recovery in the fairly near future – which in any case can be virtually ruled out – make much difference. Nationalist passions in the region have passed the point of no return. In fact, the economic situation is likely in the near future to get much worse, and with it the dangers of further instability.

Notes

1 For an excellent introduction see F. Stephen Larrabee, 'Long Memories and Short Fuses: Change and Instability in the Balkans', *International Security,* Vol. 15, No. 3, Winter 1990–1. See also, 'Welcome to the Seething South', *The Economist,* 2–8 March 1991.
2 See Milan Andrejevich, 'Crisis in Croatia and Slovenia: Proposals for a Confederal Yugoslavia', Radio Free Europe Research Background Report, 11 October 1990.
3 See Carl E. Buchalla, 'Nichts verbindet mehr als der Wunsch nach Trennung', *Süddeutsche Zeitung*, 15 December 1990.
4 Viktor Meier, 'Stabilisierung der Konfusion', *Frankfurter Allgemeine Zeitung*, 23 January 1991.
5 He became more moderate on this, as on other topics. See, for example, the following exchange with Sibylle Hamann in the Vienna *Kurier* of 10 May 1990: Hamann: 'You have repeatedly raised claims on the republic of Bosnia-Herzegovina which has a mixed population of Serbs and Croats. Might this not lead to an armed conflict.' Tudjman: 'Croatia and Bosnia constitute a geographical and political unity, and have always formed a joint state in history. The people in Bosnia should vote on what they want. We will apply no pressure.' One of the most noteworthy aspects of this exchange, of course, is Hamann's failure to mention Muslims in Bosnia-Herzegovina.
6 *Neue Zürcher Zeitung*, 8 December 1990 (Fernausgabe, Nr. 285).
7 For a personal touch, very illustrative of the Orthodox Church attitude, see Thomas Ross's article on the Serb Bishop Amphilocius, entitled 'Für die Serben', *Frankfurter Allgemeine Zeitung*, 6 November 1989. Amphilocius describes Kosovo as 'our Jerusalem'.
8 *Neue Zürcher Zeitung*, 8 December 1990 (Fernausgabe, Nr. 285).
9 Tanjug, 29 December 1990.
10 This was Alija Izetbegovic; see Carl Gustav Ströhm's article on him in *Die Welt*, 23 November 1990.
11 Tanjug, 22 December 1990.
12 See Maren Köster-Hetzendorf, 'Auch Serben Kennen die Angst', *Die Presse* (Vienna), 25 April 1991.
13 See C., Sr., 'Ohnmacht der Belgrader Bundesorgane', *Neue Zürcher Zeitung*, 6 March 1991; and Blaine Harden, 'In Yugoslavia's Conflict, Loser Has Been Federal Government', *The New York Times,* 27 September 1991.
14 See C., Sr., 'Neues Minderheitengesetz in Kroatien', *Neue Zürcher Zeitung*, 7 December 1991 (Fernausgabe, Nr. 284).

15 See Milan Andrejevich, 'Milošević and the Serbian Opposition', Radio Free Europe Report on Eastern Europe, Vol. 1, No. 42, 19 October 1990, pp. 41–2; C., Sr., 'Serbische Euphorie über die neue Verfassung', *Neue Zürcher Zeitung*, 2 October 1990.

16 *Agence France Presse* (AFP), 10 September 1990.

17 For example, Novak Kilibarda, of the People's Party, Tanjug, 23 November 1990.

18 The leaders of the new Albanian Democratic Party originally called for the 'peaceful democratic union between Albania and Kosovo'; see David Binder in *The New York Times*, 13 December 1990, quoting a student leader, Azem Hajdari.

19 See, for example, Sali Berisha, the Democratic Party's leader in an interview with the Skopje communist paper *Nova Makedonia*, 25 December 1990 (FBIS-EEU-91-002, 3 January 1991). Berisha said: 'I would recognize a republic of Kosovo in the framework, or within the borders, of the present or future Yugoslav federation or confederation, although we see the unification of the Albanian nation within the framework of demographical integrationalist processes in the future united Europe'. Speaking to a Macedonian newspaper Berisha, of course, would have to be very careful on the subject, but he still did not rule out union. Nor did Shklezen Maliqi, a Kosovar intellectual, in an interview with the much less sensitive Zagreb magazine *Danas*, 25 December 1990. If Yugoslavia broke up, he said, the Albanians could not be denied the right to consider themselves a divided nation and take steps for reunion.

20 For an excellent discussion of this, see C. Sr., 'Serbiens Traum von der alten Grösse', *Neue Zürcher Zeitung*, 30 March 1989 (Fernausgabe, Nr. 72).

21 See note 19.

22 *The Independent* (London) called it the 'theft of the century' (10 January 1991); the usually stolid *Neue Zürcher Zeitung* referred to 'Serbia self-service socialism' (16 January 1991).

23 See Milton Viorst, 'A Reporter at Large: The Yugoslav Idea', *The New Yorker*, 18 March 1991.

24 *Deutsche Presse Agentur* (DPA), 11 December 1990.

25 See Viktor Meier, 'Die Serben vor einem Scherbenhaufen', *Frankfurter Allgemeine Zeitung*, 24 October 1990.

26 See Viktor Meier, 'Jugoslawiens Teilung Vertieft Sich', *Frankfurter Allgemeine Zeitung*, 5 January 1991; also the same author's, 'Das Serben Milošević's Schafft in Sandzak eines zweites Kosovo', *Frankfurter Allgemeine Zeitung*, 25 June 1991.

27 See Duncan M. Perry's excellent history of IMRO, *The Politics of Terror: The Macedonian Revolutionary Movements, 1893–1903* (Durham, NC, Duke University Press, 1988).

28 See Radio Free Europe Research, Yugoslav Situation Report, 26 May 1989, item 3.

29 See Viktor Meier, 'Wieder die mazedonischer Frage', *Frankfurter Allgemeine Zeitung*, 22 June 1990.

30 See Milan Andrejevich, 'The Election Scorecard for Serbia, Montenegro, and Macedonia', Radio Free Europe Report on Eastern Europe, Vol. 1, No. 51, 21 December 1990, p. 39.

31 See Patrick Moore, 'The Macedonian Question Resurfaces', Radio Free Europe Report on Eastern Europe, 6 April 1990, pp. 46–9. The new IMRO leader, Ljupčo Georgievski, warned that by 1992 Macedonia would be negotiating its future with both Greece and Bulgaria; see interview with Carl Gustav Ströhm, *Die Welt*, 4 January 1991.

32 See P. S., 'Politische Aktivität der Muslime Westthräkiens', *Neue Zürcher Zeitung*, 7 June 1989.

33 This figure must be approximate, largely because of the still widespread habit of referring to Albanians as 'Turks'.

34 See Duncan M. Perry, 'The New Prime Minister: A Man for All Seasons?' Radio Free Europe Background Report, 27 December 1990. In a law passed by the Bulgarian Grand National Assembly in February 1991, which dealt largely with land restitution, an article was approved forbidding foreigners to buy land. It was mainly aimed at potential buyers from Turkey; see Rada Nikolaev, 'The New Law on Farmland', *Report on Eastern Europe*, No. 18, 3 May 1991, p. 1.

35 See *Hürriyet* (Istanbul) and *Cümhüriyet* (Istanbul), both of 12 July 1991.

36 See Viktor Meier, 'In Bukarest wächst der Druck der Nationalisten auf die Regierung: Forderungen der ungarischen Volksgruppe nach Minderheitsrechten erschrecken die Rumänen', *Frankfurter Allgemeine Zeitung*, 10 March 1990.

37 Ibid.

38 *Magyar Nemzet*, 4 June 1990.

39 Its best-known sponsor was Ernö Raffay, then state secretary for defence and a leading Democratic Forum politician. It was sharply criticized by the opposition. See, for example, *Magyar Hirlap*, 29 August 1990, and *Népszabadság*, 3 September 1990.

40 See Michael Shafir, 'The "Greater Romania" Party', *Report on Eastern Europe*, Vol. 2, No. 46, 15 November 1991, p. 25.

41 For then premier Roman's undignified role at this event, see Michael Shafir, 'Schöpflinian Realism and Romanian Reality', *Report on Eastern Europe*, Vol. 2, No. 7, 15 February 1991, p. 37.

42 *Rompress* (Romanian news agency), in English, 23 January 1991.

43 See Viktor Meier, 'Sorge wegen Sowjetrepublik Moldav', *Frankfurter Allgemeine Zeitung*, 6 November 1990.

44 Lendvai, *Eagles in Cobwebs*, p. 314.

45 See also Vladimir Socor, 'Moldavian Lands between Romania and Ukraine: The Historical and Political Geography', Radio Liberty Research Report on the USSR, 16 November 1990.

46 See Mihai Carp, 'Cultural Ties Between Romania and Moldavia', Radio Free Europe Background Report, 13 July 1990.

47 *The Times* (London), 5 November 1990.

48 See, for example, Iliescu's interview in *Süddeutsche Zeitung*, 2 November 1990. Roman later became openly irredentist on Moldavia and strongly nationalist generally.

49 On the Moldavian crisis, see *Le Monde*, 20 May 1992.

50 Ernest Gellner, *Nations and Nationalism* (Ithaca, NY, Cornell University Press, 1983), p. 1.

51 Ibid.

52 Nathan Gardels, 'Two Concepts of Nationalism: An Interview with Isaiah Berlin', *New York Review of Books*, 21 November 1991.

10 The West's Stake and Western Responses

Far off countries about which we know little – and care less? Is this adapting and updating of Neville Chamberlain's fateful rationale for Munich in 1938 the right Western response to the dangers in south-eastern Europe outlined in this book? It was the response of many; fewer, perhaps, now after the slaughter in Yugoslavia, but still a lot. Saddam Hussein also demonstrated the danger of the creeping isolationism that threatened after the demise of the Cold War and, indeed, appears to have taken on a new lease on life in America. Of course, the poverty-stricken Balkans were never as important as the oil-rich Middle East. Will instability there, war even, make much difference? Are not the Balkans, in any case, so insignificant that any instability would be self-circumscribing, or would have very few wider ramifications even if it were not? The questions themselves certainly reflect a widespread attitude, the soundness of which is worth examining on a number of levels.

Greece and Turkey

In the minds even of some of the most exclusive isolationists, Greece and Turkey are somewhat different. They are much better known in the West, both historically and currently. They are Western allies of long-standing. They are democratic countries – often only just, and occasionally not at all. But their political record is incomparably better than that of their Balkan neighbours. Their strategic importance in the eastern Mediterranean is also generally recognized. And though nominal allies in NATO, their historical enmity has, over the last 30 years, revived again. It presents, in fact, a considerable danger of conflict in the region. Greece and Turkey are taken notice of for this reason alone.

Up to now Western policy in general, American in particular, has been mainly concerned with keeping the two countries away from each other's throats and striking a balance between them in terms of both favours and signs of displeasure. (The balance has occasionally been tilted by the strength of the Greek lobby in the United States). The 7–10 ratio in arms supplies has been a case in point; so has, in a less specific way, the policy toward Cyprus. Greece and Turkey, though neither would ever be convinced of this, have been treated as equals. That, anyway, has been the intention.

It is high time for a wholesale revision of this policy. During the Cold War equal treatment may have been defensible, although the relative importance of Turkey compared with Greece was always evident. Now, however, with the huge transformation in world affairs, Turkey has become a giant and Greece has lost considerably in terms of both alliance- and of nuisance-value. Greece is marginalized; Turkey is becoming more central.

With the Soviet collapse and the growing Turkish power and influence in the newly independent Turkic/Muslim republics, Turkey could be on its way to becoming one of the *world's* key powers. It will certainly not be happy to be considered America's 'gendarme' in the region or the West's 'link' with Asia. This implies either a subordinate or a passive status. It must now be invited to play a major role in formulating Western policy toward the region, to become a full partner. It already demonstrated its crucial importance in the Gulf War; one could devise many other scenarios in which its role could be decisive. If Turkey does not become a major partner, and *feel* that it has become one, it will most likely not want to be any kind of partner, and will branch out on its own. And Turkey with a 'rejection complex' could become a dangerously introspective customer – more Islamic, less democratic; more Asian, less European.

The United States, therefore, must begin treating Turkey as equal in partnership with Germany, France, and Britain. What, then, of the European Community? If the EC is to try to shake off its exclusive Eurocentrism and become something of a world power, then it must accept Turkish membership. If it conclusively decides for Eurocentrism then there is a logic in not accepting Turkey. But if the EC takes the latter course then both it and the rest of the world has to be prepared for the dangers of a Turkey 'scorned'. It might then fall to the United States to show, in its own interest, greater preference to Turkey to try to make up for the European affront.

Yugoslav Consequences

There has been no wiser appraisal of Western difficulties in coming to grips with the Yugoslav situation than that given by Edward Mortimer in *The Financial Times* of 22 April 1992. Mortimer is worth quoting at some length:

> If you live in a part of the world that is still relatively comfortable and secure, how do you react to the troubles of less fortunate people whose homes and lives are being wrecked by conflict? One way is to try to understand, to sort out the rights and wrongs, to become emotionally involved. Sooner or later, this almost inevitably leads you to take sides. Another way is to take refuge in a general condemnation of violence, blaming the conflict on the economic backwardness or primitive political culture of the people concerned. In the former case, one will easily become the dupe of the self-deceptive and self-righteous arguments of one side, since conflicts where one side is wholly in the right and the other wholly in the wrong are rare. In the second case, one can slip into self-righteousness oneself, looking patronizingly on innocent and guilty alike, and failing to take seriously the fears and grievances of people who, in most case, do not embark on violence for fun but in the sincere belief that only by doing so can they protect themselves and their 'community' from extinction.

A good example of the second case was given by a member of a Council of Europe parliamentary group, touring the United States in 1990. He told his audience that West Europeans felt central Europe – by which he meant Poland, Czechoslovakia, Hungary and Germany – to be of direct concern to them, part of 'larger Europe' to be brought into the 'European mainstream' as soon as circumstances permitted. The Balkans, however – here meaning Yugoslavia, Albania, Romania and Bulgaria – were of 'no concern' to Europe, now or, presumably, ever. If they wanted to 'tear themselves apart', that was their business and theirs alone. What went on in the Balkans, even the direst calamity (which he considered by no means unlikely) was certainly no concern of the West European countries because it could make no impact on them.

This indifference was uttered by a man well-versed in international affairs and, in some respects, not without a certain breadth of view. If he thought that it is not difficult to imagine the blank disregard in which the Balkans are held by less knowledgeable people in Europe, not to mention the United States.

For those in the West who *were* concerned, the initial problem with Yugoslavia was similar to that with the Soviet Union: how to strike the best balance between accepting the break-up of the present system while encouraging the emergence of some new kind of coherence. The principal concern was to avoid civil war. In early 1991 most Westerners, and most

Yugoslavs, still thought that some kind of new Yugoslav association, on a confederal basis, was possible. Both the Slovene and Croatian proposals for confederation included the establishment of certain federal institutions. It was Serbia's refusal to accept these proposals that made the outlook bleak, and its insistence that if the present Yugoslav system broke up, new frontiers would have to be drawn, made it all the bleaker. So did the growing number of affirmations by senior (Serb) officers in the Yugoslav military in favour of the *status quo*.

In retrospect, many Westerners (including this author) overestimated the resilience of the Yugoslav concept. Whether this was from wishful thinking, a sentimental attachment to 'Yugoslavia', a distorted reading of history, or a readiness to forget it, a naïve belief in federations, or just an understandable unwillingness to face up to yet another problem, is difficult to say. Certainly, what the break-up of Yugoslavia demonstrated was the fallacy of the old Romantic belief that nations with ethnic and linguistic similarities could somehow be incorporated into one state and live together in relative harmony. The Yugoslav case has certainly disproved that and, at the end of 1991, it looked as if the Czechoslovak case might do the same.

Again, in retrospect, as mentioned in Chapter 3, it is now possible to see that the civil war begun by Serbia in the middle of 1991 was the logical outcome of Milošević's political victory in Belgrade in 1987. It is now also possible to see that the federal army – or, more correctly, the federal officer corps – would carry its mission of preserving the integrity of Yugoslavia to the point where its actions would finally ensure the destruction of Yugoslavia. This was mainly because of its close identification with Serbia, but also because Yugoslavia was its *raison d'être*, the purpose of its existence and the source of its power, status and privileges. (The parallel with the Red Army seemed dangerously apt.) Once the civil war started there was obviously a symbiotic relationship between it and the Serbian government. But as the war progressed it seemed that some of the interests of the federal officers were not necessarily those of the politicians in Belgrade.

Any realistic hopes that the old Yugoslavia, even in drastically revised form, could be preserved ended with the federal army's unsuccessful invasion of Slovenia in June–July 1991. And any hopes that civil war could be averted were dashed by the army's operations in Croatia immediately afterwards. The hopes then lay in the West's being able to stop the civil war. And once these efforts began the Western powers showed just how uncertain and disunited they were.

Several Western organizations were involved in the attempt, most notably the European Community. The peace conference it organized at The Hague under the chairmanship of Lord Carrington, a former British foreign secretary, had sponsored 14 cease-fires by the end of 1991, all of which had been broken. In early November 1991 there had been considerable optimism that Serbia might accept peace on the basis of proposals for a confederation that seemed to go some way towards meeting its demands regarding Serbian minorities in other states, especially Croatia. But, in the end, it was the same old story: the Serbs were demanding rights for themselves which they were not prepared to grant to others – for example, the Albanians in Kosovo. (Their specious distinction here was that *they* were a nation, while the Albanians and others were only 'minorities'.) Very soon afterwards fighting on an unprecedented scale resumed and the hope was lost.

Basically what undermined the Community's efforts was sheer inexperience in handling a crisis like this. It had neither adequate institutions nor mechanisms. Ultimately it lacked credibility because it had no effective military component. Eventually the West European Union might become one, preferably autonomous within NATO and charged with European fire-fighting. But this was going to take a long time and would be much too late for the Yugoslav crisis. As for the other European institution – the Conference on European Security and Cooperation (CSCE) – this proved to be utterly impotent in its attempts at peace-making during the summer. It was still too inchoate, too lacking in purpose or institutional coherence for it to be anything but a well-meaning talking shop.

As for the United States, its policy was for too long obsessed with the notion that Yugoslavia must be preserved at all costs. This led to a considerable degree of self-deception about the turn of events there, a refusal to believe that Yugoslavia was indeed collapsing, Washington's ideas about a solution became, therefore, part of the problem. (The British attitude had been rather similar and Lord Carrington, in the service of the European Community, persisted for too long in believing that some kind of Yugoslavia could be salvaged. He also seems to have been too trusting in his negotiations with the manifestly untrustworthy combatants on all sides.)

The United Nations came relatively late into the fray. It had been content to leave this extraordinarily difficult problem to the Europeans, but the failure of the Europeans prompted it to some kind of action. Cyrus Vance, former US Secretary of State, was made UN special envoy by Secretary-General Perez de Cuellar in October. Vance could have been under no illusions about his task. Less public-spirited men would have rejected such a likely no-win commission. But he took it on and worked with his usual resource and distinction. After weeks of patient negotiation he succeeded in achieving a cease-fire and in eventually persuading the two warring sides to accept a UN peace-keeping force. This was a promising beginning, but the situation in Croatia and in the rest of Yugoslavia was still fraught with danger.

Prior to Vance's success, the dominant issue in the West regarding Yugoslavia had been the diplomatic recognition of Slovenia and Croatia. This simply demonstrated more clearly than ever the West's lack of unity in an international crisis. Germany, which had been urging diplomatic recognition for a considerable time, now threatened to do so unilaterally. It was supported in this by Italy, Austria, and other West European states as well as by East European states like Hungary, which felt its security threatened by the war and was having to cope with thousands of refugees. But all these states preferred waiting for some general recognition rather than taking unilateral action. Britain and, to a lesser degree, France opposed recognition. The United States adamantly opposed it. It led to an unseemly disarray in Western ranks.

Among the opponents of recognition – and here the dispute affected only Croatia; everyone was prepared to recognize Slovenia – Germany was severely criticized for choosing this controversial and divisive issue to make its first big, independent, foreign policy decision since the Second World War. Bonn's motives were the subject of considerable discussion. The neurotic and primitive Serbian propaganda machine saw it as the third German attempt this century to dominate the Balkans, now, as in the Second World War, in co-operation with murderous Croatian *Ustaša*. Other, less biased observers, while discounting the *Drang nach Südosten* interpretation, did see Germany's historical sympathy for Croatia as one reason for Bonn's attitude, just as they partly ascribed the American and British attitude to historical sympathies with Serbia. History was also considered, perhaps most accurately of all, as explaining Austria's strong stand in favour of Slovenia and Croatia and for early recognition.

Historical reasons apart, there was no reason to question the German government's sincerity in arguing that recognition was a matter of both morality and realism: Croatia had opted for independence through democratic means; Yugoslavia was no more; Serbia was the guilty party; and the sooner realities were recognized the better chance a lasting peace would have. It was a perfectly honourable, reasonable attitude to take, although the German case was sometimes tarnished by the ranting and bullying tone of sections of the right-wing press, just as Austria's case was not helped by the provincial arrogance of some Viennese commentators.

The case for delay, as presented mainly in the United States, Britain and, for a time, France, had three main aspects. First, it was argued that any unilateral German recognition of Croatia would damage efforts to forge a common foreign policy, of which Bonn had always been the most consistent champion. Second, premature recognition of Croatia would set a dangerous precedent with regard to the successor states of the Soviet Union and other parts of the world. Third, in Yugoslavia itself it would spread the war because an outraged and paranoid Serbia might then use force to protect other Serb minorities, most notably in Bosnia-Herzegovina. Croatia, in any case, did not meet one of the main traditional criteria for recognition: that its government should have control over its entire territory.

Eventually Germany got its way and the European Community recognized both Slovenia and Croatia in early 1992. It appeared at first to be a successful move, confounding those who argued that it would inflame hostilities rather than dampen them. A relative peace did descend on Yugoslavia and the cease-fire negotiated by Vance was generally holding. There were two big questions now, other than whether the Croatian cease-fire itself would continue: 1) When would the United States recognize Croatia? (Slovenia presented no problem); 2) Would a new conflagration start in Bosnia? Both questions were soon to be answered. Washington, very slow – too slow in the view of most – recognized Slovenia and Croatia in April 1992. Not only that: obviously deciding that vigour rather than inactivity was now needed, it recognized Bosnia-Herzegovina at the same time, along with the European Community. It also proceeded to take a much tougher stand against Serbia in general. Three new questions now arouse: 1) Did the recognition of Bosnia-Herzegovina precipitate the outbreak of war there? 2) Had full international recognition of Bosnia-Herzegovina come earlier – say very soon after the successful cease-fire in Croatia – would it have secured peace because Serbia would have been convinced – then, though perhaps not later – that aggression did not pay? 3) In view of the outbreak of war in Bosnia-Herzegovina was the recognition of Croatia at the beginning of the year such a good idea after all?

There was considerable debate over these three questions, particularly in Europe. On the first, the timing of the major Serb offensive in Bosnia left no doubt that recognition caused it. The second and third questions are often linked. Those who earlier argued against recognition of Croatia saw themselves vindicated. Premature recognition, they maintained, would only – if not in the short, then in the medium, term – precipitate violence and solve nothing. Their opponents maintained that recognition had indeed quietened the situation in Croatia – though not entirely – and averred that a much earlier recognition of Bosnia-Herzegovina would have done the same there.

It was an argument in which very few would ever be prepared to concede they were wrong. But the whole argument may have been quite irrelevant. The real question was whether foreign recognition made much difference at all. It is here where differences between the federal army, the local Serb militias in Bosnia, and the Milošević government in Belgrade might be discerned. Milošević at least went through the motions, not of respecting foreign opinion, but of taking it into account. The federal army had much less incentive to do so, and the local militias none at all. And in Bosnia-Herzegovina it was the militias which both dictated the course of daily events and set the pace of them. The tragedy of Yugoslavia was that violence had acquired its own momentum. It was self-kindling and would have to be largely self-extinguishing.

No one knew when this would happen, when violence-fatigue would induce reason – or, at least, inactivity. But it *would* happen, and when it did, it would be time for an international conference on Yugoslavia as a whole – preferably organized by the European Community. Its principal task would be to redraw frontiers where this was absolutely essential, perhaps also arrange necessary population transfers, and organize a peace-keeping force, strong enough and with a broad enough mandate.

Immediate objections, of course, arise. Would there be sufficient international will, resources, perseverance, and stamina to mount and sustain such an operation? The only answer here is that less of everything would be needed now than in a few years time when violence could have spread much further and wider. The second objection is more profound. It would be difficult to get any international body to agree on border changes. Besides, changes to the old Yugoslav *status quo* would, for one thing, seem to be rewarding Serbia for its aggression, at least in part. Such appeasement, therefore, would be unjust and might encourage others in the Balkans (or anywhere else) to do likewise. And, as this book will have shown, there were other areas of potentially serious conflict in the Balkans. There, too, there are grievances or resentments dating back to both the end of World War II *and* World War I that need redressing or, at least, examining. Ideally, a third 20th century peace conference is needed to clean up the mess left by the first two. But the first two were only made possible by the fatigue of war on an unprecedented scale, just as the fatigue of war in Yugoslavia might eventually make a peace settlement possible there. In the other Balkan crisis spots no side at present is prepared to make the concessions needed to eliminate, or even ease, the crisis. And obviously no one – except the most irresponsible – wants the kind of conflict that has devastated Yugoslavia.

What, then, is the best way, learning from Yugoslavia, to prevent similar disasters elsewhere? To attempt precise solutions would be foolish. The most likely approach, though, would be through inter-action between NATO, the European Community, the United Nations and the United States (CSCE, particularly with the addition of the *Asian* republics of the old Soviet Union, is now hopelessly cumbersome). This inter-action could generate the necessary will, money and military force. It would also influence the sides concerned in disputes to make their own bilateral efforts – not going for one big grand settlement but chipping away at the obstacles that exist, reducing them from the insuperable to the not quite impossible. Undramatic, tedious even; often with little or no results to show. But it seems not just the best, but the only, way. Yugoslavia has shown what to avoid, not only in the Balkans but throughout Eastern Europe; in the old Soviet Union, also (if it is not too late), Yugoslavia must remain as unique in its disaster as it was, in many ways, in its apparent prime.

Bibliography

This book was based almost entirely on secondary sources. I have used extensively the FBIS (Foreign Broadcast Information Service) daily reports for Eastern Europe, and for Western Europe in the case of Cyprus, Greece, and Turkey. I have also used extensively the Radio Free Europe/Radio Liberty research reports for Eastern Europe.

Western political and scholarly journals have been used as indicated in the footnotes. Several Western newspapers have been essential: the *Neue Zürcher Zeitung*, the *Frankfurter Allgemeine Zeitung*, the *Frankfurter Rundschau*, the *Süddeutsche Zeitung, Le Monde, Le Monde Diplomatique, The Financial Times, The Economist, The New York Times, The Los Angeles Times*, and *The Washington Post*.

Various handbooks and collections of papers have been consulted. They include papers on the East European economies submitted to the Joint Economic Committee of the Congress of the United States, Direction of Trade Statistics Yearbooks, and International Monetary Fund (IMF) statistics.

The following books have been useful to me, directly or indirectly, in preparing and writing this book.

Alexander, Stella, *Church and State in Yugoslavia since 1945*, Cambridge, Cambridge University Press, 1979.

Alford, Jonathan (ed.), *Greece and Turkey: Adversity in Alliance*, Aldershot, England, Gower, 1984.

Amery, Julian, *Sons of the Eagle: A Study in Guerilla War*, London, Macmillan, 1948.

Anderson, M. S., *The Eastern Question, 1774–1923*, New York, Macmillan, 1966.

Auty, Phyllis, *Yugoslavia*, New York, Walker, 1965.

Auty, Phyllis, *Tito: A Biography*, London, Longman, 1970.

Banac, Ivo, *The National Question in Yugoslavia: Origins, History, Politics*, Ithaca, NY, Cornell University Press, 1984.

Barker, Elisabeth, *Macedonia: Its Place in Balkan Power Politics*, London, Royal Institute of International Affairs, 1950.

Biberaj, Elez, *Albania: A Socialist Maverick*, Boulder, CO, Westview Press, 1990.

Bishop, Robert, and E. S. Crayfield, *Russia Astride the Balkans*, New York, Robert M. McBride & Company, 1948.

Braun, Aurel, *Romanian Foreign Policy since 1965*, New York, Praeger, 1978.

Braun, Aurel, *Small-State Security in The Balkans*, London, Macmillan, 1983.

Brown, James, *Delicately Poised Allies: Greece and Turkey*, London, Brassey's, 1991.

Brown, J. F., *Bulgaria under Communist Rule*, New York, Praeger, 1970.

Brown, J. F., *Eastern Europe and Communist Rule*, Durham, NC, Duke University Press, 1988.

Brown, J. F., *Surge to Freedom: The End of Communist Rule in Eastern Europe*, Durham, NC, Duke University Press, 1991.

Burks, R. V., *The Dynamics of Communism in Eastern Europe*, Princeton, NJ, Princeton University Press, 1961.

Campbell, John C., *Tito's Separate Road: America and Yugoslavia in World Politics*, New York, Harper and Row, 1967.

Carter, April, *Democratic Reform in Yugoslavia: The Changing Role of the Party*, Princeton, NJ, Princeton University Press, 1982.

Chipman, John (ed.), *NATO's Southern Allies: Internal and External Challenges*, London, Routledge, 1988.

Cioranescu, George, *Bessarabia: Disputed Land Between East and West*, Munich, Ion Dumitru, 1985.

Clarke, James F., *Bible Societies, American Missionaries, and the National Revival in Bulgaria*, New York, Arno Press and *The New York Times*, 1971.

Clissold, Stephen (ed.), *A History of Yugoslavia from Early Times to 1966*, Cambridge, Cambridge University Press, 1966.

Clogg, Richard, and George Yannopoulos (eds), *Greece under Military Rule*, London, Secker and Warburg, 1972.

Clogg, Richard, A *Short History of Modern Greece*, Cambridge, Cambridge University Press, 1979.

Clogg, Richard (ed.), *Greece in the 1980s*, London, Macmillan, 1983.

Constant, Benjamin, *Foxy Ferdinand: Tsar of Bulgaria*, London, Sidgwick and Jackson, 1979.

Crampton, Richard J., *Bulgaria 1878–1920: A History*, Boulder, CO, East European Monographs, 1983.

Davison, Roderic, *Reform in the Ottoman Empire: 1856–1876*, Princeton, NJ, Princeton University Press, 1963.

Dawisha, Karen, *Eastern Europe, Gorbachev, and Reform: The Great Challenge*, second edition, Cambridge, Cambridge University Press, 1990.

Deakin, F. W. D., *The Embattled Mountain*, London, Oxford University Press, 1971.

Dellin, L. A. D. (ed.), *Bulgaria*, New York, Praeger, 1957.

Dertilis, George B., *Banquiers, usuriers et paysans: réseaux de crédit et stratégies du capital en Grèce (1780–1930)*, Paris, Fondation des Treilles, 1988.

Doder, Dusko, *The Yugoslavs*, London, Allen and Unwin, 1979.

Djilas, Milovan, *Conversations with Stalin*, translated by Michael B. Petrovich, New York, Harcourt, Brace, and World, 1962.

Djilas, Milovan, *Tito: Eine Kritische Biographie*, Vienna, Verlag Fritz Molden, 1980.

Feröz, Ahmed, *The Turkish Experiment in Democracy, 1950–1975*, London, C. Hurst, 1978.

Fischer-Galati, Stephen, *The New Rumania: From People's Democracy to Socialist Republic*, Cambridge, MA, MIT Press, 1967.

Fischer-Galati, Stephen, *The Socialist Republic of Rumania*, Baltimore, MD, Johns Hopkins University Press, 1969.

Floyd, David, *Rumania: Russia's Dissident Ally*, New York, Praeger, 1965.

Gabanyi, Anneli Ute, *Die unvollendete Revolution: Rumänien zwischen Diktatur and Demokratie*, Munich, Piper Verlag, 1990.

Gati, Charles, *The Bloc That Failed: Soviet-East European Relations in Transition*, Bloomington, Indiana University Press, 1990.

Gilberg, Trond, *Modernization in Romania since World War II*, New York, Praeger, 1976.

Griffith, William E., *Albania and the Sino–Soviet Rift*, Cambridge, MA, MIT Press, 1963.

Griffith, William E. (ed.), *Central and Eastern Europe: The Opening Curtain?*, Boulder, CO, Westview Press, 1989.

Haass, Richard, *Alliance Problems in the Eastern Mediterranean – Greece, Turkey, and Cyprus:* Part 1, Adelphi Papers, No. 229, London, International Institute for Strategic Studies, Spring 1988.

Hacker, Jens, *Der Ostblock: Enstehung, Entwicklung und Struktur*, Baden-Baden, Nomos Verlagsgesellschaft, 1983.

Harris, George S., *Turkey: Coping with the Crisis*, Boulder, CO, Westview Press, 1985.

Hiç, Mükerrem, *Weaknesses and Risks of Turkey's Economic and Social Policies*, Ebenhausen, Germany, Stiftung Wissenschaft und Politik, May 1989.

Hitchens, Christopher, *Cyprus*, New York, Quartet Books, 1984.

Iatrides, John O., *Balkan Triangle: Birth and Decline of an Alliance Across Ideological Boundaries*, The Hague, Mouton, 1968.

Ionescu, Ghita, *Communism in Rumania, 1944–1962*, London, Oxford University Press, 1964.

Jelavich, Barbara, *Russia and the Formation of the Romanian National State, 1821–1878*, Cambridge, Cambridge University Press, 1977.

Jelavich, Barbara, *History of the Balkans*, two volumes, Cambridge, Cambridge University Press, 1983.

Jelavich, Charles, and Barbara Jelavich (eds), *The Balkans in Transition: Essays on the Development of Balkan Life and Politics since the Eighteenth Century*, Berkeley, University of California Press, 1963.

Johnson, A. Ross, *The Role of the Military in Yugoslavia*, Santa Monica, CA, RAND, April 1980.

Jowitt, Kenneth, *Revolutionary Breakthroughs and National Development: The Case of Romania, 1944–1965*, Berkeley, University of California Press, 1971.

Jowitt, Kenneth (ed.), *Social Change in Romania, 1860–1940*, Berkeley, Institute of International Studies, 1978.

Karpat, Kemal H., *Turkey's Politics: The Transition to a Multiparty System*, Princeton, NJ, Princeton University Press, 1959.

Keane, John, *Democracy and Civil Society*, London, Verso Press, 1988.

King, Robert R., *Minorities under Communism: Nationalities as a Source of Tension among Balkan Communist States*, Cambridge, MA, Harvard University Press, 1973.

King, Robert R., *History of the Romanian Communist Party, Stanford, CA*, Hoover Institution Press, 1980.

Kinross, Lord, *The Rebirth of a Nation*, New York, Morrow, 1965.

Lampe, John R., and Marvin R. Jackson, *Balkan Economic History, 1550–1950*, Bloomington, Indiana University Press, 1982.

Lampe, John R., *The Bulgarian Economy in the Twentieth Century*, London, Croom Helm, 1986.

Lendvai, Paul, *Die einsame Albanien*, Zurich, Edition Interfrom, 1985.

Lendvai, Paul, *Eagles in Cobwebs: Nationalism and Communism in the Balkans*, New York, Doubleday, 1969.

Lewis, Bernard, *The Emergence of Modern Turkey*, London, Oxford University Press, 1961.

Lewis, Jesse W. Jr., *The Strategic Balance in the Mediterranean*, Washington, DC, American Enterprise Institute, 1976.

Lydall, Harold, *Yugoslav Socialism: Theory and Practice*, Oxford, Clarendon Press, 1984.

MacGwire, Michael, *Soviet Strategic Aims and Capabilities in the Mediterranean, Part I*, Adelphi Papers, No. 229, London, International Institute for Strategic Studies, Spring 1988.

Mackenzie, Kenneth, *Turkey after the Storm*, Conflict Studies No. 43, London, Institute for the Study of Conflict, 1974.

McCormick, Gordon, *Soviet Strategic Aims and Capabilities in the Mediterranean, Part II*, London, International Institute for Strategic Studies, Spring 1988.

McDonald, Robert, *Alliance Problems in the Eastern Mediterranean – Greece, Turkey, and Cyprus – Part II*, London, International Institute for Strategic Studies, Spring 1988.

Meier Jens, and Johann Hawlowitsch (eds), *Die Aussenwirtschaft Sudosteuropas*, Cologne, Verlag Wissenschaft und Politik, 1970.

Oren, Nissan, *Bulgarian Communism: The Road to Power, 1934–1944*, New York, Columbia University Press, 1971.

Oren, Nissan, *Revolution Administered: Agrarianism and Communism in Bulgaria*, Baltimore, MD, Johns Hopkins University Press, 1973.

Palmer, Stephen and Robert L. King, *Yugoslav Communism and the Macedonian Question*, Hamden, CT, Shoestring Press, 1971.

Pano, Nicholas C., *The People's Republic of Albania*, Baltimore, MD, Johns Hopkins University Press, 1968.

Perry, Duncan, M., *The Politics of Terror: The Macedonian Revolutionary Movements, 1893–1903*, Durham, NC, Duke University Press, 1988.

Prifti, Peter R., *Socialist Albania Since 1944: Domestic and Foreign Developments*, Cambridge, MA, MIT Press, 1978.

Reuter, Jens, *Die Albaner in Jugoslawien*, Munich, R. Oldenbourg, 1982.

Roberts, Henry L., *Rumania: Political Problems of an Agrarian State*, New Haven, CT, Yale University Press, 1951.

Rogger Hans, and Eugen Weber (eds), *The European Right: A Historical Profile*, Berkeley, University of California Press, 1966.

Rothschild, Joseph, *The Communist Party of Bulgaria: Origins and Development, 1883–1936*, New York, Columbia University Press, 1959.

Rothschild, Joseph, *East Central Europe Between the Two World Wars*, Seattle, University of Washington Press, 1974.

Rothschild, Joseph, *Return to Diversity: A Political History of East Central Europe Since World War II*, New York, Oxford University Press, 1989.

Rubinstein, Alvin Z., *Yugoslavia and the Nonaligned World*, Princeton, NJ, Princeton University Press, 1970.

Rusinow, Dennison, *The Yugoslav Experiment, 1948–1974*, London, C. Hurst, 1977.

Rustow, Dankwart A., *Turkey, America's Forgotten Ally*, New York, Council on Foreign Relations, 1987.

Said, Abdul A. (ed.), *Ethnicity and US Foreign Policy*, New York, Praeger, 1977.

Schwab, Peter and George D. Frangos, *Greece Under the Junta*, New York, Facts on File, 1973.

Seton-Watson, Hugh, *Eastern Europe between the Wars, 1918–1941*, New York, Harper and Row, 1967.

Shafir, Michael, *Romania: Politics, Economics, and Society*, London, Frances Pinter, 1985.

Shaw, Stanford J., and Ezel Kural Shaw, *History of the Ottoman Empire*, two volumes, Cambridge, MA, Cambridge University Press, 1967, 1977.

Shoup, Paul, *Communism and the Yugoslav National Question*, New York, Columbia University Press, 1968.

Shoup, Paul (ed.), and George W. Hoffman (project director), *Problems of Balkan Security: Southeastern Europe in the 1990s*, Washington, DC, Wilson Center, 1990.

Singleton, Fred, *Twentieth Century Yugoslavia*, New York, Columbia University Press, 1976.

Sirć, Ljubo, *The Yugoslav Economy under Self-Management*, New York, St Martin's Press, 1979.

Skendi, Stavro, *The Albanian National Awakening, 1878–1912*, Princeton, NJ, Princeton University Press, 1967.

Spain, James W., *American Dıplomacy in Turkey*, New York, Praeger, 1984.

Spector, Sherman David, *Rumania at the Paris Peace Conference: A Study of the Diplomacy of Ioan C. Bratianu*, New York, Bookman Associates, 1962.

Stanković, Slobodan, *The End of the Tito Era: Yugoslavia's Dilemmas*, Stanford, CA, Hoover Institution Press, 1981.

Stavrianos, L. S., *The Balkans since 1453*, New York, Rinehart, 1958.

Stearns, Monteagle, *Updating the Truman Doctrine*, International Security Studies Program, Working Paper No. 86, Washington, DC, The Wilson Center, 1989.

Sugar, Peter F. and Ivo J. Lederer (eds), *Nationalism in Eastern Europe*, Seattle, University of Washington Press, 1969.

Swire, Joseph, *Albania: The Rise of a Kingdom*, New York, Arno Press and *The New York Times*, 1971.

Temperley, H. W. V., *History of Serbia*, London, G. Bell and Sons, 1919.

Tönnes, Bernhard, *Sonderfall Albanien*, Munich, R. Oldenbourg Verlag, 1980.

Ulam, Adam, *Titoism and the Cominform*, Cambridge, MA, Harvard University Press, 1952.

Vali, Ferenc A., *Bridge Across the Bosporus: The Foreign Policy of Turkey*, Baltimore, MD, Johns Hopkins University Press, 1971.

Vatikiotis, P. J., *Greece: A Political Essay*, The Washington Papers, Vol. II, The Center for Strategic and International Studies, Georgetown University, London and Beverly Hills, Sage Publications, 1974.

Veremis, Thanos, *Greek Security Issues and Politics*, Adelphi Papers, No. 179, London, International Institute for Strategic Studies, Winter 1982.

Weiker, Walter F., *The Turkish Reuolution 1960–1961*, Washington, DC, The Brookings Institution, 1963.

Wilkinson, H. R., *Maps and Politics: A Review of the Ethnic Cartography of Macedonia*, Liverpool, University of Liverpool Press, 1961.

Wilson, Andrew, *The Aegean Dispute*, Adelphi Papers, No. 155, London, International Institute for Strategic Studies, Winter 1979-1980.

Wilson, Duncan, *Tito's Yugoslavia*, Cambridge, Cambridge University Press 1979

Wolff, Robert Lee, *The Balkans in Our Time*, Cambridge, MA, Harvard University Press, 1956.

Woodhouse, C. M., *The Story of Modern Greece*, London, Faber and Faber, 1968.

Woodhouse, C. M., *The Rise and Fall of the Greek Colonels*, London, Granada, 1985.

Index